W9-CZT-959

he Effect of Science on the Second World War

The Effect of Science on the Second World War

Guy Hartcup

First published in Great Britain 2000 by
MACMILLAN PRESS LTD
Houndmills, Basingstoke, Hampshire RG21 6XS and London
Companies and representatives throughout the world

A catalogue record for this book is available from the British Library.

ISBN 0–333–67061–2

First published in the United States of America 2000 by
ST. MARTIN'S PRESS, INC.,
Scholarly and Reference Division,
175 Fifth Avenue, New York, N.Y. 10010

ISBN 0–312–22833–3

Library of Congress Cataloging-in-Publication Data
Hartcup, Guy.
The effect of science on the second World War / Guy Hartcup.
p. cm.
Includes bibliographical references and index.
ISBN 0–312–22833–3 (cloth)
1. World War, 1939–1945—Science. I. Title.
D810.S2 H37   2000
940.53—dc21
                                        99–054609

This book is printed on paper suitable for recycling and made from fully managed and sustained
forest sources.

10   9   8   7   6   5   4   3   2   1
09   08   07   06   05   04   03   02   01   00

Printed and bound in Great Britain by
Antony Rowe Ltd, Chippenham, Wiltshire

For Freddie and the rest of the family

Contents

List of Plates

1. Sir Henry Tizard. Architect of the British radar chain and leader of the mission to the USA in August 1940. *Imperial College Archives*
2. Winston Churchill and F. A. Lindemann (later Lord Cherwell), his scientific adviser throughout the war. *Imperial War Museum*
3. Vannevar Bush. Head of the US Office of Scientific Research and Development and adviser to the President. *MIT Museum*
4. P. M. S. Blackett. Member of the Tizard Committee and later Chief Adviser on Operational Research in the Admiralty. *Universal Picture Press & Agency Ltd*
5. Howard Florey. Chief wartime developer of penicillin. *Wellcome Institute Library, London*
6. British nuclear physicists. *L to R*: William Penney (member of Los Alamos team), Otto Frisch, Rudolf Peierls, John Cockcroft (also director of Army radar research until June 1944). *UK Atomic Energy Authority*
7. Typical Chain Home station. *GEC Journal of Research, vol. 3, no. 2, 1985*
8. Strapped magnetron used for naval 10 cm radar. *GEC Review, vol. 10, no. 1, 1995*
9. Hedgehog ahead-throwing bomb projector against U-boats. *Public Record Office*
10. German Enigma machine with plugboard uncovered. *Dr Mark Baldwin of M & M Baldwin publishers*
11. V2 rocket being prepared to fire. *Royal Aeronautical Society*
12. Messerschmitt 262 jet-propelled fighter. *Imperial War Museum*

Acknowledgements

As so many applications of science have been covered in this book, I have been dependent on obtaining the comments and criticisms of experts. I am therefore deeply grateful to those who have read so carefully individual chapters, namely Frank Armstrong, Lorna Arnold, G. B. Carter, Ralph Erskine, Lieutenant-Commander W. J. R. Gardner, RN, Dr Norman Heatley and Professor Jonathan Rosenhead. Others who advised or helped me include Professor Ralph Benjamin, John Bradley, David Edgerton, the late Professor R. V. Jones and that nonagenarian and veteran operational researcher, J. R. Vezey. Such errors that remain are my own responsibility. I must also thank Alice Haythornthwaite who admirably did the research for the chapter on medicine.

I am also indebted to the staffs of those invaluable institutions, the Public Record Office, the Science Museum Library, the library of the International Institute of Strategic Studies, the library of the Imperial War Museum and the library of the Royal Aeronautical Society whose Librarian, Arnold Nayler, has, as ever, dug out books and answered questions at short notice.

Finally, I must thank my wife for her forbearance over the past three years while working on the book.

Guy Hartcup
East Sheen
January 1999

Introduction

The 50th anniversary of the end of the Second World War was celebrated with a spate of books reviewing the strategy, commanders and the campaigns on land, on sea and in the air. This literature merely added to the torrent of books and TV programmes on the two world wars which continue to flow, finding new material or making revisionist judgements on disputed events. It is surprising therefore that the effect of science on the war has in comparison been neglected. Everyone seems to know that science and technology made an impact on both world wars, more on the second than the first. Most people are aware of radar's contribution to RAF Fighter Command's victory in the Battle of Britain, or of the benefit of penicillin in the treatment of wounds or DDT on tropical diseases. They know that the German V2s did not alter the course of the war, unpleasant weapons though they were, but they are less aware that the V2 was the first step towards the American landing on the moon, or that the guided weapons produced by the Germans in the last months of the war led to the precision weapons that intrigued everyone who followed the Gulf War. Nor are they aware of how both sides organized their scientists, or why the Germans, Italians and Japanese – who were not lacking in scientific ability – failed to help their military, unlike their one-time colleagues in the Allied camp.

The twenty years before the outbreak of war in September 1939 was a period of intense activity in science which was to have an extraordinary effect on warfare. Five developments need to be mentioned. First, radio was transformed when spark transmission was replaced by thermionic valves, opening the way for short-wave, and later ultra-short-wave, communication which had so many military applications. Second, American and British scientists began to measure the height of the ionosphere, a belt some thirty to fifty miles above the earth able to reflect radio waves. These practical steps were a first step towards radar on which some primitive experiments had already taken place. Third, research began on new fuels such as liquid oxygen and hydrogen peroxide which would provide power for rockets and submarines, also on high temperature alloys such as nimonic later used for making jet engines. Fourth, medical research on sulphonamides began and penicillin was accidentally discovered but not yet exploited. That had to wait until the urgent requirements of war compelled action. Finally, the face of war itself was to be radically altered by a series of events in the world of physics – the artificial disintegration of the atom in 1919, followed thirteen years later by the discovery of the neutron – particles which, having no electric charge, could pass through matter without being deflected by the forces surrounding nuclei – and then in January 1939, only nine months before the outbreak of the Second World War, the discovery that the splitting of the uranium atom would release enough energy to explode a bomb.

How was all this knowledge to be translated into weapons of war and how were the scientists to be integrated into the war effort? The way in which the Allies and the Axis powers tackled this problem proved to be vital to the winning of the war.

The history of science in the Second World War has so far been disappointing. In Britain a popular account called *Science at War* was published in 1947 revealing for the first time details of radar, naval science, operational research and the atomic bomb, but there was no mention of medical research on the grounds that the public had already been told about penicillin and DDT. However, that year a proposal for a more comprehensive scientific history of the war was turned down by the Advisory Committee on Scientific Policy to the Cabinet after being told by the eminent scientist, Sir Edward Appleton, that there would only be a limited demand for such a work which would not justify the research involved.[1] In its place a volume of the civil official histories titled *The Design and Development of Weapons* was published in 1963. It surveyed the development of military aircraft (including jet-propelled), army weapons and radar and, perhaps most interesting of all, gave an account of research establishments. Even so, it did not explain why, to take one example, radar was a success while the development of the tank (a British invention) in the war was, in general, a failure.

In the United States the wartime scientific effort was given more generous recognition with the publication of *Scientists against Time* by James Phinney Baxter, first published in 1946. It covered all aspects of science in the war and was a masterpiece of compression, though, like the British version, it was a celebratory rather than a critical account.

The most interesting books on science in the Second World War were, in fact, written by the scientists themselves. There were accounts of radar by Watson-Watt who demonstrated its feasibility to the British, A. P. Rowe, head of the Telecommunications Research Establishment (TRE) and by three of his distinguished colleagues, Bernard Lovell, Alan Hodgkin and E. G. Bowen, the 'father' of airborne radar. Solly Zuckerman, eventually to become a Chief Scientific Adviser after the war, showed how an anatomist/zoologist could, by treating a military problem in the same way as he would a living organism, be able to provide an acceptable plan to hinder the arrival of enemy reinforcements on the battlefield. R. V. Jones, a physicist, was the first to give a brilliant insight into the working of scientific intelligence. In the States Vannevar Bush wrote a rambling but entertaining volume of reminiscences called *Pieces of the Action*. Accounts of the war by German scientists have been sparse though the conversations recorded by secret microphones of leading nuclear physicists interned after the European war illuminate the state of science under the Nazis.

National security was another obstacle delaying publication of books on science and the war. Officials had to be cautious, on account of the Cold War, about releasing information which, even though dated, might be valuable to a potential enemy. Thus the best kept secret of all – the deciphering of German radio communications by the British under the code name Ultra – had to wait release until the mid-1970s. The breaking of Japanese codes and ciphers known as Magic was much earlier than Ultra. They revealed another side of military science – the construction of the first primitive computers employed to accelerate code breaking. Once more, it was the personal accounts of the classical scholars, mathematicians as well as scientists, that caught the public imagination rather than the weighty but authoritative volumes entitled *British Intelligence in the Second World War* which were published from 1979 onwards.

More recently historians of science and technology have turned their attention to the effect that armed forces and weapons technology has had on society. The two world wars have provided much material to work on. Alongside these studies, analyses written from a more polemical point of view on the effect of war on society, for example the theme of British industrial decline in the twentieth century investigated by Correlli Barnett, continue to engage the attention of historians.

How then does this book fit into the scheme of things? A comprehensive history of science in the Second World War on the lines of that rejected by Sir Edward Appleton is not possible in the space available. What perhaps can be done is to bring the story up to date by comparing the Allied scientific effort with that of the enemy. Instead of describing technicalities, it will try to assess how the intervention of scientists or their devices affected particular operations. Thus radar, sonar and other underwater weapons, missiles and chemical and biological weapons (fortunately never used but which remained a threat) will be covered. Other sides of the scientific war such as operational research, the use of science in code and cipher breaking and medical research need attention. The atomic bomb is in a class on its own. It absorbed the energies of the most eminent scientists and because of it warfare was changed irreversibly. Hence it is discussed in the final chapter. What especially needs stressing is that success in the scientific and technical contributions to the Second World War went to the side which recognized the importance of close collaboration between scientists and the military, something unknown before 1939.

Finally, there is the problem of distinguishing between science and engineering. Many of the war-winning devices were the joint work of scientists and engineers. Indeed, in the development of radar, physicists often became temporary engineers. At the same time there were feats of pure engineering like the construction of the Mulberry harbours for the landings in Normandy in 1944 which fall outside the scope of this study. But there were other advances involving scientists and engineers initiated on account of the war – the long-range rocket and jet propulsion – which had limited or nil effect on its outcome but which were to change the postwar world and therefore need to be discussed.

War is much too serious a thing to be left to the military.

Georges Clemenceau

[T]heir inventions are according to right reason even if you don't approve the end to which they proceed.

David Jones, *In Parenthesis*

1
Organization of Science for War

Science in the First World War

In 1805 while Wellington's army was fighting the French in Spain, the Emperor Napoleon presented an award to the great English chemist, Humphry Davy, who travelled to Paris to receive it. No one thought it odd that a civilian from one belligerent nation should be entertained in the capital of the other. Science was an international activity; men of science studied at foreign universities and later exchanged ideas with foreign colleagues. Science, with the exception of ballistics and explosives, was not associated with the technique of warfare. But as the nineteenth century advanced warfare was transformed at an increasing rate by new technological developments. The most important were the introduction of high explosive for artillery, rapid-firing machine guns, torpedoes and mines. With the dawn of the new century came even more significant inventions such as wireless telegraphy, submarines and the aeroplane.

The military, with a few exceptions, steeped in traditional methods of warfare, failed to become aware of the new techniques. Only after the European war which began in the summer of 1914 had ground itself to a halt in the morass of trench warfare in Flanders and eastern France were they faced with grim reality. In the spring of 1915 scientific and informed public opinion urged their governments to make use of scientists, many of whom had volunteered to go to the front and more than one scientist of promise died. In Britain two events in particular demanded the participation of scientists: the introduction of U-boat warfare by the German Navy on 18 February 1915 and the first German gas attack on the Western Front two months later on 22 April. On

17 June 1915 the editor of the scientific journal *Nature* urged the government to make use of the

> hundreds of men of science in the country whose energies and expert knowledge are not being effectively used. We should possess a scientific corps with men investigating at the front as well as at home, instead of one or two committees advising officials as to possible means of offence or defence...Not a day passes but we are asked by men of science how they can devote their knowledge to national needs; and there is no ready answer. The organisation of the scientific intellect of the country is essential, yet almost nothing has been done towards its accomplishment.[1]

Action *was* taken though misunderstandings and incompatibility of thinking between the military and the scientists formed a gap which was never bridged. The Admiralty set up a Board of Invention and Research which included scientists of the calibre of Ernest Rutherford, William Bragg and J. J. Thomson. On their agenda were methods of using aircraft, control of naval gunfire and, most important, submarine detection. Some progress was made by British, French and American scientists with the acoustic detection of submarines and later by piezo-electric currents. But the Navy was reluctant to divulge information on tactics, making life difficult for the scientists, and before the end of the war the Board was superseded by a new organization within and controlled by the Admiralty.

The general staffs of the armies were no more cooperative. The leading chemists of Britain and France were mobilized, first to devise protection against poison gas, and second to evolve retaliatory weapons. By the end of the war a mass of scientific data had been accumulated. But, like naval science, the history of chemical warfare consisted of missed opportunities, slow reaction and a failure to produce countermeasures.

Chemical weapons were but one feature of trench warfare for which short-range weapons such as mortars, grenades and flamethrowers were revived and modernized. For this, and even more to assess a flood of fantastic ideas submitted by hopeful inventors, a Munitions Invention Department was set up by the Ministry of Munitions in London and staffed by prominent chemists and engineers.

The entirely novel war in the air kept scientists and engineers busy with devising new types of armament, bombsights and navigational instruments. The aeroplane, it was said, was different from previous forms of transport because it did not come to rest when its engine or part of its structure failed.[2] Most of the research took place at the Royal Aircraft Factory, Farnborough, already in existence before 1914, and where a number of bright young graduates from the universities excelled themselves. It was to provide a model for American aeronautical engineers. Protection from air attack was another new subject. There was a demand for accurate anti-aircraft artillery and sound locators for which mathematicians and physicists were called upon.

Probably the real significance of First World War science lay less in the value of gadgets or inventions but in the appreciation by Allied scientists, some of whom would find themselves engaged in another war against Germany, that collaboration between scientists and the military was a prerequisite of success.

It is doubtful whether German scientists fared any better in their relations with the military. Germany at least took the initiative by trying to end the war quickly, whether by submarine or by chemical warfare. In the latter case they had the advantage of a well-developed chemical industry and no lack of qualified scientific staff. But, as the leading German scientist responsible for chemical warfare on the Western Front, Fritz Haber, remarked, even though they lived under one roof 'there was no fruitful exchange' between generals, scientists and technologists.[3]

The interwar years

The First World War gave a tremendous boost to science, particular to aviation, medicine and radio which all had peaceful as well as military applications; chemicals and other industrial products also benefited from wartime industrial research. The governments of all the belligerents appreciated that science had to be supported. In Britain the Department of Scientific and Industrial Research was set up in 1915 to advance trade and industry; among other special bodies, it included the Radio Research Board from which British radar sprang. The French who had employed physicists and chemists extensively set up an Office of Invention. The Americans formed two state-sponsored scientific advisory bodies. The first was the National Advisory Committee for Aeronautics, established in 1915 before the USA entered the war, to direct the 'scientific study of flight'; three years later the National Research Council was created to deal with applications of science in peace and war.

Disarmament was the hopeful goal in the immediate postwar years. Military scientific establishments were cut down to the bone. In spite of this, service laboratories followed up wartime developments. In Britain

Admiralty scientists, several of whom were well-qualified physicists, worked on radio, fire control, magnetic mines and anti-submarine equipment. Army scientists grappled with the seemingly intractable problem of detecting the approach of hostile aircraft and experts on chemical warfare continued research into offensive weapons and counter-measures against them. These establishments had their counterparts in other countries, with the exception of Germany, forbidden by the Treaty of Versailles to make warlike preparations (though there was no ban on aeronautical research for civil aviation).

The Weimar Republic was not keen on spending money on aeronautics so that when the Nazis came to power in 1933 scientists and engineers found themselves being provided with unexpectedly ample funds for research. It was not surprising that the Nazis soon began to encourage research for military purposes in the universities, though some of the latter independently initiated armament research.

What was the Nazis' attitude towards science? Hitler himself took a keen interest in technology, declaring that 'technically superior weapons were decisive for the winning of any war',[4] but he never grasped the complexities of producing modern military equipment. The Nazis were not, as sometimes believed, opposed to science but favoured disciplines such as mathematics, physics and psychology that could be useful, but they frowned on theoretical physics because it did not bring quick results. Workers in the approved fields were consequently subject to the doctrine of *Gleichschaltung* or coordination which, in effect, meant the purging of non-Aryan staff.[5] Yet in retrospect it is unlikely that the Nazis set out to purge science or engineering. Einstein was, of course, the exception to the rule and, because of his fame extending beyond physics, incurred the wrath of the Nazis.

Even so, those who *were* Aryan or 'true' Germans sometimes suffered. Thus in 1938 Werner Heisenberg, ten years earlier Nobel Prizewinner for Physics and author of the 'uncertainty principle', was tipped to succeed Arnold Sommerfeld as Professor of Theoretical Physics at Munich. But because he had been vilified by the Nazi press as being Jewish 'in spirit', Wilhelm Müller, a second-rate aerodynamicist, was appointed instead. Ludwig Prandtl, known as the 'father of aerodynamics', openly and vehemently opposed the choice and protested to the Minister of Education but without success. In 1941 he wrote to Göring to draw his attention to the detrimental effects on military aviation which would result from the expulsion of Jewish scientists of merit, but again to no avail.[6]

One state-sponsored institution was created, however, the *Reichsforschungsrat* (RFR) or Reich Research Council, intended to make Germany independent of imported raw materials. But it had little effect on weapon development until taken over by Göring in June 1942 to deal with the many short-term military scientific projects on which the Germans had tardily embarked. Another factor making German science less effective compared with other countries was the inability of the state to exercise a coherent policy on technology. This was due to the Third Reich being composed of a 'cartel of overlapping, competing and contradictory power blocks [which] effectively hindered and sometimes prevented the systematic and thorough development and implementation of specific technologies and policies.'[7] The main differences between Nazi technocracy and elsewhere were: (a) German technocrats were able and willing to help further irrational and therefore un-technocratic goals and policies; and (b) clear, coherent and consequent state purposes scarcely existed.

As in other countries the German Air Force (GAF) and Navy were the services most aware of advances in modern technology. Yet it was the Army which created a truly revolutionary weapon – the long-range rocket. Rocket research began in secret as early as 1929 with the intention of developing weapons for chemical warfare. But because of the popular interest in rocket propulsion in Germany the Army was able to recruit a number of enthusiasts, notably Wernher von Braun, whose father had been a minister in a previous government. Von Braun had studied physics at Berlin University and won his doctorate with a secret dissertation on rockets. The Nazis provided financial support to this group and a laboratory was established under the *Heereswaffenamt* (HWA), the Army Ordnance Department.[8] In 1937 it was moved to Peenemünde, a remote site on the Baltic coast, where elaborate facilities were built for building and testing missiles. The long-range rocket programme, though ultimately unsuccessful, was nevertheless 'one of the first examples of state mobilisation of massive engineering and scientific resources for the forced invention of a radical, new military technology.'[9] It preceded by a decade and was not dramatically smaller in scale than the even more revolutionary Manhattan Project (the development of an atomic bomb) in the United States.

Scientists in the Soviet Union were, as in Germany, under the thumb of their totalitarian rulers. While the Soviet leaders recognized its importance in warfare, they were unable to organize and support science. In the armed forces there were a number of technically-minded officers, notably Marshal Mikhail Tukhachevskii, Chief of Army Ordnance, who laid the foundations for mechanized and airborne forces as well as encouraging the early developments of guided missiles and radar. Ironically, he was executed in a Stalin purge in 1937.[10] Only five years earlier the General Staff of the Red Army became concerned about the vulnerability of Russian cities and military to air attack from a hostile Germany. Appreciating the inadequacy of acoustic methods of aircraft detection they contacted the Physics Institute in Leningrad under Abram Joffe, a pioneer of nuclear physics, and well acquainted with scientific developments in the West. But little progress was made on radar due to the difficulties in making the necessary equipment, while the purges had a negative effect on the quality of the scientists.[11] When war came in 1941 the Institute became the first centre for scientific applications for the services. Also of great importance for the future, Joffe was responsible for encouraging nuclear physics research in the Soviet Union.

Reactions to the threat from Nazi Germany

It was not long before the aggressive intentions of the Nazis became known. Informed opinion in Britain, mindful of German air raids on London and elsewhere in the First World War, realized how vulnerable the centres of government and industry were to bombing. The outcome was the formation of the Committee for the Scientific Survey of Air Defence (CSSAD) in December 1934. Its chairman was Henry Tizard who had been a pilot and later in charge of a fighter experimental establishment as well as working on aircraft instruments at Farnborough in the First World War. He was now chairman of the Aeronautical Research Committee advising on new equipment for the RAF. At the same time he was Rector of Imperial College, London. His colleagues were A. V. Hill, a distinguished physiologist who had been a specialist on anti-aircraft gunnery in the war and now Joint Secretary of the Royal Society, and Patrick Blackett who had served as a young officer in the Navy in the Falklands and Jutland actions, after the war going to the Cavendish Laboratory in Cambridge where he became well known as a brilliant experimental and theoretical scientist. He was now in charge of the physics department at Birkbeck College in the University of London. Unlike his colleagues, Blackett was deeply involved in left-wing politics.[12] But all the members of the Committee were united in deploring the rise of Nazism. Tizard was able to ask service officers to attend the Committee. This marked the beginning of real collaboration between scientists and the military. After the war Tizard claimed it was the first time that scientists were asked to study the *needs* of the services, as distinct from their wants, and only then as a last resort.[13]

Radar was the first fruit of the Tizard Committee, as it became known. Many scientists, over and above the small group of Air Ministry physicists and engineers working on the early development of radar, were required, not only for radar but for the development of high powered transmitting valves for the Navy and the Army as well as for the Air Force. Fortunately there were a few enlightened individuals in high places who appreciated the importance of science. One was Sir Maurice Hankey, Secretary of the Cabinet and the Committee for Imperial Defence and an early proponent of the tank. In March 1936, just after Hitler had reoccupied the Rhineland, he sketched a plan for mobilizing scientists and other experts who might be useful in the event of war. Sending this to the Permanent Secretary to the Treasury, Sir Warren Fisher, Hankey noted that 'we have learned so much from 1914–18 in respect of what our needs are likely to be for a major war, that it seems we should take advantage of that experience, in the comparatively quiet times of peace and do all we can in advance of another emergency.'[14]

But not until the summer of 1938, shortly before the Munich crisis, did Hankey's plan materialize as a Central Register. The Committee of Vice-Chancellors and Principals had meanwhile made their own plan for mobilizing university graduates in an emergency. After Munich, spurred on by the increasing possibility of a European war, the National Register containing the names of chemists, physicists, medical scientists and a small group of classical scholars and mathematicians earmarked for training in cryptanalysis had been compiled. By September 1939 an archive of some 80 000 cards kept in a suburban office was ready for use.[15]

There was also a group of young scientists outside the Establishment, mostly of a leftish persuasion but essentially anti-Nazi who either had not been called upon for war work or who felt that scientific mobilization by the Chamberlain government was at best dilatory. Their views were voiced at a dining club known as the 'Tots and Quots' after a Latin tag devised by J. B. S. Haldane: *quot homines, tot sententiae* (so many men, so many opinions). Others who met there to discuss economics and the effect of science on social policy were J. D. Bernal, Lancelot Hogben, Herman Levy, C. H. Waddington and Solly Zuckerman. Even the right-wing F. A. Lindemann would put in an appearance. Writers like H. G. Wells, forward-looking industrialists like Lord Melchett of ICI, and one or two Labour politicians, including Hugh Gaitskell, came along. The government's air raid precautions policy was criticized by members drawing on experience from the Spanish civil war.[16]

When Britain stood alone in June 1940 members wrote *Science in War*. It was published as a Penguin Special and appeared on book stalls a month later.[17] It pointed out how the Germans had made use of applied science in their search for substitute raw materials and explained how medicine and proper nutrition could help the war effort. The book said little on weapons apart from a jejune discussion on anti-tank weapons. But the members of the Tots and Quots were soon to become involved in the war.

Collaboration with the United States

After the collapse of France the United States of America was the only country in the West immune from enemy attack with scientists, engineers and industry capable of producing weapons for war. It was fortunate that the States had an elite corps of physicists who had reached maturity by 1940 capable of running the laboratories for radar, atomic energy and other projects vital for winning the war. They were by no means all refugees from Nazi Germany or Fascist Italy (most of whom had crossed the Atlantic in the late 1930s) but first-generation Americans like Robert Oppenheimer and Isidor Rabi who had studied in Europe and returned to America determined, as Rabi put it, to make American physics respectable. They were more aware than most of their compatriots of the threat of fascism. The doyen of this group was Vannevar Bush, a humorous New Englander who was a pioneer of early computers and now Dean of Engineering at the Massachusetts Institute of Technology (MIT). In the First World War he had tried to help the US Navy detect submarines. Although his experiments were unsuccessful he learned, as he wrote later, how *not* to fight a war; what was lacking was close liaison between scientists and the military.[18]

With that in mind, Bush, who was no New Dealer and disapproved of state intervention but who was familiar with the political scene in Washington as chairman of the influential National Advisory Committee for Aeronautics, went to President Roosevelt in June 1940 with the summary of a plan for a National Defence Research Committee (NDRC). This would coordinate and conduct scientific research on all aspects of war. In five minutes the President, who was evidently impressed with Bush's ability to explain scientific matters in simple terms, signed the plan contained in four paragraphs and the first civilian scientific organization specifically designed for war was created.[19]

Bush made J. B. Conant, then President of Harvard, chairman of the NDRC and responsible for bombs and chemical warfare, of which he had experience in 1917; Karl Compton of MIT took charge of radar;

Frank Jewett, President of the Bell Telephone Laboratories, supervised communications. By the summer of 1941, with the US still to become a belligerent nation, young scientists had been recruited from the universities and were already at work on radio, radar and various kinds of weapons.[20] Unlike the British service laboratories which were funded by Whitehall departments, the NDRC had to rely on the President's executive funds. But with the expansion of research and development money was needed in large quantities which had to be approved by Congress. Accordingly a new organization called the Office of Scientific Research and Development (OSRD) was created with enhanced powers for Bush, its Director. A Committee on Medical Research was set up in the OSRD to initiate research programmes on tropical diseases, antibiotics and aviation medicine.

It was, however, the Tizard Mission of August 1940 that galvanized American war science.[21] Scientific collaboration between Britain and America had begun early in 1940. A. V. Hill, as we have seen, a member of the Tizard Committee, went to Washington to test the temperature and found much goodwill for Britain. He met Roosevelt who told him that a special scientific mission would be welcome. After some hesitation by Churchill and other ministers, Tizard, accompanied by John Cockcroft, the builder of the first British accelerator at the Cavendish and now in charge of Army radar, E. G. Bowen, the expert on airborne radar, and officers with recent battle experience, went to the States taking with them the most precious British secret equipment for short-wave radar, an anti-aircraft gun predictor and plans for a jet engine. Most of the detailed talks with the Americans were conducted by Cockcroft (who already knew many of the leading scientists) and Bowen. They soon discovered how far behind the Americans were; the latter in their turn were eager to learn from the British and lost no time in setting up at MIT the Radiation Laboratory (Radlab) under Lee DuBridge from Rochester University to develop on the highest priority short-wave radar equipment, which would then serve as models for mass production by American radio manufacturers.[22] The Radlab began with a staff of thirty physicists from the universities. By the end of the war there were 4000 people working for it. The British mission went on to Canada and made contact with the National Research Council of Canada, then coordinating scientific applications for the Canadian forces.

The Americans also learned from the British the importance of reaching an understanding with the services. Isidor Rabi, who became Associate Director of Radlab, believed the British were 'tremendous both technically and philosophically. We came to know a great deal, not because we were smarter, but because we were smart enough to listen to the British who had real operational experience.'[23] The laboratories of OSRD were not controlled by the military so that their association with the latter was on a voluntary basis from both sides. As Frederick Terman, head of the Radio Research Laboratories (responsible for radio countermeasures) at Havard, explained:

> We had complete freedom of action to develop what we thought the war needed, irrespective of whether or not the military at the time thought this was a good idea. On the other hand, the military people could turn to us to get help, and could do so on a rather informal basis because all they had to do to get our help was to persuade us that what they wanted done was really worth doing . . . This naturally placed a great deal of responsibility on the management of RRL as to how we allocated our efforts, and resulted in our being very independent. At the same time, we were able to make important decisions quickly and to act decisively once decisions were made.[24]

The British practice, on the contrary, was for scientists (especially those working on radar) to contact air or naval officers and discover how equipment worked on operations. At TRE, where prototypes of new radar equipment were developed, the so-called 'Sunday Soviets' were instituted by A. P. Rowe, the Chief Superintendent, at which senior officials from Whitehall and senior officers from the headquarters of RAF commands would join junior officers fresh from operations and scientists from other research establishments or engaged on operational research and discuss the shortcomings of equipment uninhibitedly regardless of rank.[25] At this stage foolish and impractical ideas emanating from the scientists could be eliminated. Rowe recalled his surprise when asked by his opposite number, Lee DuBridge, what percentage of TRE devices were eventually accepted by the user and being told that in the US it was 25 per cent.[26] In Britain most decisions on the adoption of new equipment were taken at an operational level. At the same time pressure was sometimes needed at the highest level, i.e. from the Prime Minister himself or from his scientific adviser, A. F. Lindemann (later Lord Cherwell).

Lindemann's family had come to England from France after the Franco-Prussian war. As a young man he studied physics at Berlin where he met some of the leading scientists of the day, including Einstein. In 1914, on the outbreak of war, his poor eyesight prevented him from enlisting in the Army, but in 1915 he was accepted by the Royal Aircraft Factory as a civilian scientist and it was there that he developed a recording accelerator for measuring stress on aeroplanes and an aerial rangefinder and gyroscopic turn indicator.[27] He learned to fly and became celebrated for diagnosing and curing the downward spin of aircraft (responsible for a number of pilots' deaths) by putting himself into a spin and getting out of it again. (In fact, his theory was already known to aerodynamicists, but he was ever reluctant to delegate or seek advice from others.)[28]

After the war he was appointed Professor of Experimental Philosophy at Oxford where he rejuvenated the Clarendon Laboratory. It was then that he became a close friend of Winston Churchill and when the latter became First Lord of the Admiralty in September 1939 (a post he had held in August 1914) Lindemann was invited to head a small statistical section presenting detailed information in such a way that it could easily be assimilated. But Lindemann's arrival at the Admiralty had wider repercussions. In a few weeks he challenged the authority of the official experts compelling them to back up their opinions by observational method, thus introducing the scientific approach which was to permeate all the services. Lindemann went to Downing Street when Churchill became Prime Minister and remained there as his personal scientific adviser throughout the war. No other British Prime Minister had brought a scientist into his confidence, though Lindemann had no official standing until appointed Paymaster General in December 1942, a post which entitled him to a seat in the War Cabinet. Lindemann was an aloof and forbidding figure and was at the centre of several controversies concerning radar and strategic bombing (see pages 23 and 109). His role was quite different from that of Bush who was simply a link between the President and the scientists, not as 'an oracle or an expert on all matters scientific'.[29]

The British did not have anything as clear-cut as the OSRD. Instead the direction of science in particular campaigns or battles took place within small War Cabinet committees dealing with night air defence, countermeasures against U-boats in the Battle of the Atlantic, artificial harbours and the German V weapons. At a lower level there were committees of civil servants, service officers and scientists who decided on priorities for research and development. One of these was the Radio Technical Committee dealing with radio and radar aids. Another was the Coordination of Valve Development Committee responsible for the development of valves for the three services. At the beginning of the war this committee established an intimate relationship with Birmingham University (the birthplace of short-wave radar), the Clarendon Laboratory, Bristol University, and with the leading British radio companies.

Consequently the latter were able to produce small numbers of new valves for development very quickly.[30] Also, unlike the American, the British sensibly made provision for a scientific reserve to take care of future radar development. Personnel had first to be found from the Central Register and, when that supply ran out, from graduates from the universities and technical colleges. By the end of the war over 50 000 men and women had been selected for scientific instruction and sent to the services, research and industry. The scheme, which was initiated by the omniscient Hankey, was supervised by the Wireless Personnel Committee.[31] When this resource began to run dry, Hankey Bursaries enabled qualified men and women to be trained in radar techniques.

It would be wrong to assume, however, that physicists were the only scientists sought by the government. Bacteriologists, biologists, chemists, crystallographers, statisticians and zoologists were drawn into work on chemical and biological warfare, explosives, the analysis of bomb damage and operational research. In some cases the newly-recruited scientists were surprised to find that some of the government laboratories were not as hidebound as they expected.

The development of an atomic bomb made further inroads on the reserve of chemists, physicists and metallurgists. Fortunately there were a number of émigrés from Germany and Austria living in England, not engaged on radar research for security reasons, who were enlisted into this novel and unpredictable enterprise. It was they who discovered not only that a uranium bomb was feasible but that a new element which they called plutonium would provide an equally devastating weapon. Without their insight, American scientists, initially unconvinced that a bomb was practicable, would never have been able to complete the Manhattan Project.

Two dissimilar figures were at the heart of the project, the engineer officer Brigadier-General Groves, an able organizer and forceful driver, and the sensitive physicist, Robert Oppenheimer, who sought the scientists and led the team of Americans and British who designed and armed the bomb on the desolate *mesa* at Los Alamos in New Mexico. It is noteworthy that Oppenheimer was convinced that the success of the project would be jeopardized by excessive militarization. He maintained that the

execution of the security and secrecy measures should be in the hands of the military, but that the decision as to what measures should be applied must be in the hands of the Laboratory ... It is the only way to assure the cooperation and the unimpaired morale of the scientists.[32]

In the event members of the scientific and engineering staff were not commissioned and put into uniform and the question of militarization was never raised by General Groves.

Reaction by Soviet scientists to invasion

Soon after the German attack on the Soviet Union in June 1941 Soviet scientists were mobilized by a Scientific Technical Council under Sergei Kaftanov, head of the government's committee on higher education. Leading scientists included Peter Kapitsa, who had been an outstanding member of Rutherford's team at the Cavendish until prevented from returning to Cambridge from a holiday in Moscow in 1935, Joffe and the physicist and chemist, Nikolai Semenov.

Joffe's institute in Leningrad was reorganized and priority given to research in which it had already been engaged: radar, armour and the demagnetizing of ships. Eventually 90–95 per cent of the physics institutes work was devoted to war purposes.[33] As the German army advanced, research institutes were evacuated to Kazan 300 miles east of Moscow. Here scientists who had been doing nuclear research began to develop acoustic apparatus for the detection of aircraft. Other scientists developed anti-tank weapons and powder fuel for the famous 'Katiusha' rocket artillery used with such effect in the great land battles.

One major success of Soviet technology was the development of the T34 (Josef Stalin) tank. Before the war Soviet tank technology was inferior to any armoured vehicle produced in the West. But when the T34 went into action in 1944 it proved to be superior to the German tanks, which in turn surpassed anything the Anglo-American forces put in the field. This was partly due to the material used in the turret which was made of forged steel with a high content of magnesium, on the suggestion of the engineer, Vassily Yernelyanov, and partly to the superior suspension, wide tracks and the high performance of the diesel engines.[34]

Nevertheless radar, missile development and jet propulsion lagged far behind that of the West. This is usually attributed to the lack of trust in science and scientists by the politicians. As noted earlier scientists had not escaped Stalin's ruthless pre-war purges. Nor were they to blame for their country's backwardness. Their proposals never received support until and unless they had been proved by western experience. During the war Kapitsa and Vladimir Ivanovich, a leading mineralogist, both members of the Commission on the Uranium Problem, had called in vain for collaboration with western scientists.[35] Six months after the end of the war Kapitsa in a remarkably frank letter to Stalin emphasized the weakness of Soviet science compared with the Americans.[36] Though Kapitsa was primarily concerned with the building of an atomic bomb, his strictures applied just as well to conventional weapons. The Soviet government reacted quickly. A new five-year plan was introduced early in 1946 stressing the importance of science. Stalin himself spoke publicly of the need to support science so that 'they will be able not only to catch up, but also to overtake in the near future the achievement of science beyond the borders of our country.' The new plan gave priority to the 'advanced technologies that had emerged from the Second World War – radar, rockets, jet propulsion and the atomic bomb'.[37] On 29 August 1949 the Soviet Union tested its first atomic bomb on the steppes of Kazakhstan.

The failure of German science to organize

The rapid mobilization of scientists by the western Allies was in stark contrast to what happened in Germany. Contrary to general belief, Germany was not short of theoretical scientists. As we have seen, a number of non-Aryan men of science fled or were expelled by the Nazis. But there were as many as 10 000 scientists in the universities and institutes of technology, including celebrated figures such as Werner Heisenberg, Otto Hahn, Hans Geiger, Max von Laue and Ludwig Prandtl, the aerodynamicist. But industrial scientists and electrical engineers *were* in short supply. In the period 1932–39 the numbers of students studying electrical engineering fell by about half and until 1943 there was a shortage of 50 000 electrical engineers.[38]

But Hitler's *Blitzkrieg* from 1940 to 1941 did not rely on scientific applications. His conquests were spearheaded by close-support aircraft and armoured columns followed up by lorry-borne infantry. Scientists were called up to serve in the armed forces and those left behind continued to work on their peacetime assignments.

Reverses on the Eastern Front in the winter of 1941–42 ended the *Blitzkrieg*. The entry of the United States into the war with her vast technological resources brought a volte-face in the Nazis' attitude towards science. But the great industrial combines that ran German war production and the need to obtain Hitler's approval for every important scientific project made it impossible for leading scientists to make their voices heard as was the case with a Tizard or a Lindemann, nor were there high level discussions on scientific aspects of the war such as strategic bombing, the U-boat campaign, long-range rockets and pilotless aircraft. Belated attempts were made to recall scientists and technicians from the front.

On 24 May 1943 Admiral Dönitz, commanding the U-boats trying to destroy the Allied cross-Atlantic convoys, broke off these attacks because of the increased use of Allied aircraft and their improved radar. (Another factor of which he was unaware was the breaking of the German code enabling aircraft and naval vessels to arrive quickly in the vicinity.) The previous day in desperation he had summoned an audience of some two to three hundred scientists.[39] After briefing them on the war situation they were asked to provide countermeasures against Allied radar. According to Walther Gerlach, a leading physicist and then in charge of physics in the RFR, this was the first and last time that the services and the scientists ever got together. After the meeting Göring appointed Wilhelm Osenberg, a mediocre scientist and friend of Himmler, on the staff of the Hannover Institute of Technology, to organize military research, decide on priorities and extricate scientists from the forces. Osenberg was able to withdraw about 4000 from one front or another but was unable to make proper use of them.[40] The most important scientific developments in fact took place in the naval and air force laboratories and commercial companies which became responsible for microwave radar.

The change from a war of conquest to a war of attrition, which Germany was ill-equipped to wage, gave rise to a frantic development of high technology weapons which, it was hoped, would weight the scales in favour of the Reich. They included a heterogeneous collection of guided missiles and jet and rocket-propelled aircraft. Broadly, but still without priority, under the direction of Albert Speer, the Minister of Armaments, and a close friend of Hitler, prototypes were built by the leading, and some of the less successful, aircraft manufacturers. But their development was too late to stop the pulverization of German industry by the Allied air forces. A final attempt, known as the Führer's Emergency Programme, to coordinate these schemes concentrating on the most suitable weapons like the surface-to-air missile *Wasserfall* was made early in 1945. By then the Allies were poised to cross the Rhine and the Red Army was driving on Berlin. Ironically, these missiles would provide prototypes for postwar development by the western Allies and the Soviet Union.

The Allies had always feared the possibility that the Germans would develop an atomic bomb and it was only when scientific intelligence teams discovered early in 1945 that the threat was non-existent that it was decided to drop atomic bombs on Japan. It was not only that the German scientists lacked the necessary equipment like accelerators and cyclotrons, or moderators for reactors such as graphite or heavy water, but the leader of the team, Heisenberg, failed to make a chain reaction. General Groves's comment on the German team may be apposite. 'Their trouble was their intense jealousy for each other and the lack of a strong head over all their efforts . . . we had our prima donnas [like Heisenberg] but we never allowed them to operate in any such independent fashion.'[41]

When the war ended Allied scientists, curious to discover why German science had made such a poor showing, interviewed some of the leading characters, including Gerlach and Osenberg. Their findings, recorded in some detail, have never been controverted. They had three main criticisms of the organization of German science.

First and foremost was the failure of the military and the scientists to collaborate. In its preparations for war the *Wehrmacht* did not appreciate that it needed the help of scientists. Nor did the scientists voluntarily make any attempt to offer any solutions to military problems. Universities and institutes of technology were in many cases untouched by the war and continued research on such unmilitary subjects as mass spectrographs and gamma and cosmic rays even as late as 1945.

Secondly, there was no direct contact between the user and the scientist. Telefunken, for example, which produced most of the radio equipment for the Army, never had an opportunity to observe its performance in the field. Speer alone occasionally permitted designers to go to the front and he encouraged officers to deal directly with the producers of their weapons.

Thirdly, there was no attempt to organize research teams on the Allied model. The Germans seemed to believe that a military problem could be subdivided into small sections, each of which could be assigned to individual scientists working in seclusion in their spare time and often with only a very vague idea of the basic problem. An American interrogator remarked: 'The card index mind may regard this as a miracle of the much-vaunted German planning and organisation; the sane man more rightly regards it as a monument of stupidity.'[42]

Much of war research was undertaken by the great corporations like Krupps which were very jealous of outside scientific activity. They would only turn to the scientists if they ran into a *cul de sac*, and even then would not reveal the broad phases of the problem. It was indeed remarkable that the Germans produced a series of weapons comparable to and not infrequently better than those of the Allies, e.g. in tanks, anti-tank weapons and jet-propelled aircraft.

Science in the other Axis powers

Whatever deficiencies Nazi Germany may have had in scientific organization, it was a long way ahead of its allies. In fascist Italy science was moribund. The genuine scientists, of whom the leader was Enrico Fermi (who fled to the USA in January 1939), had no contact with their foreign colleagues; at one major scientific congress in 1937 the younger scientists were segregated from their elders and made no contact with foreigners;[43] even the Italian language was a barrier as it was not used for international scientific papers. Much of Italian military technology was derived from German models.

In Japan the situation was similar. There were one or two physicists with an international reputation like Hidetsugu Yagi who had studied at the Cavendish and became famed for his radar aerial. As in Germany there was no collaboration with the military (even the services did not communicate with each other). Moreover, military projects of a scientific nature were shrouded in intense secrecy (chemical warfare was one of them).

2
Radar: Defence and Offence

Origins of radar

Although the principle of radar will be familiar to the general reader, it is worth summarising its advantages and limitations. Radar operates by projecting electromagnetic waves which reflect distant moving objects such as ships, aircraft or vehicles. The echo from these reflecting objects is measured by the time it takes to reach the observer who is watching for it. The immense advantage of radar is that it can 'see' through darkness, cloud or fog and targets cannot avoid detection by imposing radio silence. Accuracy in detection is improved by operating on shorter wavelengths. They may be used to scan an area to find an aircraft, the periscope of a submarine or a vehicle on the ground. Radar beams may be transmitted from static or mobile stations on the ground or from sets installed in ships or in aircraft. Radar can also provide a picture of a target area which is presented on a cathode ray tube or screen.

At the same time radar has a serious disadvantage. It is extremely susceptible to electronic countermeasures such as jamming, decoys and other deceiving or distorting ploys like 'chaff'. When radar is used as an early warning system aircraft must be able to identify themselves by transmitting a radio signal when interrogated.

The existence of electromagnetic waves was discovered by Gustav Herz in 1888, but he did not attempt to work out a practical application for them. In any case he died six years later aged only 36. The earliest attempts to use radiolocation were not intended for military purposes but to prevent collisions between ships or to provide warning of icebergs or wrecks. They began with experiments by Christian Hülsmeyer at Cologne in 1904.[1] Surprisingly, no attempt to develop radiolocation was made in the First World War; instead underwater soundwaves were investigated for locating submarines. In 1922 Marconi foresaw the possibility of detecting ships by projecting a radio beam which would be reflected back to a receiver screened from the transmitter. It was not until 1935 that the French liner *Normandie* was fitted with a continuous wave radio detector to provide warning of obstacles ahead. Alongside these experiments scientists in the late 1920s found they were able to measure the height of the ionosphere by bouncing radio waves against it and getting a return when they were reflected back.

War clouds gathering in Europe and the Far East in the mid-1930s caused information on radio research to dry up. Partly by chance, partly deliberately, military research establishments in the United States, France, Germany and the Soviet Union discovered that aircraft could be detected by radio waves up to a distance of about fifty miles. In Germany Rudolf Kühnold working for the Navy was able to detect ships at distances of four to five miles;[2] he formed the *Gesellschaft für Electroakustische und Mechanische Apparate* (GEMA) to expand his research. The great radio firm of Telefunken began to develop fire control sets for anti-aircraft artillery under the direction of Wilhelm Runge. The armed forces were sceptical. When General Ernst Udet, a well-known fighter pilot of the First World War, learned of these experiments he exclaimed that if they were successful 'flying won't be fun anymore'. In the United States it was the Navy that showed most interest and began to design fire control and early warning sets. The Soviet High Command, as already noted, wanted to provide an early warning system against surprise attack from a rearming Germany. But progress was significantly retarded by Stalin's horrific purges of 1937–38, though by 1938 a mobile army set had detected aircraft flying 60 miles away at a height of 10 000 feet.[3]

The first practical radar system

It was not in any of these countries but in Britain that radar for the first time in history was harnessed to a practical air defence system which, in company with the eight gun fighter, would in the summer of 1940 ensure Britain's survival. The unease over the vulnerability of London and major industrial centres to aerial bombardment began in November 1932 when Stanley Baldwin, the Prime Minister, made the alarming admission that 'the bomber will always get through'. Concern among those responsible for air defence came to a head after the summer air exercises of 1934 when it was all too obvious that the sound locators supposed to detect the approach of hostile aircraft were useless. (There was, in fact, one white elephant – an array of enormous concrete mirrors overlooking the Romney Marshes, pointing not across the North Sea but in the direction of France.) Several experiments vindicating the practicability of radiolocation were ignored by the Army and Navy.

At a meeting of senior RAF officers that autumn various methods of detection, including infra-red and supersonic sound waves were discussed and rejected. Tizard, then chairman of the Aeronautical Research Committee, who was present, said enigmatically as he left 'I think I know of something that can do the job.'[4]

Tizard knew from First World War days the Air Ministry's first Director of Scientific Research, H. E. Wimperis, the inventor of a useful course setting bombsight, since when he had become a Fabian and, like so many of his generation, an ardent believer in disarmament. He had, however, been been disturbed by his 36 year old assistant, A. P. Rowe, a specialist in air navigation who had joined Wimperis's staff in 1922. Rowe had a critical mind and an interest in strategy and had recently discovered that the Air Ministry files on air defence were quite inadequate. Wimperis thereupon wrote to R. A. Watson-Watt, head of the Radio Research Station at Slough, and responsible for ionospheric studies, asking whether sufficient energy could be directed in electromagnetic waves to act as a death ray. (Such a notion had been circulating in and out of science fiction for some years.) A. F. Wilkins, a colleague of Watson-Watt, quickly calculated that while a death ray was impractical, reflections of radio pulses from aircraft ought to be detectable. This was the seed from which British radar grew.

Wimperis, to his credit, wasted no time in forming the Committee for the Scientific Survey of Air Defence with Tizard as chairman, as described earlier. Watson-Watt sent a memorandum on the feasibility of the detection of aircraft by radio waves to the first meeting of the Tizard Committee held in January 1935. Experiments were ordered. No time was lost. On 26 February Watson-Watt's theory was vindicated when a metal-clad bomber flying up and down the short-wave beams of the BBC's Empire Radio station at Daventry was detected at a range of eight miles.

The introduction of British radar was due to two individuals, Watson-Watt and Tizard. It was Watson-Watt who appreciated that radar could become an indispensable weapon of air defence and he persisted in his belief. Tizard was the scientist who, because he knew and could talk to service officers, was able to convince the Air Staff that once radar had overcome its teething difficulties it would provide sufficient detail about the tracks of hostile aircraft.

Tizard made a second important practical contribution. He realized that an early warning system was no good without information being passed back to the controllers directing the fighters waiting on the ground to intercept enemy bombers. He therefore arranged that fighter pilots should practice intercepting bombers on the direction of their sector controllers by radio telephone using filtered plots from the coastal radar stations. At first the bombers flew on a prearranged course. Then, to make the exercise more realistic the bombers varied course and the fighters had to be redirected. A simple method of changing course was invented by one of the sector commanders. These trials were known as the Biggin Hill Experiments as Biggin Hill was the RAF station where the aircraft were based. They provided the basis for Fighter Command's control system during the Battle of Britain.

Erection of Chain Home

Events moved quickly after the Daventry experiment. The Tizard Committee recommended that large-scale experiments should be pursued. The Treasury gave permission to the Air Ministry to spend initially up to £12 300 on the development of radar (or Radio Direction Finding (RDF) as it was then called).[5] By 6 May 1935 a handful of scientists from Slough had set up a research station at Orfordness on the Suffolk coast under Watson-Watt who had been transferred from the DSIR to the Air Ministry. Later the team moved to Bawdsey Manor, a more commodious location overlooking the River Deben. Bawdsey became the first of 21 Chain Home (CH) stations which eventually gave radar cover to the British Isles from Orkney to the Isle of Wight. But Bawdsey was more than that. It was here that all the elements of radar were worked out, in theory if not in fact, including low-level early warning, airborne interception and identification of friend or foe as well as the need to provide countermeasures in the event of enemy jamming. Priority, of course, went to early warning of massive *daylight* attacks by enemy bombers.

Here too came the scientists who were to provide the back-up to the original small team to be indoctrinated in the new art of radar. Most were from the Cavendish Laboratory secretly recruited by Cockcroft (who was one of the least communicative of men) in the spring of 1939. One of those he approached recalled:

[We] thought it must be against air attack. We went through all the possible forms of sensing and finally decided that it would be just possible to bounce radio waves off a plane at 50 miles and detect the reflection. Having satisfied ourselves as to the general technique and its feasibility we went up to Cockcroft after dinner and asked if we were going to do what became known later as radar, and he said 'yes, something like that'.[6]

The object of the chain was to floodlight the sky under surveillance from four transmitters mounted on four 360 ft high steel towers emitting pulses at a frequency of 20–30 MHz; the echoing pulses from individual aircraft were returned to receivers mounted on four wooden towers 240 ft high. The aircraft's range was measured by the time elapsing between the transmitted pulse and the echo. Later it became possible to estimate the height and the bearing of approaching aircraft. On 13 March 1936 radar located an aircraft at 1500 ft at a distance of 75 miles.[7]

Another refinement was added after the outbreak of war when German low-flying mine-laying aircraft flew *under* the radar floodlight. A new radar called Chain Home Low (CHL) using 1½ metre waves was devised at short notice. These sets needed much smaller aerial arrays and could be mounted on a rotating turntable. They then scanned the horizon like a lighthouse beam. Mobile coastal defence radars were also developed to detect ships.

The setting up of the CH stations took time. Apart from the siting and construction of the high towers, special transmitters and high-powered valves had to be developed. This work was done in secrecy in the laboratories of Metropolitan Vickers, the well-known electrical engineering firm in Manchester. It was not until the spring of 1939 that the Chain Home was finally completed at the cost of £10 million which had secretly been allotted to it. Even then another year would pass before it had been debugged and the system practised over and over again so that it could be ready to meet the onslaught of the German Air Force.

It met the test brilliantly in the summer of 1940 enabling Fighter Command hard-pressed for pilots and aircraft to recuperate without having to put up standing patrols to await the enemy. The radar towers were very vulnerable but very hard to bomb. At that time most of the equipment was installed in huts under the towers. Those carrying the transmitters had curtains of wires strung between them extremely off-putting for a pilot to attack. Three stations were badly damaged but the gap was temporarily filled by mobile sets able to produce plots and tracks. Perhaps the Chain Home's value may best be judged by one of those who encountered it. General Galland, the fighter ace, wrote after the war:

From the first the British had an extraordinary advantage, never to be balanced at any time during the whole war, which was their radar and fighter control network and organisation. It was for us a very bitter surprise. We had nothing like it.[8]

The Tizard–Lindemann quarrel

One consequence of setting up the Chain Home was the notorious quarrel between Tizard and Lindemann originating from sometime before the war. As it had some important repercussions on the direction of British military science it should be noted here. Considering the novelty of radar in the 1930s it was hardly surprising that the Tizard Committee should encounter criticism. This came mainly from Lindemann, who had not been invited to serve on the Committee, though air defence had been on his mind for a long time. Lindemann was not, as often supposed, adverse to the development of radar. But he did question whether too much reliance was being placed upon it and whether experiments in heat detection of aircraft, in which he had a special interest and had encouraged R. V. Jones, one of his students at the Clarendon, to work on it, as well as less plausible ideas, such as barrages of balloons from which small mines were suspended by wires, should not be pursued as alternative forms of air defence in case radar did not come up to expectation. Lindemann, correctly, was anticipating the possibility of night bombing for which night fighters would need airborne radars which were then still in their infancy.

Lindemann, supported by Churchill, though not a member of the government, did join the Tizard Committee. The quarrels that followed leading to the dissolution of the Committee, only to be reformed later without Lindemann, have been thoroughly discussed and need not detain us here. What was significant was that science and politics had now become inextricably entangled. Lindemann was too aloof a person to have replaced Tizard with the latter's flair for understanding the points of view of both airmen and scientists. But because of Lindemann's friendship with Churchill, it was he and not Tizard who became the Prime Minister's personal scientific adviser. Would Tizard have done better? The Australian physicist, Mark Oliphant, who was associated with radar and atomic energy and an acute observer of both scientists, made an interesting comparison:

Tizard's eye was on strategy. The tactics had to fit the strategy and the ironmongery the tactics. Apart from the disastrous strategy of blanket bombing, which was his desperate bid for victory, Lindemann was obsessed with gadgetry and the overall strategy and tactics had to fit whatever weapons were available.[9]

But Tizard could be prickly and might have fallen foul of the Prime Minister and gone the way of other individualists like Wavell. Had he stayed his advice on strategic bombing, if accepted, would have differed from that of Lindemann and might have changed the objectives of the war in the air.

The invention of the cavity magnetron

The development of short-wave, or microwave, radar by the Allies was a key factor in the winning of the war, especially in the Battle of the Atlantic. In the short term microwave radar became more important than the atomic bomb itself. The power for short waves was generated by a device called the cavity magnetron.[10] Scientists from Herz onwards had attempted to generate short-wave radio waves but lacked the means. Herz in one of his experiments set up small loops of wire separated by a gap and found he could make sparks cross the gap with a generating coil placed a little way off. He thus demonstrated that there was a relationship between the diameter of the loop and the length of the waves coming out of the generator. After him the development of valves and circuits made possible the generation of both metric and centimetric wavelengths.

In 1921 A. W. Hull of the US General Electric Company made a simple magnetron. It was a vacuum tube operated by a magnetic field superimposed on the electrical field. With it Hull was able to produce an output of 8 kw at 30 Hz with an efficiency of 69 per cent. Similar experiments with primitive magnetrons were made about the same time by Czech and Japanese scientists. Other methods of oscillating microwaves were also devised, principally by Barkhausen and Kurz in Germany and by the Varian brothers in the States. In 1939 the latter with the help of a $100 grant from Stanford University made an instrument called the klystron (Greek for incoming waves up a beach). In it a beam of electrons was driven along a path involving holes or resonators in two tiny metallic boxes coupled together. Five years earlier the Standard Telephone Company made the first practical use of microwaves when it established a telephone link across the Channel whereby messages could be transmitted and received with a 17.6 cm carrier. Unfortunately the company refused to allow Bawdsey to experiment with it as a means of detection.

It was the British and more specifically the Admiralty which had for some time appreciated the importance of short-wave radio for warlike purposes. The Admiralty had to keep in touch with ships all over the world. At first spark transmitting sets relayed signals from one station to another; later silica transmitting valves were used. Since the Admiralty had the greatest need for a variety of valves it was agreed in the mid-1930s that the Signal School at Portsmouth should take over valve development for the three services. A development contract was placed with the General Electric Company at Wembley where magnetron development had been taking place since 1931.

The priority given to radar and the draining of the Cavendish to provide scientists for the Chain Home led the Admiralty to transfer the contract made with GEC to Birmingham University and the Clarendon. The naval scientists were inspired by the Admiralty Director of Scientific Research, Charles Wright, who predicted that the side that developed power on the shortest wavelength would win the war.

Oliphant, who had been one of Rutherford's students at the Cavendish, was in charge of the Birmingham team. After being indoctrinated into radar at one of the CH stations in the summer of 1939, he returned with his colleagues to Birmingham to find a suitable generator for microwave radar. Experiments were conducted both with the klystron and the magnetron, as it then existed, but neither were powerful enough to produce long-range echoes.

At that point John Randall, a Research Fellow from the Royal Society and Harry Boot, a young research student, both members of Oliphant's team, were asked to experiment with the Barkhausen-Kurz oscillator; they found it unsatisfactory. It then occurred to them to try to combine the resonant cavities of the klystron with the more favourable geometry of the magnetron. The proposal came from Randall who had discovered that summer in a bookshop an old translation of Herz's paper on the spark gap mentioned above. Randall calculated that if the loops of wire used by Herz in his experiment were extended cylindrically they should form resonators and if these resonators were drilled in a solid copper block and provided with openings into the anode/cathode space then the electrons should be forced through them to radiate powerful electromagnetic waves.

Randall and Boot, at the risk of incurring some unpopularity from their co-workers, set to work to build their magnetron in the best traditional methods of sealing wax and string.[11] Air was evacuated from the cylinder by a continuously-operated pump and the ends were sealed off by embedding halfpennies in a pool of sealing wax. A bulky electromagnet was used to provide the magnetic field and a loop of wire fitted in one of the cavities. After some delays due to lack of materials, on 21 February 1940, the magnetron was tested for the first time. It worked immediately. Two car headlamp bulbs connected to the power outlet were burned out. Larger lamps were connected with the same result. Only when low pressure neon bulbs were used was it possible to ascertain that a wavelength of 9.8 cm was being produced at a power of 400 watts – about one hundred times as much as the power output of the klystron.

The next stage was to reduce the size of the bulky magnet which was done in addition to other refinements by the GEC research laboratories under Eric Megaw.[12] Still lower wavelengths were obtained when, in September 1940, a scaled-down model of the original 10 cm, six-hole magnetron was functioning at 3 cm wavelength. As the first magnetrons were inclined to jump from one frequency to another, John Sayers, another member of Oliphant's team, found in September 1941 that by strapping alternate resonators together with short pieces of wire it was possible to overcome this deficiency. Oliphant had by then set up a magnetron production unit which between 1941 and 1943 manufactured about one thousand valves. Yet, surprisingly, apart from Oliphant, none of the Birmingham team was aware of the great contribution they were making to the war.

In fact, the magnetron taken across the Atlantic in August 1940 had already made a tremendous impact on the Americans. Cockcroft and Bowen carried the precious device in a wooden box to show to Alfred Loomis, a wealthy amateur scientist working for Bush on short-wave radar. After watching an aircraft being detected at a range of two miles, Cockcroft produced the magnetron and with the help of blueprints convinced the Americans that it was superior to the klystron. As already described, the Radlab was immediately formed and plans were made for the further development and production of ground and airborne microwave radars. All this was to take place in commercial or university rather than in service laboratories. On 18 November 1940 the Bell Laboratories in New York delivered the first 15 magnetrons to Radlab. They gave a power about five times as great as the American valves. Cockcroft later declared that 'our disclosures had therefore increased the power available to US technicians by a factor of 1000.'[13]

Back in England the magnetron was being adapted for operational use by the Bawdsey team, now much expanded and shortly to be known as TRE. After a number of vicissitudes it had found its way to the radar station at Worth Matravers on the cliffs of the Dorset coast. Although originally evacuated from Bawdsey at the outbreak of war because of its vulnerability to air attack it was now sixty miles from the German-occupied French coast. In charge was Rowe, the Secretary of the Tizard Committee who had succeeded Watson-Watt some time before the war. Unlike his American counterpart, Lee DuBridge, he had no knowledge of radio and occasionally was the butt for criticism from some of the physicists on his staff who were technically his superior. Nevertheless an attempt to promote him to a senior post in the Ministry of Aircraft Production was blocked in 1941 by the Secretary of State for Air, Sir Archibald Sinclair, who wrote 'There is no one who combines a knowledge of the technical side, of administration and of the operational use of the applications we have been developing to the same extent as he does.'[14] Rowe led TRE to its final destination at Malvern College under the shadow of the Malvern Hills. On the grounds were assembled the various radar antennae, prompting the observation that if the Battle of Waterloo, as the Duke of Wellington was said to have remarked, was won on the playing fields of Eton, the radar war was won on the playing fields of Malvern. TRE was, indeed, probably the most forward-looking research establishment formed in the war, though more powerful equipments were developed by Radlab with the backing of the American radio industry.

Rowe's microwave team was composed of scientists who would all eventually become Fellows of the Royal Society. They were Bernard Lovell from Manchester, a physicist who already had a book to his credit on *Science and Civilisation*, Philip Dee, a co-worker with Cockcroft at the Cavendish and recently released to his delight from working on Lindemann's futile aerial mines, Denis Skinner, a quiet and thoughtful though somewhat eccentric physicist from Bristol, and Alan Hodgkin, a Cambridge physiologist.

At first they worked in some dilapidated huts on the cliffs of Worth Matravers, later moving to roomier quarters in a school outside Swanage. Their antennae were three-feet diameter circular paraboloids with the transmitting and receiving dipoles at their foci, now a commonplace sight, but then used for the first time, producing a pencil-like beam.[15] One day in the mid-summer of 1940 it picked up an echo from a man cycling along the cliff. On 12 August reflections from an aircraft were obtained at a range of six miles. That November they tracked a surfaced submarine from their new quarters 250 ft above sea level.

Operational use of airborne radar: aircraft interception

Tizard and Lindemann had appreciated that as soon as the daylight raids had been defeated the Germans would resort to night bombing. Priority for microwave radar was therefore given to an airborne interception set. As early as 1937 Bowen had experimented with a 1½ metre airborne radar which was able to detect ships and aircraft at a range of two or three miles. He demonstrated his equipment to Air Chief Marshal Sir Hugh Dowding, Commander-in-Chief Fighter Command and to Lindemann. Dowding, among a number of useful criticisms, appreciated that a crew of two was needed (one to operate the radar), but Lindemann was unimpressed by the set's performance.[16] By the summer of 1939 Fighter Command had a few metric wave sets installed in light bomber aircraft.

The problem, as Bowen had appreciated from the start, with airborne radar was to make the apparatus small and light enough to fit into the nose of an aircraft. The task was made easier by using the great power of the magnetron, but the radar still had to be able to scan above and below and to the left and to the right of the aircraft. It was thus necessary to combine the transmission and reception aerials into one device, enabling the operator to obtain an all-round picture. The problem was solved by Hodgkin in collaboration with the GEC Research Laboratories, the Clarendon, other members of TRE, and the firm of Nash & Thompson. He invented a spiral scanner which was a 28 in paraboloid operated by a special switch spinning at 1000 rpm with an eccentricity varying by 30° in one second.[17]

At the same time other scientists devised a ground controlled interception (GCI) set; its cathode ray tube (similar to a TV set) enabled the controller of the night fighter to guide the pilot in the direction of his target.

Inevitably these developments took time so that it was not until March 1941 that the new type of night fighter – the Beaufighter – using the metric AI equipment went into action. It was able to detect aircraft four miles away and could close on its target only 600 ft away. By then the night *blitz* against British cities was well underway. However, when that battle ended in May 1941 and Hitler's bombers were switched to assist the invasion of the Soviet Union, 102 aircraft had been shot down and 172 severely damaged.

An improved centimetric AI set was made by Radlab which doubled the range of the British set.[18] It was also proof against jamming. It was called SCR 720 by the Americans and AI Mark X by the British, becoming available in the summer of 1943 and only discarded by the RAF in 1957.

Air to surface vessel (ASV) radar

But by 1941 the greatest priority for airborne radar was a set able to locate surfaced U-boats in the Atlantic. This was the battlefield where

Dönitz, the U-boat force commander, hoped to defeat the British by cutting off the supplies of food, raw materials, fuel and manufactured goods (particularly weapons) essential to wage war. But the standard 500 ton boats were vulnerable in two respects, one technical and one operational. When moving on the surface their average speed was around six to eight knots, but when submerged the batteries of the diesel electric engines had to be recharged on the surface at frequent intervals; one charge of batteries allowed a submarine to travel about 14 miles at eight knots, 28 miles at six knots and 65 miles at four knots. Thus whenever possible, U-boats spent as much time as possible on the surface both for voyaging and for making contact with their targets. Their second vulnerable point was their unrestricted use of radio. Beginning in June 1941, a critical period of the war, U-boats hunted in packs of eight to 20. When one boat spotted a ship, the others were called up by radio; they also received instructions by radio from Dönitz. Radio was the U-boats undoing. Their signals could be intercepted by the Allied codebreakers (Ultra) and convoys rerouted or the boats' positions could be located by high frequency direction finders positioned on the British coast. Furthermore as these large pack attacks could take up to twenty hours to assemble, air reinforcements could be brought to the scene. Curiously, the Germans did not seem to have understood the disadvantages of their tactics.

The war against the U-boats was waged by ships and aircraft, but it was from the latter that they had most to fear.[19] RAF Coastal Command was the most successful destroyer of U-boats, though an important contribution was made by the United States Army Air Force. Yet in 1939, astonishingly, Coastal Command had no anti-submarine role, for it was assumed that the Navy's underwater detection system would be effective. Indeed throughout the war it never had an aircraft specifically designed to operate against submarines. (In some types of aircraft the radar operator had to sit on the lid of the chemical toilet and leave it when wanted for its original purpose.) The Command was heavily dependent on scientists to enable it to fulfil its tasks.

At first aircrew had nothing but their eyes to search for targets so that the enemy had little to fear. The first air-to-surface radar (ASV I) was introduced early in 1940 and ASV II, an improved set, in October of that year but which could only detect surfaced U-boats at distances of about three and a half miles, allowing the boat to submerge on the approach of hostile aircraft.[20] U-boats had little to fear from shore-based aircraft until the spring of 1941 when Coastal Command received longer-ranged aircraft equipped with ASV II and more efficient depth charges.

But while the U-boats were able to operate against convoys in mid-North Atlantic largely immune from air attack, they were harried by shorter-ranged Coastal Command aircraft as they crossed and recrossed the transit area in the Bay of Biscay from and to their bases in western France. They were therefore forced to recharge their batteries at night when ASV II was ineffective. To overcome this deficiency, a searchlight called the Leigh Light was devised. The aircraft began its attack on radar and the searchlight was turned on just before the target disappeared into the sea clutter on the radar screen, enabling the attack to be pressed home.

In the summer of 1942 the Germans captured an ASV II set and from it developed a receiver called Metox with which a U-boat could detect ASV II. Metox was introduced in September 1942 and almost immediately reduced aircraft sighting by about 60 per cent. The answer to Metox was the new 9.1 cm ASV III (an adaptation of the centimetric bombing aid described below). With the transmitting and receiving aerials rotating continuously the operator was able to scan up to distances of 10 to 30 miles and targets could be detected at night.

Unfortunately Coastal Command did not begin to receive the new sets until the end of January 1943. This was due to the priority given to centimetric radar as a bombing aid against German targets. In addition the British were handicapped by the lack of long-range aircraft to cover the 'air gap' in the mid-North Atlantic (again because of the priority given to strategic bombing as well as by the inability to crack the German naval cipher for most of 1942 until the spring of 1943 (see pages 88–9). The U-boats were thus able to intensify their attacks against Allied convoys. The exchange rate of shipping sunk and U-boats destroyed from January to mid-April 1943 was 28 000 tons per U-boat sunk, or about 3000 tons per U-boat per month.

The availability of ASV III installed in some 40 aircraft and the provision of a few very long-range aircraft fitted with the Radlab centimetric set ASG (George) operating from Newfoundland and two long-range squadrons operating from Iceland and Northern Ireland caused the destruction of many U-boats (41 were lost in May 1943 alone).[21] These catastrophic losses forced Dönitz to call off the attacks on Atlantic convoys until a new countermeasure could be introduced. Hence the reason for him meeting the scientists described in Chapter 1. A new receiver operating on a wave length of 8–12 cm called Naxos was designed. But the first crude model mounted on a pole only arrived in October 1943 and not until April 1944 did a properly engineered set for U-boats become available. The only effective answer to microwave radar was to introduce a truly submersible boat with a *schnorkel* apparatus enabling batteries to be charged underwater. As will be seen (pages 74 and 76) it arrived too late to be a serious threat.

Airborne navigational aids and bombing aids

When it is considered that strategic bombing was supposed to be the central tenet of British air strategy between the wars, it is astonishing that so little was done to help air crews find their target. In theory a few pathfinder aircraft were supposed to illuminate the target for the main body. When, in around 1932, Rowe asked the then Wing Commander Arthur Tedder at the RAF Armament School how the leading aircraft were to find their targets, his answer was simply 'You tell me.'[22]

This negative approach combined with failure to make use of scientists by Bomber Command was only ended in the summer of 1941 when not only the War Cabinet and the Air Staff but the general public expressed disillusionment over the lack of success of night raids against Germany.

Lindemann therefore asked one of his statisticians, David Bensusan-Butt, a student of Keynes, to investigate. Butt discovered after interviewing aircrew and examining post-raid air photographs that less than one aircraft in three got within even five miles of the target. This scientific appraisal of failure issued in a report on 18 August 1941 was a turning point in the bomber offensive.[23]

Until Gee, the first radio navigational aid, was introduced in March 1941, navigation at night was based on dead reckoning. Target identification and bombing were entirely visual. But Gee's range was limited to 350 miles – too short for the most important cities in Germany to be destroyed under the policy of 'area bombing' and it could easily be jammed from the Dutch coast onwards. A self-contained bombing and navigational aid was needed. The answer was the centimetric airborne radar code-named H2S. (This is not to denigrate the great value of the bombing aids called Oboe [see page 111] and Gee H, but these had to be operated by ground stations.)

Several explanations, mainly mythological, have been given for the choice of H2S as a name. Lovell originally called it BN (Blind Navigation).[24] But it seems likely that bomber crews gave it the more memorable name of H2S – Home Sweet Home – because of its ability to home on to a target.

In December 1942 an operational requirement for H2S to be fitted in the new Halifax and Lancaster heavy bombers was made. The original requirement was that it should be able to pick up its target from a distance of 30 miles. This range later had to be halved. It was undecided whether to power the device with the klystron or the magnetron, the magnetron being too precious to lose to the Germans. While these trials were taking place at Malvern a tragic loss was experienced when a Halifax carrying scientists operating a magnetron crashed on 7 June 1942. The leader of the team was A. D. Blumlein, an outstanding scientist closely associated with the development of TV who had been seconded from Electrical & Musical Instruments (EMI).

However, the Prime Minister insisted that this setback should not reduce the pace of the programme. Despite opposition from Bomber Command which wanted the sets fitted in Sterling rather than in Lancaster bombers, and the apparent failure and consequent disillusionment with H2S in the States, 48 aircraft were fitted with the device by the end of 1942. There was, naturally, anxiety about the magnetron being discovered by the Germans when, as would inevitably happen, a H2S aircraft crashed over enemy-occupied territory. The policy for the operational use of H2S hinged on the war situation, specifically whether the Red Army could hold the line of the Volga.[25] This ruling delayed using H2S until 30/31 January 1943, coinciding with the fall of Stalingrad, when the Pathfinder Force raided Hamburg. Although not a success air crews were impressed with the new aid.

The inevitable happened on 2 February when a Sterling bomber crashed near Rotterdam and an undamaged magnetron retrieved from the wreckage. (The magnetron was virtually indestructible and could not be fitted with a detonating device.) The magnetron was examined by Telefunken and a duplicate called *Rotterdamgerät* produced.[26] (German scientists had been forbidden to work on magnetrons by Hitler.) But some months elapsed before German nightfighters were fitted with an airborne version of Naxos called Korfu (8.5 cm wavelength) and even then they had to home on to the bomber stream rather than on individual aircraft.

In the meantime development of an improved H2S set went ahead. Early results were not spectacular as the 'picture' on the set's screen was often difficult to interpret while the emissions from the set told the German nightfighters where the bombers were. But H2S scored a notable success in a heavy attack on Hamburg on the night of 23 July 1943. The configuration of the port was ideal for marking and bombing with H2S. In addition the first packets of Window (aluminium strips) were dropped to confuse the enemy ground radars (see page 57). Yet a heavy attack on Berlin on 23/24 August was a failure. The H2S screens were swamped by a mass of echoes among which it was difficult to recognize specific aiming points. Lovell therefore agreed with Bomber Command to produce six handmade sets with improved definition.[27] These were delivered to the Pathfinder Force in mid-November 1943 and were responsible for a series of heavy attacks on Berlin, Leipzig and other cities deep in Germany.

Later in the war the Americans, after operating their day bombers over Germany in daylight came to appreciate the value of H2S (the American version was called H2X).[28] Radlab had already embarked on a programme for a three centimetre set (as Randall and Boot had shown was feasible). It proved to be more powerful and gave better definition than the British equivalent. A few of the US sets were fitted in Lancasters and were found to be effective in raids on Berlin.

Development of H2S continued to the end of the war. But for most of the time its use was restricted to the Pathfinder Force for blind bombing and marking as it was considered to be too difficult to be used by the main bombing force. (It was not as reliable as Oboe which was dependent on ground stations.) At the same time it was of great value to the main force as a navigational aid, especially to find targets beyond the range of Gee. Thus while H2S did not meet the original operational requirement of each aircraft being its own pathfinder, it played a vital part in Bomber Command operations.

Seaborne centimetric radar

Although two of the leading naval scientists were at first sceptical about the value of microwave sets, the latter's ability to detect surfaced submarines at a range of four miles led to the TRE set being copied by the Signal School at Portsmouth.[29] As the naval sets would be susceptible to the motion of a ship, a new type of aerial was devised by Lovell. This was able to transmit a narrow beam in the horizontal but wide in the vertical position so that the target was not lost when the ship rolled.

Even before the first naval set was completed Captain Basil Willett, in charge of the Signal School, asked the Admiralty to place orders for components for 150 sets which were to be designated Type 271. The first trials took place in the corvette *Orchis* on 1 April 1941. While the ranges obtained were a little disappointing compared with the tests at Swanage, Type 271 promised well as an anti-submarine weapon.[30] Compared with the metric sets in use which were convenient for station keeping but no good for anti-submarine work because of the confusion of back and side echoes, Type 271's rotatable aerial and narrow horizontal beam was ideal as it was able to find, fix and hold U-boats on the surface at night. Even so, the set's efficiency was limited in rough weather; small targets were frequently obscured by waves and large waves gave rise to unwanted echoes.

That autumn the set was further improved by the introduction of the strapped magnetron. This made it possible to detect a submarine at five miles range and an aircraft ten to twelve miles away.[31] By then 23 Flower class destroyers had been fitted with Type 271s. The first U-boat kill attributed to a Type 271 was on 16 November 1941 when the corvette *Marigold* sunk U-433 in the Straits of Gibraltar. Contact was made at two miles range and the U-boat destroyed by depth charges.

Earlier that year radar had played a significant part in the sinking of the *Bismarck* on 27 May. Both sides made extensive use of radar. A Type 284 set (50 cm wavelength) carried by the cruiser *Suffolk* shadowed the German battleship at a range of 13 miles causing Vice-Admiral Gunther Lütjens, commander of the force, to report back to base after breaking contact and shortly before his ship was finally sunk under him, that 'the presence of radar on enemy vessels has a strong adverse effect on operations in the Atlantic. Ships were located in thick fog and could never again break contact.'[32]

Radar also proved useful in the protection of Russian-bound convoys in the Barents Sea. In December 1943 a Type 273 set (also operating on 10 cm wavelength) enabled the British cruisers to detect two pocket battleships and to make a surprise attack on one of them. According to the report made by the Commander-in-Chief Home Fleet 'the outcome of the engagement might have been very different had [radar] not been available or if it had been jammed. No useful results were obtained from optical rangefinders.'[33]

Centimetric radar for anti-aircraft artillery

Compared with the development of microwave radar to defeat the U-boats and to improve blind bombing techniques, making anti-aircraft guns more accurate against fast-flying, evasive aircraft was placed on a much lower priority. All that was available for the Battle of Britain and the night *Blitz* were rather primitive metric radars.

After the invention of the magnetron, a 10 cm set known as Gun Layer (GL) Mark III intended for the Army was delivered to the Air Defence Research Establishment, then under Cockcroft, in June 1941 for trials. But slow progress was made partly because modifications were needed for overseas service. From the start Cockcroft was insistent that the set should be able to follow a target automatically, thereby increasing speed and accuracy and making the gun crews' task easier.[34] Although this set continued to be developed, lack of trained manpower and manufacturing resources led the War Office to commission an alternative set from the Canadians. Both these sets were to be manually operated.

It soon became clear, however, that a much better equipment was being developed by Radlab. As in the case of H2S it was the work of a small team, principally Louis Ridenour from the University of Pennsylvania and Ivan Getting, an electrical engineer from MIT.[35] Again like Lovell's and Dee's device they used a parabolic dish with an antenna near the centre emitting a narrow cone-like beam of microwaves. But, unlike the British, they fitted the set with an automatic following apparatus which realigned the radar with the moving target. Such a system could plot an aircraft's elevation and azimuth, though at first range could not be determined. The purpose of the radar was to track targets with at least ten times greater accuracy to within ten yards compared with other radars.

Ridenour and Getting now designed extremely precise circuitry able to measure intervals of less than 100 millionths of a second. To achieve this work had begun early in 1941 and by that spring a prototype code-named XT-1 had been fitted to a truck with the radar dish mounted on a servo-driven platform adapted from an aircraft machine gun turret. The first automatic tracking of an aircraft took place on 31 May 1941 with a telescope attached to the mount to enable observers to see where the radar was pointing. Even when an aircraft disappeared behind a cloud it continued to be tracked, and the aircraft would emerge moments later held in the centre of the telescope.

To complement the radar an electronic gun predictor was developed at the Bell Laboratories by David Parkinson, one of the engineers. This project, known as the M9 Predictor, had originally been intended for existing radars or optical sights. But after Pearl Harbor the two teams collaborated, the M9 being adapted to operate in conjunction with the radar. Automatic rangefinding was added to azimuth and elevation and the information fed to the servomotors. The apparatus was in effect an electronic analogue computer. The combined tracking radar and gun predictor was tested by the US Army in April 1942 and dummy targets towed by aircraft were destroyed without visual contact using as few as eight rounds. A thousand sets were ordered and the radar was renamed SCR 584.

It was one of Radlab's principal successes, though difficulties were experienced in finding a suitable manufacturer to design and build a pedestal mount so that sets did not begin to enter service until July 1943. The SCR 584 went into action at the Anzio landings in January 1944, but it came into its own in the battle against the flying bombs directed against London that summer.

This was engineered by Cockcroft who had earlier appreciated the superiority of the SCR 584 to the British GL Mark III.[36] It was an unusual example where circumvention of the authorities for once paid off. Cockcroft obtained a set from the Americans on Lend-Lease arrangements but without permission from the War Office. Tests with this set using a British electrical predictor made by British Thomson-Houston (BTH) confirmed Cockcroft's predilection and he persuaded the earlier irritated and now reluctant authorities to order a few sets.

Luckily Cockcroft had learned in October 1943 of the possibility of attacks on Britain by pilotless aircraft. He appreciated that they would present an almost ideal target as they would fly at a constant speed and in a straight line. After a visit to Bush in Washington he recommended that the War Office should order at least one hundred sets. Thus when the flying bomb attacks began two weeks after D-day the SCR 584, the M9 predictor as well as a proximity fuse for shells (to be described in Chapter 3) were at hand and proved to be the only equipments capable of tracking the new enemy weapons especially in foggy weather. As a matter of extreme urgency 165 SCR 584s were ordered from the States in addition to the 134 sets demanded earlier in the year. These arrived in the nick of time for the defence of Antwerp when attacked by flying bombs at the outset of the German counter-attack in the Ardennes.

Effect of German radar on the war

So far German radar has only been mentioned in passing. As indicated earlier German scientists were pioneers in the field of radiolocation. However, unlike the Allies the German services, as we have seen, kept specialists at arm's length; their policy was to issue specifications arbitrarily and leave the scientists and engineers to fulfil them. In fact, compared with Allied equipment German radar was more like a scientific instrument in stability and precision of performance. Martin Ryle, a member of British air intelligence and later an Astronomer Royal, recalled that he was usually able to distinguish between British and German radar transmissions simply by the latter's stability.

There were two major ground radar systems used throughout the war. The *Freya* early warning set, comparable to the CH, was developed by GEMA before the war for the Navy.[37] As it operated on a shorter wavelength (2.40 metres) than CH it was mobile and only needed a small aerial which could be rotated in the direction of the target. Instead of a separate receiving aerial the set was fitted with a novel electronic direction finder which provided the target's bearing. It had a maximum range of 75 miles. Its value was proved early in the war. On 18 December 1939 the *Freya* installed on the island of Wangerooge was responsible for German fighters shooting down 12 Wellingtons of Bomber Command, half the force, in daylight when they attacked shipping off Wilhelmshaven. Henceforward Bomber Command would operate mainly at night.

The *Würzburg*, introduced in 1940, had a parabolic dish similar to the SCR 584; it was rotatable like *Freya* and could be pivoted up and down to point directly at the target, providing the measurement of an aircraft's height with some accuracy. It was used to control both the fire of anti-aircraft guns and searchlights. It had a wavelength of 5.3 metres and picked up targets at distances from 15 to 20 miles.[38] As the Allied bomber offensive intensified a *Giant Würzburg* was designed by Ludwig Dürr, the Zeppelin engineer. He modelled his paraboloids on the aluminium rings used in the construction of a rigid airship. This equipment gave extra accuracy in bringing night fighters to within striking distance of their targets.

But however efficient these systems were, they were handicapped by the lack of a comprehensive ground control system to convey information from the radars, through the control rooms to the fighters in the air. All this had to be improvised in the course of the war. Three officers in particular should be mentioned: General Wolfgang Martini, Director General of Signals for the German Air Force since before the war when he was engaged in studying radio echoes from the ionosphere, Colonel Wolfgang Falck, organizer of the night fighters defences, and General Josef Kammhuber, a dynamic leader who organized what the British (though not the Germans) named the Kammhuber Line – an intricate arrangement of radars, guns, searchlights and control centres stretching down the western frontier of Germany. Thanks to the sagacious deductions of Allied air intelligence it became possible to devise countermeasures against these formidable defences. But the Germans for their part riposted with counter countermeasures so instituting what would become radio countermeasures or electronic warfare which will be discussed in Chapter 3.

The Germans were rather slower than the British in developing airborne interception by radar. At first pilots, supported by Göring who retorted 'a fighter isn't a movie show', tended to look askance at the new-fangled equipment in their machines. The most important set was called *Lichtenstein* (60 cm wavelength) which had quite a large external aerial array.[39] After the British had introduced their jamming device called Window, *Lichtenstein* was fitted with SN2 operating on 3.7 metres wavelength which was proof against jamming. With it, the ace night fighter pilot, Major Helmut Lent, claimed to have shot down 104 Allied bombers. He himself was killed in action in October 1944.

Radar was introduced into the German Navy early in the war for early warning and for controlling gunfire. The first was *Seetakt* used as a rangefinder on German battleships. Evidence of *Seetakt* came to the attention of the British when the *Graf Spee* was examined by a member of the Bawdsey team just after she was scuttled off Montevideo.[40] Despite this discovery no attempt was made to jam transmissions of *Seetakt* which was being used to direct the fire of German long range guns across the Straits of Dover. It was only in February 1941 that the British accepted that the Germans were indeed using radar.[41]

But the greatest shock was experienced by the Germans when they discovered that the British were using microwaves. Until then German scientific orthodoxy was sceptical of their value and no priority had been given to the production of transmitting valves necessary for microwaves. In contrast to the Allied teams of scientists who were free to handle their own affairs, the German technical staffs were frightened of being proved wrong and being exposed to ridicule. As the historian of Radlab pointed out, there was 'no place where the *Führerprinzip* was less applicable than in the research laboratory'.[42]

However, once in possession of the *Rotterdamgerät* events moved quickly. Abraham Esau, a pioneer of short waves and also a Party member, was taken off Heisenberg's nuclear project in January 1944 and put in charge of microwave development. By then a magnetron had been fitted to a *Würzburg* providing a range of 18 miles and the first hand-held Naxos receiver for U-boats and *Naxos Z* for night fighters were in service. *Naxos Z* replaced the SN2 and could also be used in Pathfinder aircraft. Under the direction of Esau a number of centimetric equipments were planned for aircraft, ships and anti-aircraft guns, but the war ended before they could be put to use.

3
Diverse Applications of Radio and Radar

The proximity fuse

So far we have discussed solving the problem of *detecting* hostile aircraft and other targets. Equally important was how to hit such a small target as an aircraft flying at high speed and taking evasive action. Until 1939 there were two ways of attaining accuracy of aim; firstly, by using a predictor which mechanically calculated the right moment for the gun to fire and, secondly, a fuse in the shell timed to burst when the target was in the zone of flying fragments. Even the best anti-aircraft gun could only bring down one plane for every 2500 rounds.

Much thought had been expended on trying to improve predictors using the goniometric system which calculated the ground speed and angle of course of the target.[1] In Britain the Royal Navy evolved the High Angle Control System while the Army depended on a similar predictor for its heavy anti-aircraft guns. Far better was the tachometric system employed by the US Navy whereby using a speedometer the vertical or lateral angular velocity multiplied by the time of flight could be calculated. However, when the British Army accepted the Bofors light anti-aircraft gun, it also used the tachometric system thanks to the initiative of a scientifically-minded officer, Colonel A. V. Kerrison, responsible for liaising with the Admiralty Research Laboratory (ARL) who devised a portable electrical predictor operating in conjunction with the gun.

At the same time a few scientists believed that by using an influence fuse the shell would be made to explode on receiving an indication of the target thus saving an immense expenditure of rounds. Experiments were made with photoelectric cells sighting the target from a short distance,

39

and by acoustic and infra red operated fuses. But none of these systems offered promising results at that time.

In Britain there were two scientists who began thinking about a radio-operated fuse towards the end of 1939. One was Harry Cobden Turner, Managing Director of Salford Electrical Instruments. Apart from his scientific interests, he had served for many years as a Salford town councillor alleviating the plight of the unemployed and he was also deeply concerned about the lack of technical means to meet the threat from Nazi Germany. During a visit to Berlin with his chief development engineer, G. M. Tomlin, shortly before the war, he learned from a friend, Hans Mayer of Siemens, that the Germans were experimenting with influence fuses.[2] Speculating on how they might work on the way home, the two hit on the idea of a radio-operated proximity fuse. Their proposal, as it later emerged, was to detonate a bomb. A high frequency oscillator tightly coupled to an aerial-tuned circuit from which signals would be transmitted and received from the target causing a change in the oscillator anode current and so operating the detonator. They described this effect as a change in 'aerial impedance'. On 8 May 1940 they submitted their proposal to RAE.

(It is worth explaining at this point that Hans Mayer was the anonymous author of the Oslo Report sent to the British naval attaché in Oslo shortly after the outbreak of war and which in due course was put on the desk of R. V. Jones, Director of Scientific Intelligence at the Air Ministry.[3] It contained a wealth of information on radio, radar and rockets and also revealed the existence of Peenemünde as a military research establishment.)

The second scientist who had an idea about proximity fuses was William Butement, a versatile Australian physicist who had, as early as 1931, worked out an idea for radar on his own initiative while serving with the Signal Experimental Establishment at Woolwich, but which unfortunately failed to attract any interest from the authorities. Several years later he found himself at Bawdsey where he developed a split beam radar system for detecting targets at sea. He now had two ideas for an influence fuse.[4] The most promising required a short wave radio beam to be directed at the target, the frequency being varied continually over a narrow range. A projectile approaching an aircraft would receive two different frequencies, one direct from the ground and one reflected from the plane. The difference between these frequencies would become smaller and smaller as the projectile came nearer to the plane, producing beats which when they reached a predetermined figure would activate the fuse 100 ft from the target.

His idea depended on miniature valves rugged enough to survive being fired from a gun. A batch of these had already been received from two American companies and were tested at Shoeburyness at the end of 1939. Many of the valves emerged intact after being accelerated to 20 000 g.

After the unhappy Norwegian campaign in the spring of 1940 the need to improve the accuracy of anti-aircraft guns became urgent. For the first time British forces were subjected to the intimidating dive bombing attacks by the GAF, especially those directed against ships. Although losses of ships due to bombing were not excessive, anti-aircraft gunfire failed to deter attacks even though some ships expended as much as 40 per cent of their ammunition.

Butement was therefore instructed to go ahead with his radio fuse. He then had second thoughts after discussion with two of his colleagues, E. S. Shire, a physicist from the Cavendish and A. F. H. Thomson, another War Office scientist. They realized that a more powerful effect could be obtained through a change in current for their circuit on the Doppler principle where no modulation was necessary. Furthermore they would use the projectile as an aerial with the radio fuse inside. An insulating ring would excite the outer surface. As Butement wrote later 'No one had ever put radio apparatus *inside* its own aerial before!'

During the summer of 1940 tests were made with prototypes of Butement's fuse culminating in the successful detonation of rockets fired at a glider encased in aluminium simulating the reflecting properties of an aircraft. At the same time, unknown to Butement, independent tests were made with the Salford fuse after being examined by Cockcroft and Blackett, then working at RAE. Although told by Cockcroft shortly before he left for the States on the Tizard mission that his fuse was superfluous, Cobden Turner persisted and that autumn the Salford team's work was taken over by a small team from RAE evacuated to Exeter University.[5] Improvements were made principally by embodying the aerial in the tail and body of the bomb (similar to Butement's fuse). Subsequently Bomber Command dropped a few proximity-fused bombs on targets in Germany and Italy but the results indicated that they were not worth pursuing. Work on the bomb fuse was suspended on 19 May 1943 for this reason as well as for technical and manufacturing shortcomings.

Information and drawings of both the Butement and the Salford fuses were taken to the States by the Tizard mission. On 19 September 1940 Cockcroft visited his old friend, the physicist Merle Tuve, who was in charge of experimental work on fuses in the NRDC, and lent him details of the Butement fuse.[6] Tuve made copies and within a few days was able to demonstrate the fuse using a breadboard circuit. This was the signal for the development and production of radio proximity fuses in the States. The programme rivalled the effort put into radar. As the British electrical industry was stretched to the utmost the Americans agreed to supply fuses to their Allies.

At first development concentrated on fuses for bombs, rockets and mortars. A team under Alexander H. Ellett of the University of Iowa began work at the National Bureau of Standards, Washington. After studying the Salford fuse at Exeter, they decided to adopt the Butement fuse as it had greater power. Valuable assistance was provided by Andrew Stratton, one of the RAE scientists who designed a new circuit for which he was awarded the US Medal for Freedom. But the bombs did not come into service until the very end of the war and were used sparingly but effectively by US aircraft over Japan and Italy. The principal targets were anti-aircraft gun positions which lay beneath the path of the bombers.

After the disaster to the US Fleet at Pearl Harbor and the sinking of the *Prince of Wales* and *Repulse* by Japanese torpedo bombers off the Malayan coast top priority was given to the shell fuse being developed by Tuve's team at the Department of Terrestial Magnetism of the Carnegie Institution in Washington. Ironically Butement's design introduced by Cockcroft was apparently later superseded by the Salford fuse with some modifications. Eventually the Americans evolved their own fuse which they claimed to be superior to the Salford fuse; it was designated the Mark XXXIII circuit. But before these experiments had progressed far, miniature valves and oscillators had to be tested for ruggedness by being fired through guns as the Americans, unlike the British, had not yet done this. By May 1941 Tuve had achieved a basic design for a shell fuse separating the components into an oscillator and amplifier circuit, battery, safety device and detonator. All this, it must be appreciated, was done years before the introduction of microelectronics.

And this was only the beginning of the programme. Batteries had to be developed also able to withstand being fired from a gun; they also had to survive a reasonably long shelf life (especially important in the tropics). The provision of reliable safety was yet another task which the scientists had to fulfil. By the spring of 1942 the work required of Tuve's section had become so extensive that it became necessary to expand into the laboratories of Johns Hopkins University, eventually employing a staff of over 700.

At last the time came for the first trials of the fuse. After many prematures and duds successful tests took place in the late summer of 1941 and a contract with the Crosley Corporation for full scale production of a pilot model was placed in November 1941. In April 1942 shells hit a plane suspended from a balloon. When reliable safety devices were installed it was possible to test the proximity-fused shells under active service conditions. They took place on the cruiser *Cleveland* in Chesapeake Bay on 10 and 11 August 1942; radio-controlled target planes were shot down with the minimum number of shells. Stocks of the new shells were rushed at once to the Pacific Fleet and on 5 January 1943 the *Helena* using the new fuse shot down the first Japanese plane, the pilot thinking he was safely out of range of anti-aircraft fire.

The great capacity and resources of the American electrical industry now became manifest. Production of valves in the States before the war amounted to 600 000 a day. By the end of the war one company alone (Sylvania) was producing a total of over 400 000 a day in 23 different plants. Other companies were making rugged batteries. Some two million fuses were manufactured each month. All the work had to be done in great secrecy. Only the top management in the key companies were given basic information.

Security was also an important factor in deciding when the proximity fuse could be fired in support of land operations for it was always possible that the Germans would recover a dud and duplicate it for use against the Allies as they did with the magnetron. For the time being therefore the Combined Chiefs of Staff ruled that the fuses must only be fired over water where there was no chance of them being recovered. Proximity fuses thus played an important part in defending the US Fleet against the Japanese Air Force, especially in the final stages of the war when kamikaze or suicide attacks were launched against warships.

Meanwhile in Britain the Admiralty had been observing American progress in the development of the fuse. Probably concerned about the time needed to make the fuse operational and the Royal Navy still without adequate air defence (apart, of course, from radar-controlled guns) it somewhat belatedly decided not to rely on the American fuses and instead launch a crash programme for British firms to turn out fuses for naval guns.[7] But the need for development to start afresh, to design miniature valves and batteries, not to mention the lack of technical staff who could be 'counted in twos and threes' made it probable that production would not begin for at least two years. So the scheme had to be postponed until after the war.

Quite unexpectedly it was not the Navy but the Army that needed the fuses in anticipation of attacks by flying bombs. As we have seen,

Cockcroft had asked the Americans to send over SCR 584 radars to Britain. At the same time he discussed with Tuve the possibility of converting the American naval fuses to British shells to be used in the 3.7 in medium anti-aircraft gun to meet the flying bomb threat. Tuve agreed and the necessary arrangements were put in motion by the British scientific liaison office in Washington. On his return to London Cockcroft found the War Office unresponsive and he had to approach General Sir Frederick Pile, commanding Anti-Aircraft Command, not only an exponent of mechanized warfare but also an officer responsive to science.[8] Pile put the matter before the Chief of the Imperial General Staff, Sir Alan Brooke. On 16 January 1944 a request was made for 150 000 American proximity fuses (later increased to 640 000) for the British 3.7 in anti-aircraft guns, the backbone of the ground air defences. As the shells had to be fitted with special RDX explosive in Canada, they only arrived in England in late August/early September at the height of the flying bomb battle and after it had been decided to move the anti-aircraft guns away from London nearer the coast.

Immediately the rate of destruction of missiles went up from 24 per cent of the targets engaged in the first week the proximity fuse (in conjunction with the SCR 584 radar and the M9 predictor) was used to 79 per cent in the fourth week by which time the flying bomb launching sites were overrun by the British and Canadian armies. Like the SCR 584 the proximity fuse was used to defend Brussels and Antwerp against flying bomb attacks; Antwerp being an important port suffered especially from the missiles discharged from within Germany.

Laconically, Cockcroft wrote after the war 'Tuve undertook to develop fuses for the British 3.7 in AA shell. The undertaking was faithfully carried out.' General Pile added another tribute: 'American scientists together with American production methods, and above all American generosity, gave us the final answer to the flying bomb.'[9]

The Combined Chiefs of Staff finally agreed to release the new fuse for field artillery in Europe on 24 October 1944. The actual date of release coincided with the start of the German counter-offensive in the Ardennes. Proximity fuses set to burst 30 ft above the ground were used by American gunners to stem the German advance. But postwar investigation indicated that the claims for success were greatly exaggerated, though air bursts were fired often with murderous effect in the later stages of the war.

Despite their experiments with influence fuses (principally capacitive) begun by the Germans before 1939 they never succeeded in making a practical fuse for artillery shells though a few small bombs armed with capacitance fuses were dropped on an RAF base in the Shetland Isles in November 1939. Research on an influence fuse for guided missiles, probably employing an infra-red activator (a field in which the Germans were more advanced than the Allies) was conducted at Munster but never came into use.

When the British Chiefs of Staff assessed the value of the proximity fuse after the war, they concluded that it was a 'permanent and notable advance in artillery technique that no modern defence force can do without'.[10] It provided a remarkable increase in the effectiveness of anti-aircraft gunfire while air burst bombardment was as devastating as ground burst shooting in field artillery. Nevertheless, like all radio equipment, it was vulnerable to jamming and also, at that time, to certain atmospheric conditions such as mist and rain.

The importance of radio

Radar, being such an innovation, has overshadowed the achievements of radio for communications and radio countermeasures in the Second World War. The value of radio communications at sea, on land and in the air had, of course, been recognized by 1918 and had stimulated further development in the postwar years. By the end of the 1920s new materials were being used such as quartz crystals for stabilizing transmissions and aluminium die casting (a German innovation) in the design of electrical circuits; these were used for the construction of medium and high frequency radio sets. The Germans had also begun to investigate the use of ceramic techniques for stabilizing frequencies which in the war, when crystals became unavailable, replaced them. These technical advances were quickly assimilated and exploited by a burgeoning radio industry in Europe and North America catering primarily for the popular demand for radio receivers. Ham radio enthusiasts also stimulated the radio industry and when war came provided a valuable reservoir of technicians for the services.

Until 1939 the Germans were probably foremost in exploiting radio for war. Their strategy of the offensive relied on inter-communicating armoured vehicles on the ground, radio navigational aids in the air to guide bombers to their targets, while at sea U-boat packs were controlled from a land-based headquarters. In Göring's four-year plan for self sufficiency radio production ranked as a high priority, first for the GAF, with the Navy and Army following. Radios had to be simply made and easy to maintain for war.[11] The FUG10 designed by Lorenz for the GAF was based on modules easy to service and parts could be quickly changed by semi-skilled operators. When Allied experts examined the German radio industry after the war they discovered how much it had been handicapped by lack of raw materials. With the exception of the GAF which had priority in the use of aluminium until late in the war, the other services had to put up with zinc substitutes. Compared with the Allies, German technicians displayed less initiative and originality and consequently fell behind in high frequency radio communications.

In Britain in the mid-1930s it was the RAF which above all needed short-wave radio communications to exploit the advantage conferred by the new radar early warning system. After the Biggin Hill experiments high frequency (HF) and very high frequency (VHF) sets were needed for the new generation of fighters – Hurricanes and Spitfires. Their development was in the hands of the Radio Department of RAE. But until 1937 research on high frequency techniques was desultory; relations with the radio industry as well as with Whitehall were at a low ebb.

This unsatisfactory state of affairs was transformed by Squadron Leader (later Air Commodore) Hugh Leedham who arrived at Farnborough to take charge of radio development at the instance of Watson-Watt, Director of Communications Development at the Air Ministry after leaving Bawdsey.[12] A group of about 40 young but experienced engineers and scientists under A. C. Bartlett from the GEC Research Laboratory (a father figure, never without his smouldering pipe but well aware of all that was going on) was brought in to develop a VHF set. Working outside the perimeter of the Establishment, they were virtually autonomous (like Bawdsey) and less vulnerable to interference from the regular staff. RAF radios had hitherto been HF. VHF was superior. In peacetime it was less subject to interference from other transmissions. In war it was less susceptible to being jammed by enemy transmitters. It was able to accommodate more channels essential if Fighter Command was to expand.

Work began on a practical VHF set in 1937. As the possibility of war became more likely the Air Staff asked for 16 squadrons and eight controlling sectors to be equipped with VHF by September 1939. Two airborne transmitter/receiver sets were designed to operate on a wave band of 2.5–3.0 m. They were designated TR1133 and TR1433; the latter set was intended to incorporate improvements but in the event did not come into service until 1943 because of production difficulties due to the expansion of Fighter Command. The ground transmitter (TR1131) was designed by Robert Cockburn who had been experimenting with the properties of electronic valves at very high frequencies at Birkbeck College, London University.

The first trials with VHF took place on 30 September 1939, a few weeks after the declaration of war. The Director of Signals reported to the Chief of the Air Staff that 'There can be no doubt that even Mark I VHF opens up a completely new chapter of radio telephone communication.'[13] Production now concentrated on the airborne transmitter/receiver (TR1133). However, such was the urgency to equip at least a handful of fighter squadrons that they were provided with handmade sets. The first ground–air operational system was installed at Biggin Hill and by the early summer of 1940 the south-eastern sector of Fighter Command was sufficiently well equipped to inflict heavy losses on enemy daylight bombers. The new ground-to-air link permitting efficient deployment of the available fighter aircraft was a critical factor in the tactics ensuring the success of Fighter Command.

VHF sets were also provided to the Fleet Air Arm and to the Royal Navy for communication with Coastal Command. The Americans recognized at an early stage that the British VHF system was superior to anything available in the States. In 1942 an early prototype was sent across the Atlantic where the basic scheme was copied, only details being modified to suit American requirement.

Two factors contributed to the success of airborne VHF radio communications; first, the scientists appreciated the potentialities of a new technique rather than merely responding to a statement of operational requirements from service officers (not unlike the birth of radar); secondly, the scientists enjoyed throughout the support of the Air Staff, though the latter had to suffer their impatience when, as the possibility of war became acute, they began to consider buying ready-made foreign equipment.

High frequency direction finding

While important advances were made in inter-ship communication, the tactics of the Fleet had changed since 1914–18 and emphasis was now placed on improving VHF communication between ships and aircraft. However, one important contribution was made by British naval engineers and scientists – the development of a high frequency direction finding (HF DF) set for detecting the position of U-boats. By 1939 the introduction of radar on board ships would seem to have made shipborne HF DF superfluous for detecting enemy vessels.[14] But during the late summer of 1940 it became apparent that U-boats in the North Atlantic were being controlled by radio transmissions from their headquarters ashore. A renewed effort was therefore made to install HF DF on the escorts of convoys.

Direction finding was the responsibility of a small team of scientists under Christopher Crampton in the Admiralty Signals Establishment (ASE). An indispensable part of it was a party of Polish engineers led by W. Struszynski, formerly the head of the Polish State Communications Establishment.[15] Although shore-based HF DF stations dotted round the coasts of the British Isles were able to provide the approximate position of a U-boat by means of cross bearings, much greater accuracy could be obtained by shipborne HF DF. This was, however, as Crampton wrote, 'the most difficult technical problem in the whole field of naval directional wireless.'[16]

The first problem was finding the best place on a ship to mount the aerial where it would not be obstructed by other masts, funnels, cranes or other impedimenta. Eventually the aerial was attached to a short pole mast sited aft. Next the HF DF set had to pick up enemy signals which necessarily were transmitted as quickly as possible. Signals from the first set called FH3 were received *aurally* (the operator wearing headphones); results were, more often than not, disappointing. It then occurred to S. de Walden, one of the Polish engineers, that a set which provided *visual* signals would be much better than intercepting rapid transmissions aurally. He therefore adapted a cathode ray tube direction-finder similar to that used by Watson-Watt for his prewar ionospheric studies.[17] This was incorporated in the FH4 and proved to be more effective than its predecessor when first used in action by HMS *Leamington* in March 1942.

Another difficulty was obtaining the range of a U-boat, for the likelihood of two escorts being in the same area to make cross-bearings was rare. This problem was fortuitously solved when U-570 (later renamed HM Submarine *Graph*) was captured intact by a Hudson of Coastal Command on 27 August 1941. The strength of its radio transmissions was measured enabling a figure for the range to be determined. This was usually around 15 to 20 miles. As will be seen later (page 76) more technical information was acquired from this submarine.

The adoption of pack tactics by the U-boats took British naval intelligence by surprise but, unlike their Air Force counterparts, relations with scientists were distant. Crampton declared after the war that shipborne HF DF could have been introduced earlier had he and his group been kept in the strategical picture.[18] As it was, U-boat radio transmissions only began to be intercepted by convoy-escorting vessels in August 1941 enabling the ships to take evasive action. By the end of 1942, however, 180 vessels had been equipped with HF DF. As the number of escorts increased and their fire power became more effective, U-boats when detected could be pursued, attacks being pressed home with the help of radar and asdic detectors. Escort carriers were also fitted with HF DF enabling their aircraft to hunt and attack U-boats.

By now the naval scientists had become *persona grata* with naval intelligence and were provided with up to date information. When, after the severe losses to U-boats in 1943, the Germans were found to be developing a system of flash radio telegraphy called *Kurier* the scientists were at once told and were able to evolve a countermeasure.[19] *Kurier* (called Squash by the Allies) could transmit a seven letter message plus an introductory signal in about one-third of a second. Adapting the cathode ray detector, Struszynski and an English colleague, G. J. Phillips, found they could record a message photographically, rapid though it was. This system was ready when *Kurier* became operational towards the end of 1944.

Why did the Germans never suspect that the Allies were intercepting U-boat radio transmissions? It appears that they never believed that radio interceptions at sea were possible and they failed to appreciate that even a rough bearing on a U-boat was potentially valuable to a convoy escort. Fundamentally there was, in addition, a psychological reason. HF radio control was at the heart of U-boat tactics so that, unlike a radar countermeasure, such as Metox, a radical change in the conduct of U-boat operations would have been unacceptable.

HF DF was complemented by Ultra which, with its intimate knowledge of German radio procedure, could help the DF operators. At the same time HF DF plots could be acted on immediately without waiting for decryption. Moreover between February and December 1942 the Germans introduced a new naval code temporarily neutering Ultra. HF DF was then the only means whereby U-boat positions could be discovered. Shore-based HF DF stations were able to provided a more comprehensive picture of U-boat dispositions than HF DF afloat which was valuable both to convoys and their escorts. Recent research by German historians indicates that the U-boat defeat in 1943 was due as much to HF DF as to radar.[20]

The American benefited from British HF DF techniques and in September 1943 two US Navy ships were equipped with FH3. Such was their success that the US Navy 'encouraged further development and use of this device and by early 1945 its efficiency was comparable with the Royal Navy in plotting and bearing analysis'.[21]

Direction finding was also employed by the Allied armies. It was especially valuable in the Western Desert where 'Rommel was as likely to be east of you as west and it was extremely useful to know which. In Europe, the armies were either in contact or groping in a fog, neither of them transmitting. The gains were not so dramatic.'[22] In contrast to the Navy, some Army signallers found that optical methods of detection were inferior to aural systems, the ear being a better integrator of amplitudes over a few seconds than the eye.

Army communications

Wireless, as it was then known, had no opportunity to influence the land battle in the First World War. Reliance was placed on line communications which were at least difficult to tap by the enemy. In the early 1930s the principles of mobile warfare were being resuscitated by prophets like Fuller and Liddell Hart against opposition from senior officers who still believed that there was a role for the horse in modern war. The possibility of tanks acting as cavalry was introduced in a series of exercises on Salisbury Plain from 1931. The commander of this mobile force concluded in his report that 'radio telephony was essential to efficient manoeuvre.' Further progress in inter-tank communication was made three years later when Brigadier P. C. S. (later Major-General Sir Percy) Hobart, a fervent believer in radio control of armoured formations, took command of the 1st Tank Brigade insisting that all officers must learn how to use radio. Hobart, although not a trained mechanical engineer, was quick to grasp technicalities and together with Butement of the Signals Experimental Establishment devised a system for ensuring automatically that all transmitters and receivers in a given system were tuned to the chosen frequency.[23]

Two useful sets were evolved by Butement – the No. 9 and No. 11. Experimenting with the No. 9 in March 1937, Butement in a stationary tank demonstrated that two-way radio communication with an aircraft was possible and deduced that while moving, a range of 26 miles could be obtained.[24] In the No. 11 set good speech signals of even strength were obtainable while on the move for as long as signals could be received; there was no need to use piezocrystals except in special cases.

These developments were digested by German army observers and especially by Colonel (later General) Heinz Guderian, a signals officer and a protagonist of mobile armoured warfare who, like Hobart, had to overcome the prejudice against tanks from his colleagues, principally on the grounds that they were vulnerable to anti-tank weapons. Luckily for the Germans, they had no obsolescent equipment to scrap before building their *panzer* force and they had the support of Hitler even though he placed tanks below aircraft in priority for his rearmament programme.

In contrast to the Germans, the British did not follow through radio development for the Army after their promising start. Prototype specifications were too rigid and were followed by a lengthy period of development. The progress of the No. 19 set, the most useful wartime tank radio by Pye, spurred on by its thrusting chairman, C. O. Stanley, came into service more quickly than the Signals Experimental Establishment prototype. The Pye set was lighter than the Army model being made with pressed steel plate so avoiding using the light alloys reserved for RAF radios.

Only after the spectacular German victories in Europe in 1940 did the US Army consider creating an armoured corps. But once the decision was taken, an ambitious tank programme was launched ably fulfilled by the motor car manufacturers. Complementary to this a series of tank radios were developed by the US Signal Corps General Development Laboratories in collaboration with the Bell Telephone Laboratories and Western Electric.

In the autumn of 1940 the future of the US Army radio communications was discussed and the important decision taken to concentrate on frequency modulation (FM) rather than amplitude modulated (AM) sets.[25] The advantage of FM was, firstly, that there were plenty of channels available for a large amount of radio traffic within a radius of 100 miles (a typical battlefield scenario) for which the 1.20 Mc/s band was essential; secondly, enemy jamming was made more difficult; and, thirdly, background noise and static interference was to a large extent eliminated, making long-distance communication easier. One of these sets – the SCR 508 – designed for armoured warfare and amphibious operations took no more than seven months to develop and put into production. VHF FM sets designated AN/TRCs (colloquially known as Antracs) because they were largely immune to interference were used extensively in north-west Europe and the Pacific; they were especially valuable when General Patton made his rapid advance across France into Germany. A hundred mile system of two terminals and three relay stations could be installed in two days by 44 men whereas a land line employing a very large force of signallers took 10 days.

Although FM sets were successfully demonstrated in field tests, neither the RAF nor the British Army asked for them despite their advantages over amplitude modulation, particularly in their immunity to electrical noise. Only after the war were Antracs employed by the Army.[26] It is worth noting that the German tanks in North Africa used FM sets for communication and the British found them very difficult to jam.

Another important scientific advance was the introduction of microwave radio sets for army communications. The first (again designed by Butement) was the eight channel No. 10 set which accompanied Montgomery's advanced headquarters throughout the north-west European campaign.[27] With it he could speak to any unit in his Army Group and also hold discussions with Eisenhower, Churchill and the Chief of the Imperial General Staff, Field Marshal Sir Alan Brooke, in London. A comparable set (AN/TRC-6) went into action with the US Army in the final stages of the European war.

The birth of electronic warfare

Radar and radio, as has already been stressed, are vulnerable to jamming and other forms of interference. The more applications are introduced, the more the enemy will seek to undermine them by one countermeasure or another. This has given rise to a new form of warfare – electronic warfare.

In February 1938 the CSSAD asked Bawdsey whether signals from the new radar transmitters could be jammed. The subsequent discussion and experiments made by the Research Station made it clear that jamming was indeed possible at ranges of around 80 miles, If this was so, Chain Home could be jammed from an enemy-occupied French coastline, while should a war develop in the Mediterranean with Italy as the enemy, radar stations protecting the vital port of Malta could likewise be jammed from Sicily. Although Rowe minuted the file containing this discussion 'The worst crime we can commit is to ignore the importance of jamming'[28] nothing was done to plan a scheme for radio countermeasures (RCM) should the need arise. This may well have been an 'unconscious but deliberate mental avoidance of an unpalatable thought' for it would have bound to have sown doubts about the efficacy of radar which was then being offered as the best possible solution to the need for early warning of hostile aircraft. Indeed exposing the vulnerability of radar might have caused the Air Staff to be less enthusiastic about its introduction. It is noteworthy, too, that RCM did not appear on the agenda of the Tizard mission to the States.

That RCM were of great importance was brought home to the Air Staff in the fateful summer of 1940 when Scientific Intelligence (under R. V. Jones who had already got into trouble for suggesting the vulnerability of radar) with the help of Ultra discovered that the Germans were planning to use an intersecting radio beam system for bombing England; it was called *Knickebein*. The great men of science like Lindemann and Tizard did not believe that beams could be used for radio navigation because short waves would not bend round the curvature of the earth. How Jones convinced scientists, senior RAF signals officers and the Prime Minister that his theory was correct has been graphically told by him.[29] Apparatus for jamming *Knickebein* was immediately set up. At first medical diathermy sets were installed at a number of police station followed by high-powered transmitters installed on radar towers and designed to act as jammers (a countermeasure called Aspirin). Before long an RAF jamming organisation (No. 80 Group) was formed which made *Knickebein* (to the disgust of the Germans) useless for target indication.

A more sophisticated device than *Knickebein* called *X Gerät* was quickly introduced. But again the British retaliated with correspondingly effective countermeasures.[30] At the beginning of 1941 the Germans found it necessary to bring in a third system called *Wotan* but named *Benito* (after Hitler's partner) by the British. Like the other German radio navigational aids at that time it made use of continuous waves instead of pulses. This time instead of blanketing the enemy's transmissions so as to be unrecognisable, the signals were re-radiated back to their source so confusing the pilots who believed their bombing errors were due to the stupidity of the ground operators while the ground operators attributed the mistakes to the incompetence of the pilots. Strangely enough, it happened that the new British countermeasure went into action on the same night as *Wotan* was being used on the full operational scale.

So long as the Germans had the capacity to bomb Britain it was impossible to launch RCM in support of offensive air operations. But after Hitler's invasion of the Soviet Union became bogged down in the winter of 1941 and the GAF was unlikely to return to the attack in the west RCM could be used for new purposes. During the Battle of the Beams the purpose of RCM were to exploit German radio transmissions causing the enemy, at least for a while, to be unaware that his radio system had been made unreliable. A corollary to this countermeasure was the spoof operation in which false information was fed to the enemy. When Fighter Command began its cross-Channel sweeps after the Battle of Britain it was sometimes necessary to cause a diversion and draw enemy interceptors away from the main scene of action. A small force of aircraft was therefore equipped with receivers able to receive pulses from the German radars and return them with longer beating echoes to make it appear as if a whole formation of aircraft were present.[31] Known as Moonshine, the countermeasure met with some success. On one occasion it unintentionally diverted German fighters from intercepting one of the early daylight raids of the VIIIth US Army Air Force.

Long before this, however, an aggressive type of RCM had been initiated by Royal Naval scientists. Towards the end of 1940 German coastal batteries covering the Straits of Dover with the help of fire control radars were sinking ships attempting a night passage. A TV engineer from

Marconi, using a monitor receiver, quickly detected transmission from a *Seetakt* radar. Appropriate jammers were developed and made ready for action by February 1941.[32] Even though the Germans retaliated, requiring the naval scientists to seek new countermeasures, henceforward there were comparatively small losses to shipping sailing through the Straits. The climax of the jamming operations took place on D-Day, 6 June 1944, when a convoy sailed through the Straits *en route* to Normandy in *broad daylight* after the enemy radar installations had been totally jammed.[33]

Nevertheless the radio war did not begin in earnest until 12 February 1942 when the Germans mounted the first large-scale jamming operation to cover the escape of the battleships *Scharnhorst* and *Gneisenau* from Brest. At first undetected, they slipped through the Channel to their base in Germany virtually unscathed. Strangely enough the jamming, which began some days before the escape rising to a crescendo, did not arouse suspicion although Brest had been kept under constant surveillance from the air in anticipation of a break-out. But the effect on British radar was so far reaching that in the long run the escape of the battleships was of the greatest advantage to the conduct of the war.

An investigation was quickly put in hand by TRE and on 3 March Robert Cockburn, the radio expert who had been transferred from RAE after completing his work on VHF radio for Fighter Command, submitted an important report on the problems involved in conducting a fluid radio war. He proposed that anti-jamming measures should be accompanied by active measures against the enemy's radar and radio facilities. Cockburn's classic report established the conception of RCM as an essential requirement and laid down the principles on which electronic warfare was in future to be based.[34]

As far as the RAF was concerned RCM were devoted primarily to reducing bomber losses in the strategic air offensive against Germany which was about to gain momentum under a new commander, Sir Arthur Harris. What were Bomber Command losses at that time? An investigation made by Bomber Command Operational Research Section in May 1942 estimated that losses to bombers (operating at night) amounted to about 4 per cent of sorties despatched of which 25 per cent were due to enemy fighters, 25 per cent to anti-aircraft fire and 20 per cent to causes other than enemy action.[35] A further study made towards the end of that year concluded that non-enemy action losses were about 10 per cent of total losses while the remaining 90 per cent appeared to be equally divided between fighters and anti-aircraft gunfire. As the

German airborne radar improved in 1943–44 losses due to fighters increased compared to those caused by gunfire. Thus the aim of RCM was to deny to the enemy radar installations the information which they sought and to prevent the passing of information by means of radio. In addition, during 1943, radar search apparatus was fitted into bombers in order to provide crews with warning of imminent hostile action against them, and into night fighters used for bomber support. H2S, the bombing and navigational aid, also had an effect on the defence of bombers since it assisted in maintaining the high concentration of bombers in space and time which was found to be a powerful tactical countermeasure against the enemy defences. But it, too, could be used by the enemy to home onto the aircraft carrying it.

An important step towards formulating appropriate RCM against radar-controlled anti-aircraft guns was the capture of a Würzburg radar by a combined commando and paratroop raid on Bruneval on the French coast on 27 February 1942. Among other information it was discovered that the set could tune over a wide range of frequencies.[36]

Ever since the end of 1940 Bomber Command crews had been practising an at first unauthorized kind of RCM by leaving their IFF sets on while flying to targets in Germany; they claimed their action caused the dowsing or falling away of enemy searchlights. This provoked a dispute between R. V. Jones and the scientists of the ORS.[37] The former insisted that the enemy might deliberately encourage the switching on of Identification Friend or Foe (IFF) for ends of his own and that the use of IFF must be restrained. At first insufficient evidence was found to support Jones's argument and in September 1942 the current IFF set was modified to interfere with radiation from the Würzburg receiver. Bomber Command ORS justified this controversial decision on the grounds that in the radio war it was necessary to act quickly on judgments unsupported by inadequate evidence. But the J Switch, as it was called, proved to be too dangerous and was abandoned, as were several modifications of this apparatus. Indeed, in support of Jones's contention German scientists after the war recalled how astonished they were at the liberal amount of radio emissions made by British bombers *en route* to their targets and thus exposing themselves to the attention of fighters or guns in the vicinity.

A probably more effective RCM was Mandrel, an airborne noise jammer designed by TRE to cover the frequency band of the *Freyas*. It came into use in December 1942[38] and seemed to compel frequency changes in the German radar. Then Mandrel-carrying aircraft began to suffer higher casualties than other bombers. As it was very difficult to find out whether Mandrel had any effect on enemy radar transmissions or whether it was merely helping the enemy to locate bombers, it continued to be used and a Mandrel squadron was formed which operated on the eve of the Normandy landings against the *Freyas* on the French coast. But it was withdrawn from service as soon as the *SN2* airborne radar was introduced in July 1942.

Introduction of Window

As yet no effective way had been found of jamming the *Würzburg* radar, especially the *Giant Würzburg* used for ground-controlled interception. We have seen how the parabola of the *Giant Würzburg* had a high angular discrimination. This meant that it could only be disturbed by jammers located in the direction it was looking. The only way to jam it would be by numerous airborne jammers.

The answer was a simple one and lay not in an electrical device but in a number of aircraft dropping large quantities of strips of metal foil or dipoles cut to such a length that they would resonate at the wavelength of the radar to be jammed so producing in that radar a large number of spurious echoes. The idea was not novel for it had been suggested by Jones in March 1938, but it was then heresy to suggest that radar might have an 'Achilles heel'. Jones also told Lindemann who, as described earlier, had some reservations about radar.[39] Nothing was done, however, until early 1941 when Lindemann asked TRE to conduct trials with aircraft sowing a field of spurious reflectors. TRE gave this radar countermeasure the code name of Window (the Americans called it Chaff by which name it is known today). In September 1941 Bomber Command ORS asked for Window to be considered to help reduce the mounting losses of aircraft in the bombing offensive against Germany. Jones himself had again drawn attention to its value in a report describing measures for jamming German radar in January 1942.

But, like airborne microwave radar and the proximity fuse, Window could equally be used to the enemy's advantage. A lengthy debate between scientists and service officers now took place extending over a year and a half on the pros and cons of introducing Window. Lord Cherwell, as Lindemann had now become with a seat in the Cabinet as Paymaster-General, had changed his views and opposed Window influenced by Derek Jackson, another former student of his, a distinguished spectroscopist, but now in uniform as Chief Airborne Radar Officer of Fighter Command, after serving a period as an AI operator in a night fighter. His Commander-in-Chief was naturally concerned about the possibility of the enemy paralysing the British radar system with its own version of Window.[40] The Air Staff called for a series of trials to take place to test ground and airborne radar against the new device. It was found that Window could indeed jam the German radar defences if used in sufficient quantities. If the Germans *did* retaliate, it was believed that the American microwave SCR 584 would be able to function in spite of Window. Another anxiety was that the production of quantities of Window would make serious inroads on the nation's supply of aluminium.

At last on 2 April 1943 the Chief of the Air Staff, Sir Charles Portal, held a meeting to decide on the operational introduction of Window. Dr B. G. Dickins, in charge of Bomber Command ORS, recommended to Sir Arthur Harris, who was among the senior officers present, that there was a good possibility of saving 'one third of our losses by using this countermeasure'.[41] However, agreement still could not be reached and a further meeting was convened to allay fears that German Window would swamp the British radars. This argument was clinched when Sir Trafford Leigh-Mallory, Commander-in-Chief of Fighter Command, declared that it was more important to reduce the casualties of Bomber Command. The argument about the excessive consumption of aluminium was settled when Dickins explained that a bomber contained about ten tons of aluminium so that the saving of one or two bombers a night by Window would leave the nation's supply unimpaired. The Prime Minister now gave the order 'Open the Window!'

Window was first used in the devastating raid on Hamburg on the night of 24 July 1943. Post-raid analysis revealed that the enemy defences were completely confused and unable to distinguish Window echoes from true aircraft echoes. After further Window-supported raids the saving of bombers brought about by the use of Window 'assessed by comparison with previous experience on similar targets was estimated as a reduction of rather more than one third, a fraction in agreement with the forecast made by Bomber Command ORS in November 1942'.[42] Window was also found to be efficacious against both *Lichtenstein* and *SN2*, a special type of Window being manufactured to counteract the latter.

As was to have been expected the Germans had also considered using Window (known to them as *Düppel*) but had firmly rejected the idea. They were surprised that the British had not employed it earlier. Now that it had been released they used *Düppel* in a small bombing offensive against London in December 1943. British radar using centimetric wavelengths functioned well in spite of this countermeasure.

By 1943, however, Bomber Command was losing more aircraft to fighters than to anti-aircraft guns. This led to the introduction of jammers to disrupt HF and VHF communications between the ground controllers and the night fighter pilots.[43] The first called Tinsel was able to interfere with the HF bands used by the controllers. The Germans were thus compelled to increase the power of their ground transmitters. This move was in turn countered by concentrating a number of Tinsel transmitters on each German high power radio station.

As the bomber offensive became more intense counter-countermeasure succeeded countermeasure. A new device incorporating a cathode ray tube called Airborne Cigar was able to jam German VHF fighter communications. When the German controllers were forced to use medium and high frequency broadcasts to fighter pilots instead of communicating with each one individually, Dartboard and Jostle were introduced to jam these frequencies.

In order to provide warning of German night fighters Bomber Command fitted aircraft with several tail warning devices, one called Boozer (a passive receiver) and Monica (an active receiver) which picked up radio pulses from aircraft in the vicinity and produced clicking noises in the pilot's headphones. It was replaced by a visual apparatus with a cathode ray tube. Monica was rendered useless by the introduction of a German receiver called Flensburg able to home on to it from a distance of 50 miles. Monica was abandoned from 12 September 1944.

By then the German early warning system along the Channel had been overrun by the Allied armies advancing to the Rhine. It was thus all the more important to prevent the exploitation of Allied bomber transmission for long-range plotting by the enemy. Restrictions had to be placed on the use of H2S sets which hitherto had been switched on long before reaching enemy-occupied territory and used for navigation. Centimetric AI was able to home on to H2S. But H2S was far too valuable an aid to be cast aside. A solution was found by making use of Gee sets transmitting from ground stations set up in France and Belgium and switching on H2S in time to provide a good fix before running out of range provided by Gee. After the introduction of these new tactics there appeared to be no sign that Bomber Command casualties were increasing.

In addition to the various warning devices carried by individual bombers, RCM operations were carried out by No. 100 Group (originally No. 80 Group). These aircraft flew spoof operations involving the dropping of Window away from the main force. The long-range Mosquito night fighter (one of the most versatile aircraft of the war) equipped with AI provided 'teeth' to these diversionary attacks.

The apotheosis of Bomber Command's spoof operations was undoubtedly the simulation of an Allied assault force on 6/7 June 1944 approaching the Pas de Calais while the real force sailed towards the Normandy beaches.[44] The Navy provided a force of small craft towing barrage balloons fitted with jammers and radar reflectors. Nos 617 and 218 Squadrons flew above them executing controlled orbits and dropping clouds of Window thereby increasing the size of the seaborne force to look like a large convoy. This remarkable deception contributed to the surprise achieved by the real landings.[45]

Parallel with the growth of British RCM the American Radio Research Laboratory at Harvard had been building up its own activities under Terman. On a British suggestion, a branch of the RRL was set up at Malvern across the road from TRE. Some of the special equipments developed by RRL, such as very powerful valves, were allocated to the British to assist their jamming operations. The RRL designed an airborne jammer called Carpet to cripple the small *Würzburgs*. Carpet sets were installed in bombers of the VIIIth US Army Air Force in the summer of 1943 and were used for the first time in a daylight raid on Bremen in October 1943. To the anger of the Germans their anti-Carpet devices made them more vulnerable to Window while the anti-Window devices made them more vulnerable to Carpet. It was believed that RCM saved the American bomber force based in England alone 450 aircraft and 4500 casualties.

4
Acoustic and Underwater Warfare

Introduction of a submarine detector

Mines, torpedoes and submarines were in the possession of the navies of the great powers before the end of the 19th century. Mines and torpedoes proved their value in the Russo-Japanese war of 1904–5. But weapons that threatened the existence of the battleship were regarded with suspicion by conventional naval officers, especially the submarine which, in the words of a British naval officer, was regarded as a weapon 'unfair, underhand, and damned unEnglish'.[1] Yet it was the German Navy's submarine arm of little more than one hundred boats that nearly brought about Britain's collapse in April 1917 by sinking almost a million tons of shipping in that month alone. The belated introduction of the convoy system ensured the safety of Britain's lines of communication for the remainder of the war. But weapons for the detection and destruction of the submarine were much more difficult to implement.

Unlike radio, there were few non-military applications for which the study of underwater sound (apart from the detection of icebergs) was necessary. Very little theoretical work had been done, apart from Rayleigh's *Theory of Sound* published in 1887. Yet three years earlier the French scientist and Pierre Curie and his brother Jacques discovered that when crystals such as quartz and Rochelle salt were subjected to stress they produced a small electric charge which varied with the pressure applied. They called this reaction piezo-electricity after the Greek word meaning 'to press', Conversely, when a rapidly changing electric potential was applied to such a crystal it would begin to vibrate violently.

This discovery was first applied to underwater acoustics by the physicist Paul Langevin, a friend both of the Curie family and of Rutherford and his circle of advanced physicists at Manchester, when he began work in 1915 on an ultrasonic echo-ranging system for the French Navy to enable it to detect enemy submarines. Early in 1918, after prolonged experiments, Langevin had devised an instrument, similar to an oscillator, called a transducer incorporating a transmitter and receiver; it was made of thin slices of quartz sandwiched between steel plates looking like a box with one of the steel faces in the water. Langevin took advantage of the advanced state of French valve technology; using an eight valve amplifier he was able, with his earphones, to obtain echoes from a submerged submarine at ranges of between 600 and 1000 yards.[2]

Langevin passed on the results of his research to British naval scientists. They constructed a similar apparatus at the Admiralty Experimental Station at Harwich and obtained echoes from a submarine in March 1918.[3] To preserve its secrecy, this echo-ranging system was called asdics after the initials of the Anti-Submarine Division (*ics* being added at the end). A few sets were fitted in a destroyer and some small craft but the war ended before they could be tested in action. American naval scientists were also working on devices for submarine detection but preferred to use Rochelle salt crystals instead of quartz.[4] Oddly enough the French, despite their pioneering experiments, abandoned work on submarine detection after 1918.

Interwar research on anti-submarine detection

In spite of drastic cuts in British defence expenditure after the war and two attempts by the politicians supported by pro-battleship naval officers to ban submarines as weapons of war at the Washington Conference in 1921 and the London Naval Conference in 1930, research on asdics continued due to the persistence of officers in the Anti-Submarine Warfare Division who remembered the threat posed by the U-boat in 1917. Research and development took place at HMS *Osprey*, a shore establishment at Portland, the naval base on the Dorset coast which housed the Anti-Submarine School commanded by a captain RN. The scientific team was led by B. S. Smith, an electrical engineer then aged 40. The principal members were A. E. H. Pew, the chief designer, N. Shuttleworth, in charge of the asdic section, who was later succeeded by J. Anderson who also became responsible for sea trials. Some of the fundamental research was provided by the Admiralty Research Laboratory (ARL) at Teddington.

Unfortunately Smith's team, unlike the radar scientists in the Air Ministry, was closely supervised by naval officers and was unable to conduct theoretical research beyond that directly related to tactical

problems. On one occasion Smith incurred the displeasure of his immediate superior when he complained in a report that there was

> little opportunity for systematic research on the fundamental condi-
> tions that control the asdic method of detection...very little is
> known of the causes of reverberations, attenuation, inconsistency and
> non-submarine echoes. As these phenomena are peculiar to under-
> water acoustics very little assistance can be obtained from outside
> sources.[5]

In the row that followed Smith (admittedly neither an easy man nor an
efficient administrator) was to some extent exonerated by the Director
of Scientific Research at the Admiralty. While an official investigation
acknowledged that asdics were still in an experimental stage it did
nothing to define the responsibilities of the naval and civilian staffs.
Scientists were never allowed to attend important meetings at the
Admiralty but had to be content with briefing the Captain Anti-
Submarines and his Experimental Commander. This was to have
serious repercussions in the war to come.

Nevertheless during the period 1927 to 1934 two important contributions to asdic technology were made by Smith's team. The first was the
streamlined retractable steel dome housing the transducer which was
installed in the keel of the submarine hunting vessel.[6] It became the
standard equipment in the Royal Navy until the end of the Second
World War. Although at first its design was considered to be mainly an
engineering problem, a great deal of theoretical and practical work had
to be done to improve its acoustic properties. One important trial was
carried out by the cruiser *Devonshire* with Anderson aboard conducting
observations from a separate dome underwater often with the ship
steaming at speeds up to 30 knots. He found that the asdic dome should
be sited as far forward as possible on the centre line where it would not
be affected by streams of aerated water.

The second innovation was the electrochemical range recorder. Hitherto ranges had to be determined by calculating the interval from the
moment of the transmission of the beam to the reception of the echo.[7]
This instrument was based on the Fultograph used in the early days
of the transmission of pictures by radio. It consisted of a roll of starch
potassium iodide paper which is discoloured each time a current runs
through it. In this way a picture could be built up. The track of the submarine in relation to the ship was automatically drawn and from it the
correct time to release the depth charges or fire a projectile could be

accurately obtained. Asdics now became an efficient submarine hunter, the device becoming especially valuable when ahead-throwing weapons were introduced. For the time being, however, the depth charge was the weapon used in conjunction with the asdic. When a submarine was detected the hunting vessel sailed directly towards the target releasing its depth charges from the stern when over the suspected area.

By 1939 *Osprey* had provided the Navy with a number of workable asdics suitable for destroyers, trawlers and other small craft while defensive, or passive, sets were fitted in cruisers and other large warships like aircraft carriers. The most advanced set was the Type 127 with a retractable streamlined dome designed for destroyers while the Type 129 set was designed for submarines and used both for detection and as a listening aid similar to the hydrophone.[8] In all these cases asdics operated on the same basic principles. A sound beam, like a searchlight beam, was produced and an echo from the target received by a piston type quartz steel transducer operating at a predetermined ultrasonic frequency. Its maximum range under favourable conditions was 2500 yards but this was rarely achieved. But during the Second World War as the equipment was improved and experience gained submerged submarines could be detected at ranges up to about 2000 yards.[9] Asdics were naturally extremely susceptible to rough weather conditions and, equally importantly, to variations in sea water. However, the science of oceanography at that time was hardly understood.

The Royal Navy was then probably more technically advanced in submarine detection than other navies. The US Navy's experiments had been carried out on similar lines with the exception that it had developed magnetostriction* transducers as an alternative to quartz. (The British had also worked on magnetostriction but had decided to stick to quartz transducers on the grounds of expense and lack of trained manpower.) At the outset of the war most American warships and submarines were fitted with the QC set which had the transducer housed in a spherical container mounted on one side of the vessel. It had a range of 3000 yards.[10]

The German Navy was, unsurprisingly, well aware of the existence of asdics but as it had embarked on a submarine construction programme in 1933 (albeit on a small scale) in defiance of the Treaty of Versailles, it was not concerned with developing *anti*-submarine weapons. Two

---

* A phenomenon in which magnetization of a ferromagnetic material such as nickel produces a small change in its linear dimensions, or conversely an enforced change of length develops a change in its state of magnetization.

years later the Germans signed a treaty with the British restricting their naval construction to no more than 45 per cent of the British submarine tonnage. The Admiralty approved this surprising concession to German naval power on the grounds, firstly, that it did not believe that the Germans would launch another unrestricted U-boat campaign but instead would rely on powerful surface raiders like the pocket battleships *Deutschland* and *Admiral Graf von Spee* to prey on merchant shipping. Secondly, it believed that asdics would defeat any submarine offensive, forgetting that in the First World War most of the U-boat attacks were made on the surface and under cover of darkness. But asdics and depth charges were only effective against *submerged* submarines; moreover, the British anti-submarine force had neither been equipped nor trained in night tactics.[11] Clearly this was a serious misjudgement by the Admiralty of future naval strategy.

Dönitz appreciated that since asdics presented a serious threat to submerged submarines he should train his force to make surface attacks, at the same time taking advantage of modern long range radio communications to control every U-boat from his land-based headquarters. The Germans did, however, work on passive listening devices to give U-boats information about merchant ships, although it was appreciated that electrical emissions from the submarines might well be intercepted by the enemy. Their naval scientists at Kiel developed a group listening apparatus which was installed on the sides of the pocket battleships and proved to be extremely effective.[12] U-boats were also equipped with groups of receivers. Active echo-ranging gear began to be developed after the Anglo-German Agreement of 1935. Unlike the British and American sets, the Germans did not have a range recorder or a streamlined dome for the transducer and echoes were displayed on a cathode ray oscillator. Their attack set was inferior to the British equipment and it was only later in the war that comparable sets began to be developed, but they never got beyond the experimental stage.

Lack of adequate British anti-submarine warfare techniques

So confident were the British in the efficacy of asdics at the outbreak of war in September 1939 that even Lindemann, not usually given to making optimistic statements, declared that:

> Investigations carried out with every resource of science, and with the whole prestige and drive of the Royal Navy behind them, have to a great extent debunked the submarine. The instrument which threatened

to bring us to ruin in 1917 is now regarded as comparatively innocuous provided we have an adequate number of smaller craft properly fitted out with appliances and weapons to cope with them.[13]

Yet in June 1941, when the U-boat campaign had really got underway, R. H. Fowler, Professor of Mathematical Physics at Cambridge and a colleague of Rutherford, reported that *Osprey*, which had been evacuated to Fairlie on the Clyde because of its vulnerability to air attack or raiding parties from across the Channel, had become obsessed with the improvement of asdic gear to the detriment of research on *offensive* anti-submarine weapons. There was therefore, as we shall see, a pressing need for an ahead-throwing weapon working in conjunction with asdic as an effective alternative to the stern-released depth charge. Fowler went on to criticize the lack of fundamental research on underwater sound, the lack of which Smith had complained about to the Admiralty 12 years earlier.[14]

Investigations into the other Admiralty scientific establishments revealed that there was a lack of cooperation between naval officers with sea experience and the scientists ashore. New weapons like the homing torpedo were being neglected, as Lindemann had observed shortly after becoming scientific adviser to Churchill, then First Lord of the Admiralty. In the resulting enquiry the Director of Torpedoes and Mines advised the Controller of the Navy, responsible for armaments, that he was not in favour of the homing torpedo (admittedly a complex weapon) and did not recommend research on it. To which the Controller responded: 'We have previously said that the acoustic mine is of little value, but now we are finding it is a torment. Do let us try something new.'[15]

Strengthening of science at the Admiralty

In fact, apart from the development of radar at *Vernon* very little was being done to devise new weapons. But in the early summer of 1941 shipping losses were averaging about 400 000 tons per month mainly due to U-boats which had begun to operate from the Biscay ports in July 1940. These sinkings and the lengthy turn round of ships at ports and the time wasted at repair yards due to air raid warnings were having a drastic effect of Britain's food supplies. For example, in mid December 1940 UK stocks were only:

Wheat:	enough for 15 weeks;
Meat:	two weeks only (ration of one shilling a week per person);
Butter:	eight weeks (on ration);

Margarine: three weeks (on ration);
Bacon: 27 weeks (on ration);
Imported
   fruit: finished.[16]

On 30 May 1941 an Admiralty Advisory Panel was set up to improve the application of science. The principal members were Sir Edward Appleton, the chairman, who had made important contributions to the study of the ionosphere and who had recently been a member of the Tizard Committee, Ralph Fowler, Charles Wright, the Director of Scientific Research at the Admiralty, and his deputy, Frederick Brundrett, an expert on short-wave radio. One of the Committee's most valuable achievements was the introduction of Blackett to the Admiralty.[17] He was then in charge of the Operational Research Section at Coastal Command and it was suggested that he should be brought into the Admiralty to introduce methods used in operational research. This proposal was strongly supported by Captain George Creasy, the Director of Anti-Submarine Warfare. Blackett arrived at the Admiralty on 31 December 1941 and assumed the title of Chief Adviser on Operational Research responsible to the Assistant Chief of Naval Staff (Weapons) and the Controller of the Navy.

A small group of scientists was selected to support him covering anti-submarine warfare, signals and gunnery. Edward Bullard, another Cavendish physicist who had turned to specialising in geophysics, had joined the RNVR before the war and had recently built up a team to counteract German magnetic mines, became Blackett's deputy. This group was to make a number of valuable contributions to the conduct of naval operations which will be described in Chapter 6.

At the outset of the war the Admiralty had made provision for an additional 40 scientists; by the end of the war nearly 4000 were engaged in one capacity or another. A number of them, mainly from the RNVR, were recruited into a new organisation called the Directorate of Miscellaneous Weapons Development. Its founder and deputy director was Charles Goodeve, a Canadian physical chemist. Like Bullard, he had been working on countermeasures to the magnetic mine (see below) and then had been asked by Vice-Admiral James Somerville, another officer appreciative of science, who had been appointed Inspector of Anti-Aircraft Weapons and Devices, to recruit a team to work on unorthodox weapons.

DMWD was a quasi-scientific body, more familiarly known as the 'wheezers and dodgers', or the 'electrical gentlemen' in which physicists rubbed shoulders with engineers and a handful of somewhat eccentric inventors. Their disrespect of convention did not always work to their advantage; they were set up as a temporary wartime department and their independence meant that they had no links with those responsible for naval production and inspection and therefore they had no control over the fate of their designs once these had left the Department. One of their most important contributions was the ahead-thrown weapon called Hedgehog which, as will be seen, was dogged by interminable teething difficulties which not only delayed its introduction into the Fleet but continued to plague its operators for sometime afterwards.[18]

While DMWD got underway other civilian scientists from the universities were sent to provide fresh blood for *Vernon*, the Admiralty Research Laboratory and the Mine Design Department.

In the meantime something was done to rectify Wright's complaint of a 'failure to appreciate the place which scientists and engineers hold in matters of defence.'[19] The answer was to create a new post called the Assistant Controller, Research and Development. His main purpose was to coordinate research and development to ensure that scientific opinion was adequately represented and all due weight given to it. Goodeve was chosen to fill the post in October 1942 and he held it successfully until the end of the war.

Performance of asdics in the Battle of the Atlantic

Neither the German U-boat arm nor the Royal Navy were ready at the outbreak of war either to wage an all-out offensive against shipping or to conduct anti-submarine warfare. Dönitz had no more than 30 U-boats capable of extended seagoing operations. The British had only about 140 destroyers of varying age, some 20 anti-submarine trawlers and about 30 patrol craft. They were reinforced by the new corvettes and the 50 aging US destroyers fitted with asdics by April 1941, after an agreement between Churchill and Roosevelt, later followed by frigates specially designed for anti-submarine warfare.

As we have seen, the early metric ASV radars because of their lack of range (though much greater than that of asdic) and because of the lack of suitable aircraft to carry them, did not begin to get results until early 1941. The first seaborne centimetric sets began to operate in the autumn of that year. Thus much depended on the asdic detection of submarines which, in turn, was not effective until the U-boats were forced to submerge by ASV-carrying aircraft.

Asdic detections were most successful in the period March 1941 to July 1942 using Types 127 and 128. Reports of U-boats diving deeper than 700 ft in mid-1943 led to the rapid development of the Q attachment to the transducer. This device produced a narrow, vertical wedge-shaped beam; it was mounted beneath the main transducer and extended the angular depression of the asdic contact from the 10° of the main beam to 45° (ultimately to 60°). It enabled contact to be made with U-boats at close range at depths between 300 and 700 ft. It was introduced in July 1943.[20]

The most sophisticated asdic, however, was the Type 147 which was equipped for the first time with a depth recorder designed by I. G. Morgan, one of the early members of *Osprey*, who had a flair for mechanics. The greatest U-boat depth measured by the Royal Navy in the war was 780 ft. A Type 147 was first installed on HMS *Hadleigh Castle* in September 1943. However, the first successful use of the depth-determining gear was by HMS *Spey* when she sank two U-boats with three depth charge patterns. Forty Type 147 sets were supplied to the US Navy while its own depth-recording equipment was being prepared.

Although the Germans, after the fall of France, were able to examine British asdic gear supplied to the French Navy and later examined a British submarine captured by the Italians, they never developed effective tactics against the Allied anti-submarine forces. After the war some German authorities blamed this on the absence of a tactical unit or operational research group, similar to that of the Allies, in the U-boat command.

German acoustic countermeasures were equally ineffective. Several kinds of decoy were put into operation without much success.[21] However, the Germans were ahead of the Allies in developing sound absorbing coatings on the hulls of submarines. One of these codenamed *Alberich*, after the dwarf in German legend who wore a helmet which made him invisible, consisted of a layer of synthetic rubber which entrapped bubbles. The sound reflected from submarines was reduced by between 60 and 85 per cent, depending on depth and other factors. The drawback was that the layer tended to tear away from the hull while the submarine was travelling at high submerged speeds.

What was the value of asdic in the Battle of the Atlantic? Asdics effectively detected the standard U-boats in favourable conditions but were outdistanced by faster and deeper diving boats. Their range was limited compared with radar. But they were invaluable in enabling an escort vessel to press home an attack after a U-boat had been detected by radar or HF DF. Radar and Ultra were undoubtedly the key factors in the defeat of enemy submarines in the Atlantic and in the Pacific. Rear Admiral

Creasy, then Flag Officer Submarines, aptly summed up the contribution of asdics when he wrote after the war:

> We entered the war with blind faith in one instrument, the Asdic, which proved practically impotent to deal with the fast-moving surfaced U-boat; we defeated this tactic with another mechanism, radar, which in its turn was largely neutralised by the introduction of the *schnorkel*.[22]

As with other British scientific contributions to the war effort, the Americans benefited from the close liaison between the two nations. Pew, the asdic expert, who had been transferred to Ottawa to supervise the manufacture of asdic gear in Canada, kept the American naval scientists *au fait* with fresh developments in Britain. The Americans for their part only began to influence British asdic equipment after the war. But they did introduce into the military vocabulary the word sonar – *So*und *Na*vigation *a*nd *R*anging – to make it the acoustic equivalent of radar. The term was invented at the Harvard Sound Laboratory which had become a centre of acoustical research. It was accepted by the British with reluctance as they felt it was a slight against the small band of enthusiasts who had worked so hard, frequently against naval orthodoxy, since 1918. Nevertheless the American term was eventually adopted by the Royal Navy in the early 1950s.

Airborne devices other than radar

The Americans did, however, make several useful contributions to airborne search equipment. Soon after the formation of the NDRC Bush made sure that the detection of submarines was put on a high priority. The US Navy was fortunate in that it had at its disposal the renowned Woods Hole Oceanographic Institution which conducted fundamental research on underwater sound. In addition special laboratories were set up to conduct research on underwater warfare in the Atlantic and Pacific. The former was located at New London and was operated by Columbia University.

Two airborne devices were introduced which, while on a much smaller scale than radar and sonar, were better able to detect more silent and faster U-boats as they were not affected by temperature layers and rough seas. The first device was the magnetic airborne detector (also referred to as the magnetic anomaly detector). Although it was not an acoustical device it was used in association with asdics. During the first winter of the war Blackett and a fellow scientist, E. J. Williams, used magnetometers installed on an aircraft to detect the metal hull of a sub-marine.[23] Their idea was communicated to the Americans by Tizard and the former enthusiastically developed MAD principally at the Bell Laboratories. A limited number of MAD equipments were fitted in American aircraft and were used for locating U-boats which had sub-merged on sighting and for patrols over restricted waters such as the Straits of Gibraltar. It was in those waters on 24 February 1944 that the first succesful contact was made with a U-boat resulting in it being destroyed with the help of British destroyers. MAD, however, suffered from its extremely short range which never progressed farther than about 600 ft.[24]

Towards the end of the war MAD was largely supplanted by the cheap expendable radio sonobuoy used mainly by the Americans. Again, the original idea was Blackett's who suggested that buoys containing asdic sets or directional hydrophones dropped by low-flying aircraft could give radio warning of U-boats preying on convoys.[25] At first the inten-tion was to drop the buoys over the side of a convoy ship; they would then pick up any waterborne sound from a vessel approaching from astern and transmit a radio warning to the convoy. The New London Laboratory took this proposal a stage further by designing the expend-able radio sonobuoy. This was a very small frequency-modulated receiver fitted with a parachute which was dropped by aircraft flying about 500 ft above the sea.

The passive sonobuoy provided an opportunity for an anti-submarine patrol to listen to the engines of a submarine after it had crash-dived to safety following an initial sighting. Sonobuoys had a range of about 2000 yards in a calm sea and they were able to function for four hours. They were also used to investigate suspicious signs of submarine activity like oil slicks, disappearing radar blips or MAD indications. Expendable radio sonobuoys were used extensively by the Allied air forces. Coastal Command was equipped with a small number of sonobuoys in August 1943 which were used sparingly until the end of 1944. They were limited, however, by being unable to provide either range or bearing of the target. Thus a pattern of buoys had to be dropped and the sound output from each group compared. Accuracy was difficult to obtain because the buoys often differed in sensitivity while the sound emitted by the target varied, thus making tracking difficult. After the war the British introduced a directional passive sonobuoy which enabled the searching aircraft to obtain a bearing on the target. These sets were sub-sequently produced for the Americans.[26] The great value of the sonobuoy was that it provided a method of keeping in touch with a submerged submarine proceeding at above silent speed, the previous position of which had been known.

Weapons for attacking submarines: airborne depth charges

The most effective destroyer of the U-boat was the depth charge (invented in 1907) and launched from a ship in the First World War or, in addition, dropped from an aircraft in the Second World War. At the outset of the latter bombs were dropped but they proved to be more dangerous to the aircraft than to the submarine. They detonated either on the surface or after a short interval following entering the water. Fragments from the bomb were thrown upward sometimes striking the aircraft. (On one occasion an Anson of Coastal Command was forced to ditch in the sea after being hit by bomb splinters; the crew were later picked up by a naval vessel.) In due course bombs were replaced by 250 lb depth charges detonated either by a very short time fuse or by a hydrostat initiated at a depth of 100–150 ft. They were not powerful enough to cause mortal damage to a U-boat (see also pages 105–6).

After being pressed by the ORS for a more powerful explosive, Headquarters Coastal Command asked the Air Ministry to supply it with RDX fillings (the latest explosive devised by the Armament Research and Development Establishment). Blackett, then head of Coastal Command ORS and Scientific Adviser to the Air Officer Commanding-in-Chief, after hearing that Minol (a less powerful explosive) was to be provided, complained to his Chief:

> What worries me is that such a vital matter as the best filling for depth charges should be left to be raised by me as a result of the accident that I heard, by chance, that the new design of the anti-submarine bomb was to be filled with Minol. Then is Torpex definitely to be excluded on supply grounds? Why shouldn't we have the best?[27]

The sequel was that torpex-filled depth charges (50 per cent more efficient than amatol and TNT) became available to Coastal Command in July 1942 making it a truly anti-submarine warfare weapon. The incident was also 'a good example of one of the less official functions of an ORS [see Chapter 6] – that of being grease in the works; grease which only rarely feels called upon to point out that the frictions which it helps to overcome should not be there in the first place.'

Ahead-thrown weapons

Improving the performance of depth charges discharged from anti-submarine vessels was a far more difficult task. For there was a time lag after the moment of detecting the U-boat involving the vessel being put into a favourable position to launch the depth charge and, most important, the blind run of the final 200 yards before the attack when asdic contact had been lost (it could be as long as a minute). Further, the slow sinking of the depth charges added to the blind time, especially if the U-boat had dived deep. More powerful explosives were introduced but the conclusion was reached that better results would not be obtained until a depth charge or a bomb was fired *ahead* of the anti-submarine vessel.[28]

In fact, bomb projectors had been on the agenda of *Osprey* since 1924 but had been neglected due to the importance attached to detection. Shortly before the war the matter was raised again and in 1940 the decision was made to build the Fairlie Mortar. It was to consist of two sets of ten mortar barrels fitted on either side of the forecastle of a ship. Projectiles would be thrown at the target in a circular pattern. On account of his reluctance to delegate, Smith rarely sought advice from other Admiralty departments on the design of the projector and soon fell foul of the Director of Naval Ordnance.

Meanwhile in the spring of 1940 DMWD had become interested in developing a bomb-thrower after Bullard had told Goodeve that work on the Fairlie Mortar had run into difficulties. The inspiration for the DMWD projector came from a light anti-tank mortar called the Blacker Bombard after its ingenious inventor, Stewart Blacker, a retired Indian Army Lieutenant-Colonel working on explosives and special weapons for the Director of Military Intelligence at the War Office.[29] The base of the bomb was fitted round an electrically-actuated steel rod called a spigot which fired the projectile. The advantage of a projector like the Blacker Bombard over the Fairlie Mortar was that it was light, not too complicated to install on the deck of a ship and be made seaworthy, while the projectiles would sink much more rapidly and quietly than depth charges.

Working under extreme pressure with scarce resources, DMWD evolved a projector pointing upwards which fired 24 bombs in six rows like the quills of a hedgehog (after which the weapon was named). Each row would be tilted up to about 20° to compensate for the ship's rolling, and each spigot was slightly offset so that the projectiles made a circular pattern about 130 ft in diameter, the spacings being somewhat less than the mean beam of a U-boat. Most of the recoil was used to reset the weapon and little remained to be absorbed by the mounting and the ship's deck. To reduce the impact of the recoil still further, the projectiles were fired in pairs in rapid succession. Unlike releasing depth charges, asdic contact with the target was not lost as the bombs only exploded on contact. Moreover, if the attack was abortive, another attempt could be made by another unit as the water would not have been disturbed by useless explosions.

The projectile itself took a long time to develop as so little was known about the best shape for or the behaviour of a projectile when underwater. The most difficult component to design was the impact fuse. A number of alternative schemes were considered by scientists both in and outside DMWD. The best solution, after much trial and error was designed by P. H. Lindley, a rocket expert. It was set in motion by a small propeller rotated by the motion of the water. It was also difficult to estimate the lethality of the bomb which had to penetrate the pressure hull of the U-boat. With the help of a photograph extracted by Naval Intelligence from an Italian magazine showing a dockyard worker standing up to his waist on the hull of a U-boat, it was possible to estimate the distance between the surface of the deck and the pressure hull.

After two years of strenuous work Hedgehog at last became operational at the end of 1941. But it did not sink a U-boat until December 1942 by which time the critical stage of the U-boat war was almost over.[30] There were a number of reasons for this frustrating delay. In the haste to get it into service the weapon was often fitted badly causing accidents to the crew; it was not serviced properly; there was no instruction manual issued to crews because of the extreme secrecy which surrounded the project. It was not surprising that Hedgehog was unpopular with ships' captains and crews. There was also the effect of morale; crews were used to seeing a 'big bang' when a depth charge exploded. Hedgehogs with their impact-detonated bombs were much less impressive to watch. Only towards the end of 1944 did the success rate reach the expected level.

By that time a successor to Hedgehog called Squid was in action. It was a three-barrelled mortar (not unlike the Fairlie Mortar) with a range of about 300 yards. The projectiles fired were more powerful than those of Hedgehog; they sank more rapidly and could strike submarines as deep as 900 ft. Squid's most novel feature was the automatic setting of the depth charges by the latest Type 147 depth-determining asdic set. It was more popular with the Navy because the projectiles exploded when they reached their depth setting and thus, it was argued, at least damaged the morale of the U-boat's crew. Two types of this weapon were produced – the Single Squid for small ships and the Double Squid for larger vessels. Squid proved to be the most efficient anti-submarine weapon as shown in Table 4.1 and after the war provided the model for the much more flexible weapon called Limbo.

In parallel with the British, the Americans worked on ahead-thrown weapons. The California Institute of Technology developed a lighter projector than Hedgehog called Mousetrap – a rocket projectile weapon. It was much used in the Pacific war but never entirely displaced the conventional depth charge attack. When Squid emerged, the Americans enthusiastically took it over as it stood and US Navy vessels were fitted with it from October 1944.

The German response

After the U-boats had withdrawn from the North Atlantic at the end of May 1943, Dönitz recognized that if his force was to continue to inflict grievous harm on Allied shipping he would have to bring faster boats with better underwater performance into service. Until then the basic design of his submarines had hardly advanced since 1939. It was necessary to improve both the hydrodynamic performance of the hull and the power plant.

He therefore decided to reconsider the advice of Helmut Walther, head of Germania Werft, the shipbuilding firm in Kiel, who as early as 1937 had proposed an improved hull form and a revolutionary power plant which utilized a turbine driven by powerful but very unstable chemicals such as hydrogen peroxide. His design was shelved because of lack of money. Although it was revived as the Type XVIII, time was too short for development and production.[31] Instead he concentrated on diesel-electric driven boats with very high performance, but even these failed to materialize in time due to unexpected teething troubles and accurate attacks by Bomber Command against production centres, movement of prefabricated components, and interruption of crews trying to train in the Baltic.

Instead the existing types of U-boat were equipped with the *schnorkel* – a combined air intake and diesel exhaust outlet apparatus which enabled them to remain underwater while recharging batteries. The *schnorkel*, a Dutch invention, was already known to the German Navy, but only after the mid-1943 crisis was its value appreciated. The 'submersible' now became a submarine in the true sense of the word. The *schnorkel's* great asset was that it made radar detection very difficult as it

Table 4.1 Relative performance of three main A/S weapons, 1943–45

Period	Depth charge			Hedgehog			Double Squid			Single Squid		
	Attacks	Successes	%	Attacks	Successes	%	Attacks	Successes	%	Attacks	Successes	%
1943 (1st half)	554	27½	5.0	53	4½	8.5						
1943 (2nd half)	401	15	3.7	49	4	8.2						
1944 (1st half)	404	30	6.5	70	10	14.3				3	0	–
1944 (2nd half)	98	5½	5.6	37	13	35.1	6	2½	*	17	4	23.5
1945 (Jan–May)	107	7½	7.0	59	15½	26.3	21	8½	40.3	3	2	*

½ = Attacks shared with aircraft.
* = Too few attacks to make percentage calculations meaningful.

was almost impossible to distinguish between sea returns and those of the target.[32] On the other hand, the device was not easy to operate; it prevented the U-boat from increasing speed to chase a convoy; living conditions on board, already hard to bear, became almost intolerable. A more important tactical handicap was that the commander had to rely on the limited view provided by the periscope when searching for a convoy. As *schnorkel* boats in 1944 usually operated in coastal waters around the British Isles where targets were plentiful, this limitation was not so important. Nevertheless while the U-boat was made safer by the *schnorkel*, it had become less effective as an anti-ship weapon.

Acoustic torpedoes against submarines

There was, however, one weapon that could threaten the *schnorkel*-equipped submarine – the air-launched acoustic torpedo homing on its target through the noise of the propellers. It was left to the Americans to evolve and manufacture such a weapon. The British, as we have seen, were slow in appreciating the importance of acoustic offensive weapons and although a good deal of progress had been made in designing and testing airborne homing torpedoes, they had to concede that it would be impossible with their limited resources to bring a viable equipment into operation in time. Instead they concentrated on solving problems of background noise to help the Americans.[33]

The Harvard Underwater Sound Laboratory and the Bell Telephone Laboratories began to develop an acoustic airborne torpedo at the end of 1942. Such was the extreme secrecy surrounding the project that it was called the Mark 24 'Mine'.[34] On reaching the water it ran at a speed of 12 knots at a fixed depth in a wide circle until it picked up the sound source. It had an endurance of 15 minutes and sank if it failed to find the target. The Mark 24 Mine was first deployed on 17 May 1943 but its use was limited by the Americans as they did not want a specimen to be captured by the Germans and turned against them. It was forbidden to be used in the Mediterranean and other restricted waters in case it accidentally ran aground.

It was employed in small numbers (following tests using ex-U-boat *Graph* as a target) by Coastal Command where it was known as Fido. Their first success was also in May 1943 when a Liberator sank a U-boat in the Atlantic. Towards the end of the war Coastal Command believed that the Mark 24 Mine used in conjunction with the sonobuoy were the most promising weapons to enable aircraft to regain their ascendancy over the U-boat.

Acoustic torpedoes against surface craft

By sheer coincidence the Germans began using acoustic torpedoes in the Atlantic about the same time as the Allies. Their purpose was, of course, to cripple merchant ships. Frustrated by their inability to penetrate the screen of escort vessels surrounding the convoys, the U-boats sought to inflict damage by firing homing torpedoes outside the defensive perimeter.

The German Navy had always taken torpedoes seriously. The Chemical and Physical Experimental Establishment at Kiel, where torpedo and mine research took place, was one of the few service laboratories where scientists instead of service officers were in charge.[35] The chief scientist held the equivalent rank of an admiral. Electrically-powered torpedoes were used against Allied shipping in 1917–18. Although, compared with the orthodox torpedo driven by compressed air turning a small turbine, the electric torpedo was slower, it had the advantage of being trackless. (The British did not introduce an electric torpedo until after 1939.)

German torpedoes were by no means always effective. In the 1940 Norwegian campaign, for example, they sometimes failed to explode. But by 1943 a major effort was being made to develop an acoustic torpedo at Atlas-Werke in Bremen, specialists in underwater acoustics. The principal one was called *Zaunkönig* (Wren) and was named Gnat (German naval acoustic torpedo) by the Allies because of its nuisance value to escort vessels.[36] The ship's bearing was determined by comparing the amplitude of the incoming sound. Hydrophones were located in the nose of the torpedo connected in alternating pairs. A special electronic device compared their output one hundred times a second and the rudders steered the torpedo to the side receiving the strongest sound. The torpedo was able to travel at 25 knots.

Allied countermeasures against acoustic torpedoes

By the time Gnat was deployed, U-boats had been forced to attack escort vessels at the expense of sinking merchant ships. A combination of high speed U-boats and Gnat would have seriously threatened Allied convoys. The possibility of acoustic torpedoes had already been foreseen and a group from the Minesweeping Division under M. N. Hill (the son of A. V. Hill) were working on countermeasures. They were three in number: the easiest was to slow down the vessel in order to reduce the noise of the propellers; alternatively, noise could be increased by towing a noisemaker to divert the torpedo; finally, the vessel's speed could be increased to outrun the torpedo.[37]

Slow speed was not exactly a popular measure when U-boats were known to be in the vicinity. More acceptable were noisemakers and a large scientific effort was devoted to designing various kinds. The British favourite was a mechanical noisemaker appropriately called Foxer. Two parallel steel pipes held in a frame struck each other constantly when towed at speed creating a high frequency sound much louder than the cavitation noise of ships' propellers. But they were clumsy to operate and interfered with asdic reception, quite apart from providing a warning to U-boats 20 miles away. A single towed noisemaker developed by the Royal Canadian Navy was lighter and could be towed faster.

Experiments were also made with various types of explosive noisemakers, or 'squawkers' as Churchill described them, which would attract or distract acoustic torpedoes. One of these was called Publican – a chain of exploding cartridges fired from a projector.[38] But they were not loud enough and the programme was cancelled. In fact, Gnat was not such a devastating weapon as had been expected. Probably about 640 acoustic torpedoes were fired; they sank around 25 escort vessels and 20 merchant ships. This total was kept down by Foxer and other devices.

Outcome of the anti-U-boat campaign

The threat to the Allied supply lines by the German submarine arm could well have been critical. Altogether 1162 U-boats were commissioned during the war and were responsible for sinking 14 687 000 tons of Allied shipping. Over half the sinkings occurred in the crucial North Atlantic area, the Arctic and British coastal waters. But the Allied response was vigorous. Five measures contributed to its success. First, the introduction of the convoy system which compelled the U-boats to reach their targets by penetrating the screen of escort vessels on the sea and the searching aircraft above. The other four measures were asdic, radar, Ultra and HF DF. The sinkings of U-boats by ships and aircraft were approximately equal and amounted to 67 per cent of the total U-boat losses, the rest being sunk by carrier-borne aircraft or destroyed in raids on U-boat pens by Allied bombers.

The human losses on both sides were grievous. A total of 22 800 merchant seamen are believed to have perished in ships sunk by U-boats. At the same time some 28 000 members of U-boat crews died.[39]

Looking at the campaign dispassionately, the outcome ended in stalemate. The Germans hoped to evade the increasing effectiveness of radar through their adoption of the *schnorkel*, but this invention did not permit them to regain the ascendancy they had in 1942–43. At the same time the Allies could not counter the *schnorkel*. Luckily for them the liberation of north-west Europe restricted the number of U-boat bases. Yet the ability of the submarine to remain submerged made it continue to be a highly dangerous weapon, even more so when, in 1954, the first nuclear submarine was launched.

Combating the mining menace

At the beginning of this chapter the sea mine was noted as being one of the new weapons revolutionizing naval warfare. In 1939–45 it was to account for 16 per cent of shipping sunk. Up to the end of the First World War it was a fairly primitive contraption moored in the sea, only exploding when in contact with a ship and usually causing no more than local damage. But by 1918 both the Allies and the Germans possessed mines capable of being activated by a steel ship's magnetic field and even when resting on the sea bed their explosive content could blow a ship out of the water.

On the approach of war in 1939 Admiralty scientists recognized that non-contact mines were likely to be used and planned possible countermeasures. But a suitable antidote could not be made operational until an enemy mine had been examined and its method of activation discovered. This soon occurred on 23 November 1939 when a mine dropped by an aircraft was washed up on a beach near Southend. Albert Wood, Chief Scientist at the Mine Design Department who had researched in atomic physics under Rutherford before 1914, pronounced that it operated on a change in the vertical magnetic field in the direction of the north pole downwards.[40] Therefore in order to make ships immune to the mine's activating mechanism, they could either be *remagnetized* so as to have no north pole downwards (i.e. in northern latitudes) or, alternatively, be *demagnetized* by winding an electric cable round them producing an equal magnetic field in opposition to that of the ship. Within a few days of Wood's analysis degaussing of ships began in all major British ports. As Goodeve later claimed:

> Although in technical achievement and human effort [the Battle of the Magnetic Mine] was not in the same class as the radar or U-boat battles, it was the first technical battle in which we won a decisive victory over the enemy; but more important still, it was one which brought science fully into the war in the very early days.[41]

Although, as noted earlier, the Admiralty was convinced that acoustic mines were unlikely to be used, mines equipped with microphones were recovered in the autumn of 1940. Wood had to remind his superiors that 'acoustic mines had been designed, tested and were ready for use in the First World War.' It was not long before combinations of acoustic and magnetic mines were introduced by the Germans usually fitted with anti-sweep mechanisms and booby traps. In order to counter this potentially dangerous threat to shipping, a large scientific group was formed (initially under Bullard), not just to devise suitable countermeasures but to anticipate future strategems, That often demanded a great deal of abstruse scientific investigation which needed to be completed before the new threat materialized. The headquarters of the Sweeping Division was established in April 1941 at Fettes College, not far from the Firth of Forth.[42]

As was to be expected, the Germans made a determined effort to cripple shipping supporting the Normandy landings in 1944. Pressure or 'oyster' mines were the chosen weapon. They were motivated by suction when a ship passed over them in shallow water. Once again luck attended the British scientists when two of the latest German pressure mines were recovered intact off the beachhead on 19 June, 13 days after D-day. Having discovered the sensitivity of the firing mechanism the antidote was a simple one. If ships travelled below a certain speed, the suction effect would be too small to activate the mine. Shipping was thus ordered to proceed at slow speed in shallow water off the beachhead. Pressure mines were found to be almost unsweepable and they accounted for some 30 vessels of various kinds during the assault phase. The sea itself proved to be the best sweeper when the Atlantic swell coming up the Channel exploded many mines.

The Allies, too, became proficient at mining. Wood appreciated that new kinds of mine-firing units could be assembled quite easily without resorting to sea trials as regulations demanded. Although his proposal was anathema to the Admiralty,[43] it was put into effect by his successor at MDD, Harrie Massey, an Australian physicist and yet another student of Rutherford at the Cavendish. Before he was translated to America to work on the atomic bomb, he set up the MX (X standing for the unknown) Group led by Francis Crick, the future Nobel Prizewinner. Batches of mines with varying actuating circuits were prepared and despatched to airfields where they awaited despatch by Bomber Command to strategic points in the Baltic and west Atlantic. Like the German minelayers, a number of mines fell accidentally on land enabling their secrets to be unravelled.[44] It is no reflection on the ingenuity of the

MDD scientists that the main reason for the success of Allied mining in the final stages of the war was found to be due more to the shortage of German sweepers as a result of air attacks on shipping in ports than to the lethality of the mines.

5
The Acquisition of Signals Intelligence

The birth of modern signals intelligence

Radio emerged in the First World War as an essential method of communication between headquarters and their subordinate units or formations, especially at sea (the static nature of land warfare only needed telephone lines which were more secure than radio). Radio transmissions could easily be intercepted and therefore codes were vital to ensure secrecy. For the first time in warfare codebreaking, hitherto regarded as an erudite art, became a necessity. Although all the belligerents employed cryptanalysts, the British Admiralty's Room 40 achieved the best results. It was manned by a handful of classical scholars and linguistic experts drawn from universities and schools. Helped by the capture of several German naval codebooks, their codebreaking provided valuable information to the Naval Staff. A more outstanding success was their interception of the famous Zimmerman Telegram, partly responsible for the entry of the United States into the war.

At the same time Room 40 depended on the system of interception stations set up, first on the Western Front and then around the British Isles, to pick up German Army and Navy radio signals.[1] H. J. Round, who had worked under Marconi, was responsible for developing this network, while Russell Clarke, barrister, pioneer radio enthusiast, and able to speak German, devised methods of safeguarding the interception of enemy signals. Unfortunately the novelty of this new technique in warfare was not appreciated by the Naval Staff which failed to take advantage of the information that Room 40 was able to provide until the latter part of the war when better cooperation with the cryptanalysts was at last achieved.

Coding and codebreaking expanded after the war, not only among the military, but also for diplomatic communications which were being conducted increasingly by radio. These messages were transmitted in *code* which substituted groups of several letters or digits for words, phrases, or sentences, the meanings of which were known to both sender and receiver. A more secure system was to send messages by *cipher* machines which replaced individual letters by manual or mechanical means according to a key which could be changed at intervals.

One of the first to perceive the value of cipher machines was Arthur Scherbius, a German electrical engineer, who invented a mechanical encryption system. In the spring of 1918 he informed the German Navy of his machine which

> would avoid any repetition of the sequence of letters when the same letter is struck millions of times ... The solution of a telegram is also impossible if a machine falls into unauthorised hands since it requires a prearranged key system.[2]

His idea was rejected both by the Navy and the Foreign Office But Scherbius was not daunted and in 1923 became a director of the *Chiffriermaschinen Aktien Gesellschaft* (Cipher Machine Company) formed for the purpose of marketing his invention. It was appropriately named Enigma and was intended for commercial purposes. After some publicity in the commercial and technical press its design, in the following years, became more sophisticated. In 1925 the German Navy, impressed by learning how effective Room 40 had been during the war, changed its mind and invested in a number of machines from Scherbius's company. When the German Army took up Enigma it incorporated a plugboard (see below) which made the machine far more secure. In 1934 the Navy decided to adapt the plugboard.

As the operation of the Enigma machine has already been described in detail elsewhere, a summary of its working must suffice.[3] Enigma turned plain text into cipher text one letter at a time. It was operated by three or more rotors connected by electrical wiring. One of the rotors was a reflector and did not turn but allowed both decipherment and encipherment to take place. Each rotor was encircled by a ring bearing the 26 letters of the alphabet so that with the ring fixed in position each letter would label a rotor position. From the outside the machine resembled a portable typewriter in a wooden box. It had 26 tiny round windows each displaying a letter of the alphabet and illuminated by light bulbs in three rows behind the keyboard. Above the glass windows were the three rotors. The military version, as just noted, had a small plugboard which operated like a telephone switchboard.

Pressing a letter on the keyboard connected a circuit between a battery and one of the 26 light bulbs. The lighting of the letters was determined by the relative positions of the rotors and the arrangement of the plugs in the plugboard. For example, the G key might illuminate the Z bulb, or any other bulb with the exception of its own. Once a key had been pressed, one or more of the rotors turned a notch so that when the letter G was pressed again another letter besides Z would light up. The machine was operated by two signallers: one typed in the message; the other noted where the letters lit up. When the whole message had been enciphered it was transmitted by ordinary international morse code or teleprinter. As the setting of the rotors could be changed daily or more frequently, anyone not knowing the setting would have to choose from 150 trillion solutions. Even if the machine was captured the makers were confident that it would not reveal its secrets.

As international relations began to deteriorate after the end of the 1920s, the cryptanalysts of the major powers were kept busy. In Britain, Room 40's staff had been taken over by the Foreign Office and given the codename of the Government Code and Cipher School (GC&CS).[4] It was responsible to the Head of the Secret Intelligence Service. Leading members of the staff were Dillwyn Knox, a classical scholar and one-time Fellow of King's College Cambridge, and Oliver Strachey, elder brother of the celebrated writer, Lytton Strachey. The Americans, however, adhering to their policy of neutrality, had, in 1929, abolished the State Department's 'Black Chamber' (the equivalent of GC&CS). Henry Stimson, Secretary of State, years later justified this decision with the retort 'Gentlemen do not read each other's mail'.

German rearmament, the Abyssinian war and the Spanish civil war generated a large amount of mainly diplomatic radio traffic. Although GC&CS enjoyed some success in breaking early non-plugboard versions of Enigma, by the late 1930s it had no luck with the military version.

Polish solution of Enigma

Meanwhile the French Intelligence under General Gustave Bertrand, with the help of a German agent, had managed to obtain a quantity of secret instructions on the setting of the Enigma keys among other documents. Neither the Czechs nor the British to whom Bertrand disclosed his information showed any interest. But to the Poles, sandwiched as they were between two dangerous neighbours – Nazi Germany and the Soviet Union – the information came as 'manna in a desert.'

Unlike other cryptanalysts, the Polish Cipher Bureau under Francizek Pokorny had approached the problem of decipherment mathematically.[5] In 1932 Pokorny bought a commercial model of Enigma. This was analysed by his team of three cryptanalysts, of whom the most important was 27 year old Marian Rejewski who had studied mathematics at Göttingen. Their aim was to decrypt German military signals intercepted by the Polish monitoring system.

With the help of the instructions and later the keys provided by the French, Rejewski began to elucidate the wiring and, later, the keys of the military Enigma. Before the end of December 1932 he had solved the working of the machine. By 1935 the Cipher Bureau was installed in a communications and signals intelligence centre at the village of Pyry outside Warsaw. Assisted by replicas of Enigma built by the AVA Radio Company in Warsaw, Rejewski and his colleagues were able to decrypt German Enigma signals until 15 September 1938, when the Germans changed their keying system.

The answer was to build an equivalent machine to attack Enigma. The Poles devised what they called a *Bomba*, named either after an ice-cream with a round top, eaten when discussing the idea, or after the ticking noise made by the mechanism. The *Bomba* consisted of six Enigma machines coupled together. When driven through all their positions, the *Bomba* would stop when it came to a possible solution. The key would then be read and tested on an Enigma replica. If it read plain text it was right; otherwise the machine would be restarted for another attempt.

German signals were once again decrypted, but on 15 December 1938 the Germans added two more rotors to Enigma. Thanks to mistakes made by the Nazi security services, it was possible to reconstruct the wiring of the new rotors. But instead of six *Bombas* the Poles now required sixty, far more than their budget allowed.

Not only lack of funds but the realization that breaking Enigma was more difficult than they had anticipated led the Poles to seek help from their potential allies – the British and the French. But this had to wait until the British guaranteed support to Poland on 29 March 1939 should Hitler invade. During a visit to Pyry on 24–25 July by Commander Alastair Denniston, the head of GC&CS, Dillwyn Knox, and Commander Humphrey Sandwith in charge of the Admiralty's interception and direction finding service, as well as by Bertrand, the Poles, to the astonishment of the British, revealed their copies of Enigma and agreed to hand two over. The British copy was brought to London on 16 August by Bertrand in person.[6]

The British use of Enigma

After the conquest of Poland in September, Rejewski accompanied by two of his colleagues fled to France where they collaborated with Bertrand's team which, in turn, had begun to work with GC&CS in England. From now onwards, however, the British took the lead in breaking Enigma. Shortly before the outbreak of war GC&CS was evacuated to Bletchley Park, a rather dilapidated Victorian mansion conveniently situated between Oxford and Cambridge and within easy reach of London. Among a recent intake from the universities were two Cambridge lecturers in advanced mathematics, Alan Turing and Gordon Welchman. Both believed they could develop a British Bombe that was greatly superior to the Polish version.

Turing, only 26, was already recognized as the author of a paper entitled 'Computable Numbers'.[7] It offered a solution to the *Entscheidungsproblem* (decisive problem) then exercising the minds of a circle of European and American mathematicians. Most of them believed that the problem was insolvable. But Turing visualized a machine able to replicate the computations of a human brain by using a punched tape. His machine, in effect, anticipated the modern computer. With an aptitude for mechanical work, Turing was thus well qualified to tackle the intricacies of Enigma. Welchman, aged 33, was a specialist in algebraic geometry. He was also a 'very practical visionary', believing that at the end of the 'phoney war' the Germans would rely on Enigma for military communications. More mature than Turing, he appreciated the need for an expansion of GC&CS and its equipment and he had the courage to press his demands on higher authority.[8]

Meanwhile the British had to resort to a method of reading Enigma texts without using the Bombe. They used a method devised by the Poles which entailed assembling 60 sets of 26 perforated heavy cards marking the 105 456 rotor positions. When placed one on top of the other a matching of the pattern would occur when light passed through all the cards – a lengthy process hardly likely to provide information rapidly to a battle front.

Turing's answer was to improve the Polish Bombe by adapting the replication he intended using in his 'Turing Machine'. Early in 1940 he had completed his design.[9] The blueprint was sent to the British Tabulating Machine Company at Letchworth. Accustomed to making office calculators in which electrical relays performed simple mathematical functions, the firm now made relays perform the switching operation whereby the Bombe recognized a position when consistency in the Enigma settings occurred and stopped.

Welchman had been given the task of analysing the structure of the German army and air force communications system. His investigations stimulated thoughts on a way of solving Enigma signals. As soon as he heard about Turing's Bombe and digested its design, he appreciated, through his study of encrypted signals, that Turing's Bombe could be made to run much more quickly by changing the wiring system and installing a simple electrical circuit which became known as a 'diagonal board'.[10] After studying a rough diagram made by Welchman, the astonished Turing agreed that it was an improvement on his own design and within a short time a new prototype Bombe had been made at Letchworth incorporating the diagonal board. Not only had Welchman made a remarkable breakthough, he had made it soon after understanding the characteristics and operating procedures of Enigma. He was later appointed Assistant Director of Mechanization at GC&CS.

The first Bombe (without a diagonal board) was installed at Bletchley Park on 18 March 1940. However, as construction of the Bombes was on a low priority only 16 three rotor Bombes had been delivered to GC&CS by December 1941, of which only 12 were serviceable.[11] But by the end of August 1942, as the value of Ultra was more appreciated, the number had risen to 30 and to 49 by the end of that year. The machinery was contained in bronze-coloured cabinets about eight feet high and seven feet wide. On the face of each machine were the analogues of the Enigma rotors, each bearing a large number in the middle and the letters of the alphabet around its circumference. The machines were tended by hard-worked members of the Women's Royal Naval Service. To minimize damage from air raids the Bombes were dispersed in country houses in the vicinity of Bletchley Park.

Until the Bombes were ready GC&CS had to solve Enigma signals by using the perforated cards. During the Norwegian campaign in the spring of 1940 they were amazed to find how much the German high command relied on Enigma when transmitting orders. Radio silence had been expected. Then during the evacuation from Dunkirk the first GAF Enigma key (which included army–air cooperation) using a single encipherment was broken and from 22 May until the end of the war GC&CS were able to read its settings with few interruptions and little delay.

During the Battle of Britain there were few opportunities to break Enigma – the nature of short-range air operations did not require its extensive use. But as the war spread beyond Europe in 1942 and intelligence from Enigma (known as Ultra) became more available, the German army keys were solved on the eastern front and in the Mediterranean before the end of 1941. Probably the most valuable intelligence was derived from reading the German naval Enigma signals in the Battle of the Atlantic. The naval Enigma had been the most difficult to crack, not only because the Navy used Enigma more carefully than the other services, but because the naval Enigma rotors were selected from eight rather than the five used by the army and air force. Moreover, the capture by HMS *Bulldog* of U-110 in the east Atlantic provided GC&CS with the Enigma settings for June 1941.[12] With one (almost disastrous) exception between February and December 1942 and for the early part of 1943, the two most important naval keys known by GC&CS as Dolphin and Shark were read for the rest of the war. As we have seen, this made it possible not only to reroute convoys (probably saving 300 ships) but also to take offensive action against U-boats and their supply system.

Even so, GC&CS had been starved of manpower in the autumn of 1941 to such an extent that there were delays of at least 12 hours before the naval keys were found every day. There were insufficient staff to take advantage of the large amount of enemy tactical radio traffic circulating in the Western Desert, while the staff at Letchworth making the Bombes had become liable to call-up for military service. So frustrated were the members of Hut 6, which included Turing and Welchman responsible for evaluating German army and air force activity, that they took the highly irregular step of writing personally to the Prime Minister on 21 October 1941 (Trafalgar Day) listing their complaints.[13] Churchill, who had recently visited Bletchley Park, took action at once and by 18 November all the requirements of GC&CS were being met.

The breaking of Shark

The inability to read Shark mentioned above during most of 1942 had to some extent been foreseen. Towards the end of 1941 GC&CS discovered that the Atlantic U-boat Enigmas were to be issued with a fourth rotor.[14] A high-speed four-rotor Bombe would therefore be needed to break the settings. But before the new Bombe came into service two codebooks, by a remarkable chance, were recovered from U-559 just before it was sunk in the Mediterranean on 30 October 1942.[15] Three members of the crew of HMS *Petard*, Lieutenant Anthony Farson, Able Seaman Colin Grazier and 16-year-old Tommy Brown, a civilian working in the ship's canteen, boarded the submarine to remove the documents. Sadly the two Royal Navy crew were drowned when the U-boat suddenly capsized. One of the books was the short weather code, previously broken by GC&CS but which had been changed early in 1942. As the weather reports were transmitted with the fourth rotor in neutral, making the machine into a three-rotor Enigma, GC&CS found it could break the four rotor settings. This was accomplished on 13 December 1942. But on 10 March 1943 the weather report code was changed again.[16] Worse still, the Germans had temporarily broken the British code for controlling convoys. Such was the skill of the British cryptanalysts that the Shark settings were again broken after only nine days and, after 20 March the reading of Shark traffic was resumed intermittently until the beginning of August when regular readings became the norm.

The four-rotor Bombe intended to break Shark was delayed for a number of reasons. First, its development. Only one scientist could be spared for its design. As usual the alternative was to persuade the Americans to design and manufacture the machine. But its complexity caused problems across the Atlantic while, in June 1942 the British were reluctant to agree to the Americans building more than 100 machines. Consequently the first British Bombe was only delivered in June 1943 because of the shortage of high quality materials and the lack of skilled workers. The American-built Bombes entered service in August and were found to be more serviceable than the British machines.[17] The political side was cleared up on 17 May 1943 when the British and the Americans reached a more satisfactory agreement on the exchange of Army and Air Force intelligence which persisted until after the end of the war.

By the end of 1943 the British were decrypting 90 000 Enigma messages of all kinds a month – a level that was maintained until the end of the war. The Allies were thus able to put together a detailed and immensely valuable picture of many German activities. But after the North African campaign and the Battle of the Atlantic the intelligence value of many Enigma signals tended to be of little importance, being mainly routine messages from one unit to another.

The breaking of the German Army cipher machine

Up to the end of 1943 intelligence about the German army had been difficult to obtain. With the Allied plans for invading enemy-occupied Europe afoot, it became imperative to gain information on appreciations and reports emanating from the German high command. For some time the army had been encoding teleprinter messages in plain text for high level messages between Berlin and headquarters in the Middle East. Encoding was performed by an apparatus developed by the firm K. Lorenz known as the *Schlüsselzusatz* (cipher attachment) of which there were two types – the *SZ40* and *SZ42*. They were attached to separate teleprinters, one of which was the T52.

For some time before the war British police and Post Office engineers had found that they could intercept coded non-morse German tele-printer traffic.[18] Around July 1942 GC&CS, taking advantage of this expertise, had been able to break the *SZ40* attachment which was given the name of Tunny. (The codename Fish stood for all kinds of encrypted radio teleprinter messages which were called *Sägefisch* – sawfish by the Germans.) From mid-1942 Tunny links began to proliferate between Germany and the army commands in Europe from six in July 1943 to 26 early in 1944, each link using different cipher settings. At the same time the security of the ciphers was constantly being tightened. Only a high speed machine would enable the codes to be broken.

An engineer and a mathematician were mainly responsible for the development of a machine that, in its ability to break Tunny, was the forerunner of the modern computer. They were Maxwell Newman, the leading exponent of the branch of mathematics known as topology and whose lectures at Cambridge had been attended by Turing, and Thomas Flowers, an electrical engineer, who had been exploring the uses of electric valves for telephone switchboards at the Post Office Research Station at Dollis Hill in north London.[19]

The actual working of the *SZ40/42* was straightforward. Messages typed in plain language at the keyboard were transmitted by the machine in cipher, and enciphered messages received in the machine came out printed in plain language, all automatically without effort on the part of the machine operator, other than setting the machine to certain initial mechanical conditions specified in a list of key settings before sending or receiving a message. Incredibly, due to a mistake made by an operator of a Tunny machine, GC&CS not only discovered the number of rotors (12) in the machine and the number of pin settings on each rotor, but also how they moved in relation to one another as a message was enciphered.

Newman came to Bletchley Park late in 1942 on the recommendation of Blackett. It was the task of himself and his colleagues to determine the patterns round the circumferences of all the 12 rotors at a particular time, as the Germans regularly changed the pin setting patterns. Then they had to work out the settings of the rotors at the start of each message. The first problem was called rotor breaking; the second rotor setting. The attack on Tunny, according to the official historian of British war-time intelligence, had to surmount intellectual, technological and organisational problems of a still higher order than those presented by the Enigma machine, and even those which GC&CS overcame in breaking the four rotor Enigma by the end of 1942.[20]

Newman proposed using two paper teletype tapes to be read by the same machine. One tape stored information of the inner workings of the *SZ40/42*; holes in that tape would represent the 12 rotors and the unique way the rotors were constrained to rotate, relative to each other, as they encoded the messages. The other tape would hold the encrypted message.

The first machine to perform these tasks was called Heath Robinson after the British artist well known for his entertaining drawings of complicated machines performing essentially simple functions. Its principal designer was C. E. Wynn-Williams of TRE, who had already designed the four-rotor Bombe, assisted by a team of Post Office engineers.[21] The first Heath Robinson (several were made) began to operate at Bletchley Park in September 1943 but was soon found not to be up to the job. Speed of operation had been the overriding objective and the reliability of certain subsections was overlooked. As the paper tapes were driven at speeds about a hundred times faster than the tapes in normal teleprinter usage they often tore. The machine began to overheat from time to time. Even so, it was possible to read 2000 characters per second on the Heath Robinsons.

At this point there was some despondency among the Newman team. But Flowers, who was working on a bigger machine called Colossus, suggested that the Heath Robinson tape holding the fixed unchanged data on the Tunny machines be replaced in Colossus by an electronic subsystem. With only one tape to be read at high speed the overall reliability of Colossus, compared with that of the Heath Robinsons, would be greatly improved.[22]

Flowers' suggestion was greeted with some scepticism on the grounds that the large number of valves required, with the likelihood that many of them would fail, made the machine too unreliable to be of any use. Flowers responded by arguing that thousands of valves were used by the Post Office in its communications network and, provided the power was not switched off, valve failure was rare.

With the date for the Allied return to north-west Europe rapidly approaching, the need for Colossus became extremely urgent. After 11 months' labour the Dollis Hill engineers (financed by the Director of the Research Station as GC&CS was not prepared to fund the initial cost) completed the first Colossus in December 1943. Unlike the Heath Robinsons, Colossus was entirely electronic. It contained 1500 valves but the limited speed at which the paper tapes could be driven, on account of tearing, was not more than 5000 characters per second.[23]

Flowers therefore modified his design, increasing the number of valves to 2400 and supplementing them by 800 electromagnetic relays. Using processors operating in parallel and shift registers (similar to a modern computer), an effective speed of 25 000 characters per second was obtained. (One of the cryptanalysts working on Tunny later reflected that the running of paper teleprinter tape at a speed of 30 miles per hour without tearing was one of the greatest secrets of the Second World War!)[24] The message that emerged was not fully plain text but an intermediate variety which had to be completed by hand by skilled specialists, often taking them two days and, in the latter stages of the war, as long as seven days to read.

Anticipating that more Colossus machines would be urgently needed if the first was successful, Flowers' team had already begun redesigning and incorporating improvements even before the first machine was finished; and certain complicated parts were manufactured in advance. Towards the end of February 1944 Flowers was instructed to have 12 Colossus IIs ready for operation by 1 June. The reason for this sudden demand stemmed not only from the success of the existing Colossus but from the enemy's increasingly widespread use of teleprinted messages and from improved German operating procedures.

Although Flowers said that the demand was impossible to meet in full, he promised that at least one machine would be in service by the required date. The remainder would hopefully be delivered at the rate of one per month, provided the first machine worked properly. After another period of intensive work, the first of the new machines was operational on 31 May. Recovering from a mild hiccup, corrected that night, the machine was in service the following morning. Eleven months later ten machines were in operation and the eleventh was due to be commissioned when the war ended.

Colossus I made the first break into Tunny in March 1944.[25] Although the pre-D-day decrypts were not numerous, they included detailed returns supplied by the Commander-in-Chief West from corps and divisions as well as strategic appreciations sent by von Rundstedt to Berlin, the first being decrypted on 6 April. One disturbing piece of information was that rather larger than expected reinforcements were being sent to the Cherbourg peninsula; the news came in time for last minute adjustments to the invasion plans and for modifications to be made to the deception plan.

Ironically, not long after Colossus II had been commissioned, changes to the Tunny links prevented regular decrypts being made. By that time, however, the Allies had established themselves in the beachhead. Not until October, when the Anglo-American forces had reached the German frontier, were all the links consistently read again. The improved security of the German ciphers was offset by the arrival of more Colossus IIs. As the German landline and telephone communications deteriorated through interruption by Allied bombing, so more and more reliance was placed on teleprinter transmissions. Yet the Germans remained confident that their teleprinter system was immune to hostile interception. As late as March 1945 Fish decrypts were higher in number than in any other month of the war, especially on the Eastern Front. In the west the growth of radio teleprinter links and the increase in Fish decrypts were 'the outstanding developments in signal intelligence during the last seven months of the war.'[26]

At that stage the breaking of German army ciphers clearly had a higher priority than the breaking of the GAF *T52* machine, known as Sturgeon, as the threat from the air had so much diminished. To this date it is still not known whether or not Sturgeon was ever broken by GC&CS.

Before leaving Colossus it is worth recording that it had most of the essential features of the modern computer, e.g. it was the first application of logic controlled by an alterable programme; it was able to interrupt so as to prevent overloading of the printer; it introduced the optical reading of paper tape; and it was the first machine to make use of a shift register.[27] Colossus was comparable to the American ENIAC (Electric Numerical Integrator and Calculator), until the disclosures about the former, regarded as the first electronic computer; it came into service on 16 February 1946. It was also used for a special purpose – the solution of differential equations occurring in ballistic problems, though it could, of course, be used for other computations.

The breaking of Japanese codes and ciphers

The second great cryptographic victory of the Allies was the American breaking of the Japanese cipher machine codenamed Purple. In many respects this was, from a cryptanalytical point of view, perhaps a greater feat than the breaking of the Enigma machine (though not Fish) as an actual machine never came into the hands of the Americans. Thus its structure had to be deduced by making 'cribs' from radio intercepts. This was done by identifying recurrent characteristics of messages such as the title of the recipient and guessing part of the message's ending.

In 1930, after Stimson had abolished the Black Chamber, the US Army quietly transferred its activities to a new unit in the War Department known as the Signals Intelligence Service (SIS but not to be confused with the British Intelligence Service). The head was a Colonel of the Signal Corps and his unit included a small team of civilian cryptanalysts, the most important being William Friedman, a biologist, and Frank Rowlett, a teacher who was fluent in Japanese. Friedman had been a codebreaker during and after the First World War; one of his feats had been the breaking of the Hebern cipher machine invented in 1922.[28] He wrote several pamphlets on codebreaking and was a pioneer in applying statistical methods to cryptanalysis.

As Japanese imperial ambitions became more threatening in the mid-1930s, the Americans set up radio interception stations to cover the Pacific as well as the Atlantic. But because of the US policy of neutrality, interceptions were made under the cover of training exercises and were limited to breaking high-grade radio traffic between the Japanese Foreign Office and its diplomatic missions overseas rather than intercepting Japanese naval, military and air force radio traffic.

By 1935 the Japanese suspected that the Americans had been reading their diplomatic radio traffic and switched to a new machine with rotors, similar to the non-plugboard Enigma called *Agooki Taipu A*. To the Americans it was known as Red. In 1936 the SIS was able to read these messages. Red remained in service until 1937 when a more secure machine containing a plugboard known as *97-Shiki O-bun In-ji K* was introduced. The Americans called it Purple on the grounds that it would be unwise to use another primary colour as a codename. Purple was installed in many Japanese embassies by the end of the 1930s.[29]

Purple was far more difficult to break. After much painstaking work, making logical deductions from the form and patterning of Japanese messages (luckily they were transmitted in roman letters), it became possible to construct a copycat Purple machine. The SIS was then able to list a variety of possibilities relating to the setting of the machine and the pattern of messages. Purple was at last broken in August 1940 after over a year and a half's intensive analysis.[30] When a real Purple machine was studied after the war, it was found that out of all the thousands of soldered connections only two wiring connections had been interchanged. The intelligence obtained from breaking Purple was called Magic (the equivalent of the British Ultra).

SIS immediately began to manufacture a number of Magic machines. Several were given to the Navy and one was under construction at Hawaii when the attack on Pearl Harbor was made. In January 1941 the British received a Magic machine; it arrived in the battleship *King George V* accompanied by two Army and two Navy cryptanalysts. So far the Americans had not been told about Enigma, but from that summer onwards they received information derived from Ultra. After Pearl Harbor a British Magic machine was probably sent to Singapore but was removed to New Delhi before the capture of the island.[31]

The US Navy had been operating its own cryptographic service in Washington for some time. It was called OP-20-G (the G section of the 20th Division of OPNAV – the Office of the Chief of Naval Operations). But lack of liaison between the two service (at that time the air force was part of the US Army) meant that the two codebreaking agencies operated in separate compartments. It was hardly surprising, therefore, that the attack on Pearl Harbor was a disaster for American intelligence. Several days before the attack Japanese troop and ship movements were identified, but Magic did not clearly reveal the intention to destroy the US fleet. As an American historian later wrote:

> The signals lay scattered in a number of different agencies; some were decoded; some were not; some travelled through rapid channels of communication; some were blocked by technical or procedural delays; some never reached a centre of decision.[32]

After Pearl Harbor the Americans reacted with characteristic resilience. Cooperation between the services improved. The SIS became less isolated and assumed the name of the Signal Security Agency. It was never an inter-service institution like GC&CS.

The Japanese forces were heavily dependent on high frequency radio communications because of the great distances separating the theatres of operation ranging from China, Burma and Malaya to scattered islands in the Pacific. While they may have possessed either German or home-made Enigma machines, though probably without a plugboard, little use was made of them, probably because of the difficulty of distributing the machines and training staff to use them. Nor was any attempt made to decode Allied messages.

The Americans rapidly formed Ground Combat Intelligence Units which were sent to bases in the Pacific to break Japanese service ciphers. One of the most important was the main naval code known as JN25 to the Allies.[33] This was broken in time to influence the Battle of Midway in June 1942, described by Admiral Chester Nimitz as 'essentially a victory of intelligence'. The losses inflicted on the Japanese fleet were a turning point in the Pacific war. The reading of JN25 also led to the shooting down by US fighters based on Guadalcanal of the aircraft carrying Admiral Yamamoto, Commander-in-Chief of the Combined Japanese Fleet, on a visit to units in the Solomon Islands on 18 April 1943. While this action was undoubtedly a coup, it might well have alerted the Japanese that their cipher had been broken.

To return to Magic – information derived from it was extremely useful to the Allies in the last year of the war in Europe. The lengthy despatches of General Oshima, the Japanese ambassador in Berlin and a confidant of senior members of the German government, to his masters in Tokyo provided, among other things, an account of a German jet fighter, German troop strengths in the Balkans and even details of a tour of the coastal defences of north-west France in the spring of 1944 – fruitful grist to the Allied intelligence mill.[34]

GC&CS's contribution to the defeat of Japan

Finally, a brief mention must be made of GC&CS's contribution to the winning of the war against Japan. Its reaction was swift. By the middle of 1942 small groups of young, mainly classical, scholars had been taught the rudiments of Japanese and after training at Bletchley Park were sent overseas to begin analysing Japanese radio traffic in the Indian Ocean. After a short stay in Kenya, a permanent headquarters of one group was established at Colombo with links in Melbourne and Brisbane, while cooperation was maintained with OP-20-G in Washington. Towards the end of the war the Colombo group was visited by Admiral Mountbatten, Supreme Commander South-east Asia, who told them they were worth ten divisions.[35] Another section disguised as the Wireless Experimental Centre operated from New Delhi and dealt with Japanese army and air force codes being employed on the Burmese front. A major achievement of the British was the breaking of the Japanese merchant shipping code (JN42) by a team under Brian Townend, seconded from the Foreign Office, in November 1942.

Effect of Magic and Ultra intelligence on the war

While Magic undoubtedly contributed to the defeat of Japan, probably the most significant innovations in cipher breaking were made in the war against Germany. It is tempting, after the long-delayed unveiling of the secrets of Ultra, to exaggerate its influence on air, land and sea operations. Four questions are relevant.

(1) Was Ultra decisive in the conduct of certain campaigns? Indisputably, as has been repeatedly stressed above, Ultra in conjunction with airborne and seaborne centimetric radar, HF DF and very long-range aircraft were the technical innovations that contributed mightily to the victory over the U-boats. Space has not permitted an account of the contribution of Ultra to the ding-dong battles in the Western Desert. Suffice it to note that the information, derived from the breaking of German and Italian ciphers about cargoes, times of sailing and destinations of Rommel's supply ships was a potent factor in denying fuel for his vehicles and tanks and helped to stem the Afrika Korps' advance to the Egyptian frontier in the summer of 1942.

In Europe the Normandy landings were the first in which the Allies were countered by German armoured divisions. It was information on the strengths of individual units and their attempts to reach the battle area provided by Ultra that enabled the Allied planners to make very fine adjustments in the limited number of troops and their administrative echelons that could be landed in the opening phase of the assault.

(2) Was the information supplied by Ultra exploited sufficiently? There were occasions in the early part of the war when information supplied by Ultra could not be implemented because of inadequate forces. Crete was such a case. Plans of the German airborne assault were known in detail but the forces needed to contain it were inadequate. (Nonetheless the Germans never attempted an airborne operation of similar magnitude again.) Conversely, there were instances where insufficient attention was paid to Ultra decrypts. In the summer and autumn of 1944, for example, the drastic effect of the oil shortage (due to Allied bombing of oil refineries) on German air operations, training flights, as well as movement on the battlefield as revealed by signals to economize on fuel consumption, did not appear to have been digested by Sir Arthus Harris, absorbed with his *idée fixe* of destroying German towns.

(3) Did Ultra, as has been claimed, shorten the war significantly? Ultra reached the height of its effectiveness at the moment when the strategic initiative had passed to the Allies, i.e. after the Eighth Army's victory at El Alamein and the German surrender at Stalingrad, when planning of the invasion of the German heartland could begin. As just observed, the value of Ultra was minimal when there was insufficient force to take advantage of it. It is impossible to calculate in terms of months or years how much Ultra shortened the war. What cannot be ignored is that prolonged delay in defeating the U-boats would have

caused the postponement of the launching of the assault on enemy-occupied Europe. That, in turn, would have given more time for the perfection of the V weapons, the construction of high performance submarines, while jet-propelled fighters would have played havoc among the streams of American heavy day bombers.

(4) Why did the Germans not change Enigma during the war? As we have seen the Enigma keys were changed frequently. Although there were some doubters confidence in the impregnability of Enigma continued. Indeed, hardly any changes to the mechanism were made during the war. When leaks in intelligence occurred the Germans attributed them to the activities of spies or to members of the Resistance. Furthermore an immense amount of resources was invested in Enigma. Changing the system would have required quantities of copies of a new machine together with new procedures which might have led to operators' mistakes and have been discovered by the Allies. Moreover, the Germans did not suspect that the British were using their weather codes to assist analysis. There was a lack of interest in codebreaking at high level. Unlike Churchill, Hitler displayed no interest in codebreaking. Nevertheless none of this was known to GC&CS and until the very end of the war there was always the possibility that Ultra would dry up.

Although of great importance, Ultra should not be allowed to overshadow other methods of acquiring intelligence. Rated next in value was the development of high altitude photographic reconnaissance and the interpretation of aerial photographs. Third, 'Y', or radio, intelligence developed by all services, was derived primarily from messages in plain language and medium and low-grade codes and ciphers as well as from DF and message traffic analysis. Without 'Y' and the weather reports the naval Enigma would not have been broken, while air force 'Y' intelligence was often of greater tactical value than Ultra and provided warning of enemy aircraft taking off and indicated their targets. In 1944 ground-based listening stations were complemented by American airborne interception equipment.

Finally, other intelligence organizations should be mentioned. The Operational Intelligence Centre (OIC) at the Admiralty kept a plot of U-boats and enemy surface vessels in the Atlantic and the positions and routes of Allied warships, convoys and independently-routed vessels. Also working closely with GC&CS was the British Air Ministry's scientific intelligence directorate under R. V. Jones (which was the brain child of Tizard) and which, as we have seen, provided important technical information on German navigational aids, reports on coastal radar stations in the English Channel and the V weapons. Neither of the other services adopted similar scientific intelligence sections, due to the obduracy of the Admiralty, though Crick was moved from the MX Group to be a scientific adviser to the Director of Naval Intelligence.

6
Birth of a New Science: Operational Research

Origins and nature of operational research

So far we have discussed the impact of science on the war in relation to the development of new weapons or equipment which contributed to victory. There was another kind of scientific work which became known as operational research (OR). For the first time in the history of warfare scientists of varied disciplines were brought in to apply scientific methods to the problems facing commanders engaged in battle. Most of these problems, particularly in air and sea operations, could be reduced to numerical terms. More often than not, the scientists had to discover for himself the fields in which scientific analysis would be profitable.

> With no operational sorties at his back, never having flown an aircraft or dropped a bomb, he had to divine what were the crucial limitations on military efficiency, when professional opinion was good sense and when it was mere tradition, when obstruction was simple obstructionism, when to let a matter slide, or when to press the relevance of a piece of algebra against all the gold braid on the Staff.[1]

Blackett has justly earned the title of Father of OR being largely responsible for introducing it to all three services as well as defining its general principles.[2] When the Tizard Committee ceased to be active after the outbreak of war. Blackett worked on bomb sights at RAE, Farnborough. During the Battle of Britain he was introduced by A. V. Hill to General Frederick Pile, commanding Anti-Aircraft Command, then experiencing difficulties in operating the new gunlaying radar sets coming into circulation. Blackett assembled a small group of young scientists (dubbed as Blackett's Circus) to work on the gun sites and iron out the technical problems that arose. Pile recognised in Blackett the 'quick intuition of a freshman.' To Pile's chagrin when anxieties were mounting about the threat to merchant shipping from U-boats in 1941, Blackett was moved to RAF Coastal Command. Again he collected a team of scientists called an Operational Research Section (ORS) and he himself became personal scientific adviser to the Commander-in-Chief. We have seen how in 1942 he was translated to the Admiralty to become Chief Adviser on Operational Research.

In his first paper entitled 'Scientists at the Operational Level' (originally circulated privately because of its 'rather facetious character'),[3] Blackett explained that the scientist's main function was to analyse the data found in an operations room such as signals, track charts, combat reports, meteorological information, etc. Using this information he would be able to assess the value of one weapon against another, often relying on a probability formula like Poisson distribution to solve the problem. Blackett had found that when an equipment did not work, it was often abandoned for a new gadget which 'would spring like Aphrodite from the Ministry of Aircraft Production'[4] quite unnecessarily. A numerical estimate of an alternative equipment could avoid the consequences of making too rapid a changeover.

In a second paper on the methodology of OR, Blackett considered two ways of approaching a new problem.[5] In the *a priori* method certain important variables were selected for their suitability for quantitative treatment; the remainder were ignored. Solutions were obtained through forming differential equations. In the *variational* method an attempt was made to find, both by experimental and by analytical methods, how a real operation would be altered if certain of the variables, e.g. the tactics employed or the properties of the weapons used were varied. As will be shown, Blackett demonstrated the variational method most effectively, and controversially in anti-submarine warfare.

Evolution of operational research

Men of science from Leonardo da Vinci onwards have attempted to solve military problems by quantitative methods. In the seventeenth century Sébastien le Prestre, Marquis de Vauban was acknowledged as a master of siegecraft and the science of fortification. He collated facts like a true operational researcher while 'his scientific turn of mind led him to throw his observations, where possible, into quantitative form'.[6] Two hundred and fifty years later, warfare again demanded a scientific approach. In the First World War the physiologist A. V. Hill, then an infantry captain with no knowledge of ballistics, was put in charge of a small group of mathematicians and physicists to investigate the ability of rather primitive anti-aircraft guns to defend London against Zeppelin attack.[7] Known as 'Hill's Brigands'. This party was sent to France to improve the accuracy of artillery fire, thus becoming the first ORS in action.

The creation of a tiny long-range bomber force in 1917 to attack targets in Germany led Viscount Tiverton, the son of Lord Halsbury, a one-time Lord Chancellor, and then a major in the RAF serving on the British Aviation Commission in Paris, to consider navigational aids for finding the target, the advantages and disadvantages of day and night attacks and, most important, the selection of targets that would hurt the enemy most.[8] It was a tragedy that his analyses were forgotten by the Air Staff when preparing plans for using Bomber Command in a future war.

In the 1920s it was left to the far-sighted and imaginative military critic, Basil Liddell Hart, to lament the lack of scientific analysis of weapons, tactics and strategy in the British Army. He urged that an operational research group (he may well have coined the term) be created in all the services. He himself prepared some useful statistical analyses, including the effect of age on commanders in various types of campaign.[9] In the Munich crisis of 1938, when an unofficial adviser to the war minister, Hore-Belisha, he commented on a proposal made by Julian Huxley, J. D. Bernal and Solly Zuckerman, all members of the 'Tots and Quots' Club to make use of scientists in national defence. Their initiative was ignored until June 1940 when, as described earlier, members of the 'Tots and Quots' published *Science in War* explaining how science could be applied to the national effort.

But at Headquarters Fighter Command the Air Staff had to operate a new technology – radar. In 1938 two teams were formed from the staff of Bawdsey Research Station. One under E. C. Williams, a 21-year-old science graduate from Birmingham University, evolved a system for assessing and passing on rapidly the information which came through the Chain Home stations; in other words, the process of plotting, filtering and telling. These analyses were made at Headquarters Fighter Command, Stanmore during the summer air exercises of 1938 and 1939 and were one of the earliest examples of operational research. The second team was led by G. A. Roberts, formerly a Post Office engineer concerned with switchboards. It was sent to the operations rooms of fighter groups where it observed the controllers dealing with the information provided by the radar chain during the summer air exercises. Improvements were suggested for the procedures of the reporting and aircraft control system, the equipment of the operations rooms and the technique for controlling aircraft during an actual interception.[10]

So useful was the work of these two teams that on the outbreak of war, Sir Hugh Dowding, Commander-in-Chief Fighter Command, moved them from Bawdsey and established them at Stanmore under Harold Larnder, a radio engineer who had joined Bawdsey from the International Standard Electric Corporation. First of all known as the RDF Section, in 1941 it assumed the name of Fighter Command ORS. The RAF's acceptance of civilians at an operational headquarters was largely due to three qualities possessed by Larnder. He caused his staff, a number of whom were intellectually his superior, to work effectively together; he had a gift of anticipating what was to be required in six months time; and above all he got on well with service officers of all ranks, won their complete confidence and led his staff to work closely with them.

Fighter Command ORS was characteristic of most other sections. Apart from engineers, there were physicists, a biologist, a minerologist who became an expert on gun harmonization, graduates in English and geography, a statistician and several botanists, added to whom were a handful of women graduates. Although, unlike some other sections, there were no Fellows of the Royal Society, Fighter Command ORS provided the officers-in-charge of six other ORSs attached to RAF commands at home and overseas. (Larnder himself became head of Coastal Command ORS in 1943 and Eric Williams formed an ORS in the Middle East which covered the North African campaign and then went on to Italy.)

OR and air defence

Perhaps Larnder's most significant piece of advice was given to Dowding when the latter opposed Churchill's determination to send fighter squadrons to support the crumbling French defences in mid-May 1940. He gave Dowding a graph which he had prepared with Williams showing the figures of fighter wastage and replacement in France.[11] Dowding took it to the War Cabinet meeting on 15 May. Although fighter squadrons continued to be sent to France for another four days, when it appeared that the collapse of France was inevitable, if Dowding's warnings had gone unheeded the numerical deterioration of his Command would certainly have resulted in defeat in the Battle of Britain. When Dowding, ever a supporter of his scientists, was retired from Fighter Command at the end of the year, he returned Larnder's farewell letter with the following note 'Thanks. This war will be won by science thoughtfully applied to operational needs. H. D.'[12]

A more complicated piece of research was set in motion towards the end of the Battle of Britain. On several occasions the radar reporting system almost reached saturation point. Anticipating that raids would be intensified, a comprehensive investigation was put in hand by the ORS. Eric Williams, Leonard Huxley – an Australian physicist – and F. L. Sawyer, a young mechanical engineer from Cambridge took part in discovering the weaknesses of the system. The report published in November 1940 was basically a study of information handling and proposed 15 measures 'that must be taken' to improve the reporting system.[13] Nearly fifty years later Sawyer recollected

> One of the measures was summarised as the 'proper selection, training and education of personnel' – good resounding stuff when you look back on it . . . But the Service took it all, and they went on to involve us heavily in follow-up action. There were meetings with the Command staff, with TRE, and with equipment manufacturers. There were countless individual discussions and exchanges of minutes. There were further operating experiments, and we helped to write operating procedures. We were directly involved in carrying out procedures for the 'proper selection and training of personnel'![14]

As the preparations for the Normandy landings drew to their climax, members of Fighter Command ORS formed new sections to work with Headquarters Allied Expeditionary Air Force and the 2nd Tactical Air Force supporting the British 21st Army Group in the field. Larnder was appointed Scientific Adviser (OR) to Air Chief Marshal Sir Trafford Leigh-Mallory, the Air Commander-in-Chief, and Michael Graham, a distinguished marine biologist, led the section dealing with tactical air operations. Studies were made of air defence problems over the battle area. An unsuccessful attempt was made to extend night fighter support for Bomber Command raids over Germany as 2nd Tactical Air Force night fighters were well within range. As Sawyer recalled, 'We were possibly being a bit presumptuous into going into such matters of strategy, but we did know what we were talking about in relation to the electronic warfare that was going on at that time.'[15]

OR against the U-boats

Blackett believed that an ORS should be kept to around 20 members. Small though Coastal Command ORS was, it contained a galaxy of talent – no less than six of the staff either were or would become Fellows of the Royal Society and two of those were Nobel Prize winners. The original members consisted of three physicists, one physical chemist, three radar experts, four mathematicians, two astronomers and about eight physiologists and biologists. Their most important attribute came less from making rough estimates than from asking the right question.

Camouflage of aircraft

Blackett himself admirably illustrated this quality trying to improve the camouflage of aircraft. Looking at a map of estimated U-boat positions shortly after his arrival at Coastal Command, he calculated that from the number of hours flown by anti-U-boat patrols they should be sighting four times more submarines than was actually the case. From estimates of the time U-boats spent on the surface he concluded that in three cases out of four the U-boats must be sighting the aircraft and diving before the aircraft spotted them.[16]

Coastal Command aircraft were then painted dull black, appropriate protection against searchlights. But the U-boat usually saw the underside of an aircraft which was usually darker than the sky. Tests were then made with white under-surfaces; it was believed that this would lead to some 40 per cent more U-boats being sighted before they themselves spotted the aircraft and dived. A definitive paper was written by the ORS and was accepted by the Commander-in-Chief, Sir Philip Joubert, and put into general use. In the latter stages of the war deteriorating standards in the training of U-boat crews contributed to even more U-boats being sighted on the surface.

Depth charge setting

Coastal Command ORS's insistence that attacks on U-boats should be made with depth charges rather than with bombs has already been described. The ORS then discovered that the setting of the depth charge was based on the assumption that a U-boat would sight an aircraft and dive, on average, two minutes before the attack.

An outstanding paper was written by E. J. Williams, who succeeded Blackett as head of the ORS, showing that the comparative failure of anti-U-boat attacks was caused by neglecting a few simple considerations. Williams, the son of a Welsh stonemason, had worked under Rutherford and Niels Bohr and at the age of 35 had become Professor of Physics at the University College of Wales, Aberystwyth. He had the gift of simple exposition. 'If you must use mathematics,' he told his staff, 'put them in an appendix.' On one occasion, however, he forgot to write the appendix. In the case of the depth charge setting the crux of the matter was, as Williams explained, as follows:[17]

> In as many as about 40 per cent of all attacks the U-boat was either visible at the instant of attack or had been out of sight for less than a quarter of a minute. It is estimated from such statistics, and the rate at which the uncertainty in the position of a U-boat grows with time of submersion, that the U-boat which is partly visible or just submerged is about ten times more important a target potentially than the U-boat which has been out of sight for more than a quarter of a minute. The very small percentage of U-boats seriously damaged or sunk in past attacks is probably largely the result of too much attention having been given to the long submerged U-boat.

Whatever the filling of the depth charge its lethal radius was only about 20 ft so that a depth setting of 100–150 ft was too low. As a first step the setting was ordered to be changed from 100 to 35 ft. Williams believed that this was still too deep and as new fuses became available the settings were changed to 25 ft. This setting came into general service in the summer of 1942, the change being accomplished by a steady rise in the lethality of attack. In fact, captured German U-boat crews believed that the British had introduced a new and much more powerful explosive. Blackett later wrote 'There can be few cases where such a great operational gain had been obtained by such a small and simple change of tactics.'

In another classic paper of OR Williams predicted the countermeasures that the Germans would introduce when Coastal Command was equipped with centimetric radar, all of which were tried out at one time or another with results very much as Williams had suggested.

Shortage of aircraft: the organization of flying

In the spring of 1942 Coastal Command received a peremptory note from the Prime Minister instructing it to increase the number of patrols over the Bay of Biscay, though no additional aircraft were to be provided. Getting the most out of aircraft within existing resources was not an entirely new idea to the RAF. In the early days of the war Flying Training Command embarked on an intensive flying training programme without any increase in the number of aircraft or servicing personnel. It adopted a system of centralized or 'garage' maintenance, which was introduced by Wing Commander E. C. Cuckney against considerable opposition from the Headquarters of the Command.

This system was further developed by Cecil Gordon, a recently-joined member of Coastal Command ORS, who was asked by Williams to find out how the number of Coastal Command U-boat patrols could be increased.[18] Gordon had entered London University in 1931 after taking degrees in mathematics, chemistry and zoology followed by a degree in physics at Cape Town University. He then embarked on research in genetics. He was, and remained, a committed Marxist which combined with his abrasive personality and careless appearance endeared him to his friends but aroused feelings of distaste in others. But his persistence in developing new ideas flourished in the atmosphere generated by the war.[19]

In his first paper Gordon came to the obvious conclusion that if Coastal Command were to fulfil an increased offensive against U-boats it would have to be given a larger supply of aircraft. Gordon then went on to discover how to make the best use of the men and aircraft available. He treated Coastal Command 'as though it were a colony of his pet *drosophila* (the banana fly).' He identified the aircraft states in the cycle from one major inspection to the next and discovered that its length could be usefully divided into flying days, days spent on maintenance, days spent awaiting maintenance, and days when the aircraft was serviceable but did not fly. The number of days spent in each of these states were necessarily related to the number of flying hours undertaken before a major inspection was required, and to the number of hours flown per day (the sortie length). Some of these factors could be regarded as fixed, but others were at least partially controllable. The interrelationships were explored, both theoretically and in practice.

After a few weeks work Gordon had recast the problem as one of flying hours per maintenance man since the shortage of skilled labour was found to be the key bottleneck. This upset the RAF's criterion of serviceability that the proportion of aircraft flying or available should be maintained at a level of 75 per cent. But the more an aircraft is flown, the sooner it will need repair or maintenance. A *reductio ad absurdum* solution to ensure the serviceability of all aircraft would be never to fly at all.

Gordon tested his theory, assisted by J. J. Vincent, a statistician, and T. E. Easterfield, a mathematician, on the performance of No. 502 (Whitley) Squadron. It was ordered to disregard the serviceability percentage and fly on routine anti-U-boat patrols whenever the weather was fit. In order to make sure that the maintenance organization was fully employed the flying was increased gradually by one sortie per fit-for-flying day, until there was always one aircraft awaiting manpower. When this point had been reached the state of the aircraft in the Squadron was noted every half-hour; this took one observer only. From these individual aircraft histories the number of days spent on maintenance and the number of days awaiting spare parts and tools for Whitleys could easily be calculated.

The trial ran for five months, and during three of them, when conditions had reached an equilibrium, the Squadron exceeded the best average of any squadron over a similar period by 75 per cent. This could largely be attributed to the planning of the flying, since little change was made to the maintenance organization beyond keeping it fully employed by flying the Squadron to capacity. To the aircrews Gordon was known as 'Joad' (after the philosopher who appeared on the BBC Brains Trust) 'for his oddities of appearance and behaviour and for his intellectual arrogance. On one occasion they unrolled a prayer rug in front of him.'[20]

Known as Planned Flying and Planned Maintenance, Coastal Command ORS, since it alone had experience of operating the system, introduced it into the Command as a whole. As Blackett later pointed out PF and PM 'was of very great importance in making available increased flying during the critical period of 1943 when Coastal aircraft contributed so much to the final defeat of the U-boat campaign.'[21] Meanwhile Gordon went on to spread his system throughout the RAF by 'sheer force of character', jumping the hierarchy to take issues to the top if necessary to win his point.

Contradictory advice on the strategic bombing offensive

In contrast to the Battle of the Atlantic, the OR contribution to the bombing offensive against Germany was more controversial. The strategy of area bombing (the destruction of German cities) had for long been laid down and approved by the Air Staff. It was strongly endorsed by Cherwell who had the ear of the Prime Minister. Yet very different conclusions had been reached by Bernal and Zuckerman who had joined the Research and Experiments Division of the Ministry of Home Security on the outbreak of war.[22] Virtually no research on high explosive weapons and their consequences had taken place in the interwar years; what had been done was mainly about gunnery and armour-piercing shells. The scientists attached to this Ministry were required to discover the nature and scale of air attacks likely to be expected; the number of civilian casualties in the early stages of the war and the extent to which these numbers could be reduced by building or finding air raid shelters for everyone, and particularly for London which was assumed to be the main target. This was in effect another form of OR though not named as such.

Bernal, an X-ray crystallographer at the Cavendish Laboratory, known to his friends as 'Sage', joined the Division on the recommendation of Zuckerman, though his Chief warned the Minister of Home Security that as Bernal was a Marxist he might be a security risk. Sir John Anderson, the Minister, replied that 'even if he was as red as the flames of hell' he wanted him as an additional adviser. It so happened that Bernal in his recently published book *The Social Function of Science* had provided a vivid outline of the historical connections between science and war; he had also strongly criticized the government's policy for air raid shelters. He now became head of the operational side of the Division. Zuckerman was gaining a reputation in his research on the social life of apes but, like Bernal, he had wide interests outside the academic circle and after Munich had formed his own Extra Mural Unit at Oxford for the purpose of investigating the effects of bomb blast on human beings.

At the request of Cherwell, Bernal and Zuckerman prepared a report on two towns, Birmingham, a typical industrial centre, and Hull, a port which had suffered extensively from enemy bombing and about which they had a mass of data. This report was issued on 8 April 1942 and contained some unexpected results on the bombing of the civil population.[23] In the raids on the two towns they calculated that one ton of bombs had killed four people and that for every person killed 35 people were bombed out. More damage to houses was caused by fire and not by high explosive bombs. Their most significant conclusion was that they found 'no evidence of breakdown of morale from the intensities of the raids experienced.' (The maximum intensity of bombing was 40 tons per square mile.)

Cherwell drew a very different conclusion. In a much-quoted minute to the Prime Minister on 30 March 1942 on the subject of strategic bombing policy, he declared that the bombing of 58 German cities by a greatly expanded Bomber Command over a period of 18 months would cause the 'great majority of their inhabitants to be turned out of house and home.' He continued 'Investigation seems to show that having one's house demolished is most damaging to morale.' He concluded that compared with the bombing of Hull 'we should be able to do ten times as much harm to each of the principal 58 German towns. There seems little doubt that this would break the spirit of the people.'

But both Blackett and Tizard challenged the numerical assumptions of Cherwell's minute. Blackett thought the estimate of the number of houses which could be destroyed in 18 months was six times too high and Tizard independently assessed the destruction as five times too high. Neither scientists believed that area bombing could produce decisive results in such a limited period in view of the likely trends in aircraft production, the supply of trained aircrew and other valid demands on the supply of long range bombers.

While Cherwell's minute, according to the official historians of the strategic bombing offensive, was not 'decisive', his calculations were used in a highly selective way in order to support a preconceived conclusion. Zuckerman was probably right in stating that 'without it the impetus to sustained area bombing would have been less urgent and certainly less compelling.'[24]

On the tactical level regular scientific advice was not available to Headquarters Bomber Command until 1 September 1941. The Butt report had already revealed the inability of bomber crews to find and hit their targets. B. G. Dickins, a member of the staff of the Director of Scientific Research at the Air Ministry, had for some time been investigating the causes of bomber losses (before the war he had helped Tizard with the Biggin Hill experiments – see page 21). He now took charge of the new ORS. Dickins was usually present at the Commander-in-Chief's daily planning conferences but never became a personal scientific adviser like E. J. Williams or Larnder. Although he had access to the Commander-in-Chief at all times, he and his section were placed under the Deputy Commander-in-Chief. Dickins was a highly competent civil service scientist, but did not have the stature or independence of mind of Blackett or Williams, or the abrasiveness of Gordon.

A junior member of the ORS, Freeman Dyson, who after the war became a distinguished physicist in the United States, recalling his wartime experiences, asserted that the guiding principle for civil servants in the ORS was to tell the Commander-in-Chief only things that the Commander-in-Chief wanted to hear. The Section was

> too timid to challenge any essential element of policy . . . Our Commander-in-Chief [Harris] was a typical example of a pre-scientific military man. He was unimaginative, but at least he was human and he was willing to take responsibility for what he did.[25]

Successful interventions by Bomber Command ORS

Despite Dyson's denigration of his ORS for failing to find a solution to enemy nightfighters attacking from below a Lancaster bomber with upward-firing machine guns and overcoming the difficulty of baling out from the narrow hatch of the Lancaster, there were a number of positive achievements by members of Dickins's team. These included a study of collisions between aircraft over the target area and the accidental dropping of bombs on friendly aircraft. The ORS's support of the introduction of Window has already been mentioned. Another example was its strong support of a specialist force 'to initiate raids and to introduce fires' from December 1941 onwards. There were cogent objections to the creation of a pathfinder force both from Harris and his predecessor, Sir Richard Peirse. The controversy culminated on 16 April 1942 when Harris stated at a meeting attended by members of the ORS that he was 'entirely against anything that would result in the creaming-off of squadrons owing to its effect on morale.'[26]

But evidence that bomber crews properly trained in navigation and night vision could find an aiming point without suffering undue casualties was demonstrated by No. 77 Squadron commanded by Wing Commander Donald Bennett, a protagonist of special markers, and who, promoted to Air Vice-Marshal, became commander of No. 8 Group, the Pathfinder Force, in August 1942. Its birth was precipitated by the crisis which arose as a result of the enemy's jamming of Gee (the first radio navigational aid). By that November the ORS found that a third of the attacks by the Pathfinders were successful.

Much better results were obtained with the introduction of Oboe (a precise radio bombing aid using range measurements from two ground stations) and capable of reaching targets in the Ruhr. The technique of target marking using Oboe and coloured indicators, originally suggested by Dickins, the details being worked out by G. A. Roberts who had transferred from Fighter Command ORS, was first used successfully in the raid on Essen on 5/6 March 1943. The most suitable aircraft for carrying Oboe was the recently-introduced unarmed Mosquito bomber. It was able to carry four of the new target indicators which, when dropped in a salvo, provided a very distinctive mark. The use of Oboe (especially with the centimetric model first used operationally in the autumn of 1944) for target marking was probably the greatest contribution to the increasing effectiveness of bombing operations.[27]

OR and the size of merchant shipping convoys

While Blackett's group at the Admiralty was asked to solve a variety of problems, for example, on gunnery and signals, its greatest impact on the war was in evolving methods for protecting the vital trans-Atlantic convoys carrying supplies of all kinds from the US to Britain. This became all the more urgent with the preparations for returning to the continent. Early in 1943 Blackett was asked by the Anti-U-boat Committee to determine the marginal values of both escort vessels and aircraft. Investigating the statistics for the past two years, the apparent conclusion emerged that the number of casualties in a convoy, in an attack on a given scale and with a given number of escorts, had been roughly independent of the size of the convoy. Apparently a convoy of 40–50 ships suffered no heavier losses, on average, than a convoy of 30 vessels.

This assumption was confirmed by examining several possibilities such as the effect of weather, more efficient escorts, or more air cover for large convoys which might show it was incorrect. All these possibilities were discarded. Further research showed that the length of the convoy's perimeter which had to be protected increased only very slowly with the number of vessels in convoy. Finally, the handling of large convoys was examined. A collection of commodores' reports revealed that while large convoys had been more unwieldy than smaller ones, they had not been unmanageably so.[28]

Blackett's conclusions were challenged by senior British and American naval officers, mainly on account of difficulties in handling the convoys and controlling the escorts.[29] However, Blackett was able to persuade the Admiralty to alter the ruling about convoy size. From April 1943 the number of ships per convoy was increased to 40 and to 50 in October; and the average of 60 was reached and exceeded in June 1944. The increase in convoy size was accomplished without having to introduce new weapons or special training. Blackett later regretted that he had not tackled the problem earlier, but explained that he needed a strong OR group with access to all the relevant facts. This had not been possible before mid-1942.

His group also examined the effect of speed on the safety of ships from U-boat attacks. A long study was made of many individual voyages of ships sailing independently at various speeds and the potential U-boat threat. The effect was finally measured in the following terms: 'proportion of independently-sailing vessels of given speed hit by U-boats per 100 miles of voyage per unit of U-boat density'. The conclusions were that at low speeds a ship was extremely vulnerable to U-boat attack. Fast vessels, on the other hand, were very safe and the degree of safety increased still further as their speed increased. In the intermediate speed range, the safety depended critically on the speed made good, a small increase in the latter making a marked increase in the former. After a

1 Sir Henry Tizard. Architect of the British radar chain and leader of the mission to the USA in August 1940.

2 Winston Churchill and F. A. Lindemann (later Lord Cherwell), his scientific adviser throughout the war.

3 Vannevar Bush. Head of the US Office of Scientific Research and Development and adviser to the President.

4 P. M. S. Blackett. Member of the Tizard Committee and later Chief Adviser on Operational Research in the Admiralty.

5 Howard Florey. Chief wartime developer of penicillin.

6 British Nuclear Physicists. *L* to *R*: William Penney (member of Los Alamos team), Otto Frisch, Rudolf Peierls, John Cockcroft (also director of Army radar research until June 1944).

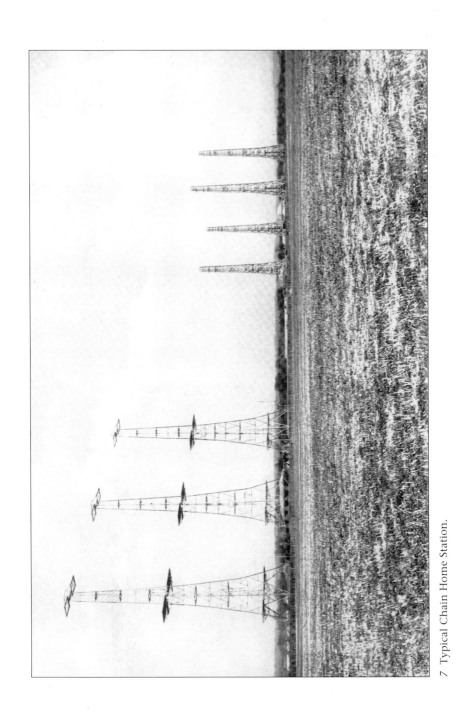

7 Typical Chain Home Station.

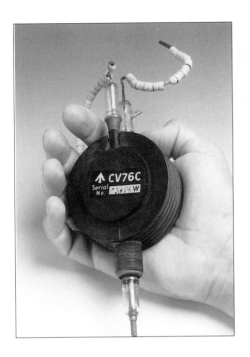

8 Strapped magnetron used for naval 10 cm radar.

9 Hedgehog ahead-throwing bomb projector against U-boats.

10 German Enigma machine with plugboard uncovered.

11 V2 rocket being prepared to fire.

12 Messerschmitt 262 jet-propelled fighter.

number of studies of attacks on independent ships, it was found that the 'critical speed was in the region of the maximum speed which a U-boat would be prepared to maintain for several hours.' From these deductions it was possible to consider questions to which quantitative answers had not previously been feasible. These included the value of defence against torpedoes and the value of zig-zagging. In the case of the former, certain devices might protect a merchant ship but would slow down the vessel. In the latter, this tactic made a ship more difficult to hit but reduced the mean speed of advance.

Opposing views on the Bay offensive

Much more controversial were papers prepared for the Anti-U-boat Committee in March 1943 by Blackett and E. J. Williams (who had followed the former from Coastal Command towards the end of 1942) on whether priority should be given to long-range aircraft covering convoys in mid-Atlantic rather than to aircraft attacking U-boats crossing the Bay of Biscay from their French bases en route to their hunting grounds. The crux of the matter was the distribution of aircraft and whether a proportion of long-range bombers could be diverted from the bombing offensive against Germany. Blackett, supported by naval officers in the Admiralty, contended that there were not enough aircraft for the Allies to be strong enough on every front and that while air cover to threatened convoys might temporarily be the most effective way of employing VLR aircraft, it was unlikely to be the decisive method of defeating the U-boat. He maintained that at least 200 aircraft were needed for the Bay.[30] Williams in a supporting paper on the allocation of aircraft for day and night operations, taking into account the introduction of centimetric radar, but perhaps unaware that the first sets were only received by Coastal Command at the end of January 1943, estimated that 100 centimetric radar-equipped aircraft would be required by day and around 250 aircraft by night. The Admiralty case for intensifying the Bay offensive rested on these two papers.[31]

When Air Marshal Sir John Slessor, the new Commander-in-Chief, Coastal Command, a clear thinker and formidable strategist, read the Admiralty paper he was very angry. He shared Sir Arthur Harris's view that the war would be won by area bombing and that his Coastal Command was essentially a defensive organization, which should 'draw as little as possible on limited resources'. He did not agree that an additional 190 long-range aircraft were needed for the Bay. About 60 VLR aircraft would anyway become available by 1 July. In a forthright letter to the First Sea Lord, Admiral Sir Dudley Pound, on 4 April, he criticized the method of calculating the number of aircraft needed to patrol the Bay.[32] He continued:

> Please do not think I am an enemy of the scientists – very far from it – I have the deepest respect for them and think their work is of vital importance to us. But these last few days especially have impressed on me the feeling that strategy by slide rule is not a working proposition. In particular, the one thing the scientists obviously cannot tell us is what the enemy is going to do – what tactics or strategy he is going to adopt, how he is going to react to heavier casualties, or even what technical countermeasures he is going to produce.

The primary objective, he argued, was to prevent Allied ships being sunk and concluded 'We should tackle this problem from a less scientific but perhaps more realistic angle.'

The outcome went against the scientists.[33] An agreement was made between Pound, Admiral Harold Stark commanding the US naval forces and Slessor that between 30 and 40 long-range aircraft should be added to Coastal Command bringing it to a front line strength by 1 July of 187 long-range aircraft of which between 50 and 60 would be equipped with centimetric ASV and Leigh Lights for operating at night. The Americans were asked to contribute an additional 72 aircraft to join Coastal Command over the Bay.[34]

'Slide rule strategy' survived this fracas, but Blackett, while continuing to provide advice to the Admiralty on a variety of topics until the end of the war, nevertheless no longer enjoyed the confidence of some of his naval colleagues and at the time of the Normandy landings was even denied access to the war room of the joint Army–Navy headquarters at Portsmouth.[35] Williams, his brilliant deputy, tragically developed cancer after a useful visit to North Africa in January 1944 and died 18 months later. He believed that his analyses of U-boat warfare were of comparable interest intellectually to his study of physical problems.[36]

American OR

The Americans, as usual, were quick to see the value of OR for anti-submarine warfare. In April 1942 a small group of scientists was recruited by Columbia University and assigned to the Atlantic Fleet. After overcoming strong opposition from Admiral King, the US Chief of Naval Staff, scientific methods were further extended in May 1943 by the establishment of the US Tenth Fleet which liaised with OSRD and the Air Force.[37] Its main unit was the Anti-Submarine Warfare Research Group (ASWORG) under the direction of P. M. Morse of MIT. William Shockley (who subsequently invented the transistor) acted as his Director of Research. The programme of work was similar to British OR studies and included optimum size for convoys, patterns for depth charges and ways of combating the German acoustic torpedo.

The British were greatly impressed by the speed with which the Americans accepted new ideas or put a prototype into production. An American officer told a British admiral visiting Washington to study the US scientific effort: 'We give you full marks for original thought, but in putting your ideas into production we beat you every time.'[38]

An OR/analysis group was formed about the same time in the VIII US Army Air Force at the request of General Arnold, Commanding General USAAF, to study problems of the daylight bombing offensive against Germany. At first composed of four scientists and two lawyers, one of whom later became a Supreme Court Judge, it was initiated into the mysteries of OR by the scientists in Bomber Command; both sections keeping in close touch for the remainder of the war.[39] Similar cooperation between American and British scientists was established when a small operational analysis section went to North Africa to assist the US long-range bomber force operating over the Balkans. Americans were also attached to the Research and Experiments Division of the Ministry of Home Security to study the effects of bombing German targets. Among them was Charles Hitch, later an influential member of the Rand Corporation which began to study the effect of nuclear bombs after the Cold War began. In the 1960s he held an important post in the Department of Defense.

OR and the return to Europe

The intervention of scientists before and after the Normandy landings proved to be even more controversial than the arguments over the Bay offensive. The planners feared that in the race to build up reinforcements in the beachhead the Germans might win by a factor of three to one. Zuckerman was to play a leading role in finding a solution. In doing so, however, he ceased to be a pure operational analyst and became an advocate of the policy he was convinced was right. For it was possible to draw two different conclusions from the same piece of evidence.

Both he and Bernal were removed from the Ministry of Home Security at the request of Admiral Mountbatten when he became Chief of

Combined Operations in October 1942. They were to advise on the technical aspects of commando and larger force raids on the coasts of enemy-occupied Europe.[40] The third member of this so-called 'Department of Wild Talents' was the eccentric Geoffrey Pyke recommended by Leo Amery, Secretary of State for India. Pyke had no scientific qualifications but was an independent and sometimes brilliant thinker, and according to Mountbatten, was 'something of a genius'. While Bernal busied himself in analysing the composition of beaches suitable for landing armoured vehicles (the beach chosen for the disastrous Dieppe raid was composed of round pebbles into which the tank tracks ground making progress impossible), Zuckerman, among other things, prepared a fire plan for a projected assault on Alderney, one of the Channel Islands.

Early in 1943, on the suggestion of Tizard, who appreciated that the Eighth Army's advance in North Africa provided the first opportunity to examine the effects of Allied weapons on enemy equipment and installations, Zuckerman and Bernal were flown to North Africa to discover the effect of Allied (and enemy) air raids on Tripoli which had recently been taken by British troops. After only a few days Zuckerman was left on his own, as Bernal decided to go to Canada to work on an ill-conceived scheme of Pyke's for making a giant aircraft carrier of reinforced ice. His decision precipitated an all-night row with Zuckerman who tried in vain to persuade him that Habbakuk, as the project was called, was nonsense (which it proved to be). This put an end to the partnership of the two scientists.

Zuckerman now resumed his analyses on the effect of bombing which included the raids made by the RAF. In his report on Tripoli, with assistance from Army and RAF operational researchers, he demonstrated that the raids had had little effect; less than 10 per cent of the bombs had fallen within about two miles of the point at which they had been aimed. Moreover, the RAF bombs were less effective than the American or German equivalents.

Zuckerman had in the meantime attracted the attention of the Air Commander-in-Chief Middle East, Air Chief Marshal Sir Arthur Tedder, and soon became implicated in the air side of the planning for the invasion of Italy. It was essential that the enemy's movement in southern Italy should be delayed. Zuckerman, who had been reinforced by four colleagues from the Ministry of Home Security, discovered that 'the more we concentrated our bombing attacks on those nodal points in the railway system which regulated major traffic and which were responsible for the maintenance of rolling stock, the greater the return in terms of the dislocation of troops and military supplies.' His conclusion was borne out by examination of the Sicilian and Italian railway records. Zuckerman's clear and detailed report convinced Tedder that this was the right method of dislocating communications. In January 1944, after handing over his bombing analyses to E. C. Williams's section to be continued, Zuckerman returned to England to advise on the bombing of rail communications in north-west Europe. He became a Scientific Adviser to Leigh-Mallory in addition to Larnder because as the latter explained, 'there is no single scientist who could of his own knowledge and ability tender the best scientific advice on all points which might arise'.[41] Zuckerman's experience in the Mediterranean was to form the basis of the extremely controversial 'railway' or 'transportation' plan to be executed by the Allied strategic and tactical air forces in the two to three months before D-day.

Zuckerman found that the current plan to delay enemy reinforcements was quite inadequate.[42] Some twenty points on the railways stretching in an arc inland for about fifty to sixty miles were to be bombed less than a month before D-day. A number of the targets were bridges or viaducts or signalling systems. To Zuckerman's astonishment no account had been taken of the possibility of unfavourable weather conditions curtailing the plan or the lack of opportunities for visual bombing which might prevent precise bombing attacks.

In contrast, he proposed attacking between seventy and eighty railway centres where maintenance of locomotives and assembly of rolling stock took place. These centres were selected not only around the projected battle area west of the Seine, but also in north-east France and Belgium, thus disrupting both the transport of troops and equipment *and* the enemy's industrial capacity, especially the movement of stocks of coal, vital both for smelting iron and for producing synthetic oil. In addition he included a number of tactical targets to be attacked shortly before D-day. In defending his plan he would resort to biological analogies.

In order to incapacitate a man it is not necessary to wound him everywhere . . . The fact that one part of the body could continue to have a circulation did not materially help another, whose main arteries had been critically damaged.

The new plan came under fierce attack from a number of quarters. Firstly, from the military transport authorities and C. D. Ellis, Scientific Adviser to the Army Council, as well as from American economists, the latter arguing that it would be impossible to reduce the capacity of locomotives in the time available before D-day and that the plan would have no effect on the movement of troops. The vulnerability of any rail system to even minor breakdowns did not appear to have occurred to them. Even evidence from Ultra that attacks on rail communications were, in fact, being effective was either suppressed or ignored.

Secondly, there was intense opposition from the strategic bomber commanders, both British and American, supported by the Directorate of Bombing Operations at the Air Ministry, who believed that they were on the point of bringing Germany to her knees and that a substantial diversion of the heavy bomber effort to targets in France would only postpone that day.

Finally, there was powerful political opposition led by Churchill who was very worried about the inevitable casualties that would be bound to be inflicted on the French civilian population living in the vicinity of the targets, most of them in built-up areas. He favoured a modification of the original tactical plan, probably drafted by Cherwell.

But both Eisenhower, the Supreme Commander, and his Deputy, Tedder, supported the plan as did the Chief of Air Staff, Sir Charles Portal. Their conclusions were endorsed by the Combined Chiefs of Staff who, at the same time, put Eisenhower in charge of the strategic air forces with Tedder coordinating their operations for the critical period of the invasion. Grudgingly, both Harris and the American commander, General Spaatz, obeyed (though not always), Bomber Command being particularly effective with its precision attacks made with Oboe.

The success of the railway plan did not become fully apparent until records of the pre-D-day French rail traffic were discovered and showed that a 'railway desert' had been created in the north and north-eastern railway system and that in the whole of France by the end of July 1944 the *total* volume of rail traffic had fallen to about 20 per cent of its January level. The effect on military movement was perhaps rather less than anticipated. Nevertheless, to take an example, two panzer divisions posted to Normandy from Poland were forced to detrain over 400 miles from the beachhead. Similarly, formations from the south of France had to abandon their trains and proceed by road where they were subjected to straffing by the Allied tactical air forces. For the German high command the railway system had lost all reliability.

OR in the land battle

The problems facing OR scientists in the land battle were very different from those in air and sea warfare. In the latter, it was usually impossible to check results of attacks visually. (There would have been no difficulty in depth charge setting if it had been possible to spot a submarine 150 ft below the surface of the sea.) But in ground operations results were more easily identified and weapons could be modified or adjusted accordingly.

Army OR was nourished by Blackett's Circus which found a home at Petersham outside London where it could check the accuracy of anti-aircraft batteries located in the adjacent Richmond Park. Before long OR spread to other arms.[43] The difficulties encountered by tank crews working in a hot, confined space, their radios often breaking down, demanded urgent attention. The effect of trigger pressure when firing from a stationary tank at a moving target was the subject of another investigation. Other scientists studied mine detection and clearance; geologists applied their knowledge of soil mechanics to ensure that tanks did not get stuck in soft terrain. The growth of airborne operations presented unexpected problems such as the need for an equipment bag to be dropped separately from an aircraft instead of being strapped to a paratrooper's leg.

On account of these activities the Army Operational Research Group (AORG) was formed and made responsible to the Ministry of Supply.[44] Separate ORS's provided by AORG were formed to go overseas but were controlled by the War Office. The most important was No. 2 ORS which was attached to 21st Army Group commanded by General Montgomery – the British contribution to the liberation of north-west Europe. When asked whether he would like a small team of scientists to observe his battles, the General was reported to have replied tersely, 'I observe my own battles.'[45] However, Montgomery did not object to a scientific adviser being attached to his staff nor to the establishment of an ORS in the field. The Scientific Adviser chosen was Basil Schonland, a South African physicist who had studied at the Cavendish and was then Superintendent of AORG. He was given the rank of Brigadier which put him on a equal footing with the operations and intelligence staff officers at Headquarters 21st Army Group. Wisely, he insisted on being able to summon any member of AORG in England, provided he was in uniform, for a particular job.

No. 2 ORS was led by Patrick Johnson, an Oxford physicist who was the first of his team to land on D-day and observe the siting of the Army radars on the beachhead. After a few weeks he had to find a way of locating German mortar positions which were causing an inordinate number of casualties. The answer lay in adapting the new centimetric gunlaying radar which was able to pick up an echo from the bomb after leaving the mortar; from this it was possible to obtain a bearing on the mortar position. Perilously dug in in front of the forward troops, the radar proved to be the most precise method of locating enemy mortars. German prisoners of war testified to the speed and accuracy of the British counter-mortar fire.[46]

As the beachhead expanded, No. 2 ORS became increasingly occupied with observing the effects of air support either by the heavy bombers or by the bomb/rocket carrying Typhoons of 2nd Tactical Air Force. A report on Bomber Command's massive attack on enemy positions around Caen on the evening of 7 July 1944 indicated that the destruction caused did more to impede the British advance than to accelerate it. After studying the report Headquarters 21st Army Group ordered the ORS to analyse subsequent heavy bomber support. As a result the Army planners were able to develop a more sophisticated approach to the use of heavy bombers over the battlefield.

The value of the recently-introduced airborne rocket projectile was the cause of a prolonged dispute between the Army and the 2nd Tactical Air Force operational researchers.[47] In a desperate attempt by German armour to cut off the American advance after the breakout from the beachhead on 7 August at Mortain, 2nd Tactical Air Force, operating in conjunction with American fighter bombers, claimed to have knocked out nearly ninety tanks and a large number of other vehicles. But Johnson's team discovered that while rockets had indeed knocked out a number of tanks and caused great confusion among the enemy, thus speeding the collapse of their counter-attack, most of the tanks claimed to have been destroyed from the air were, in fact, disabled by US artillery and by infantry firing bazookas.

A few weeks later, when the German army was trapped in the Falaise 'pocket', the Army ORS found that the air forces had accounted for only one-third of the soft-skinned vehicles abandoned. Friction was eased after a formal agreement was negotiated between Schonland and the 2nd Tactical Air Force which provided for joint investigations of air operational against ground targets. This arrangement worked quite well in the Ardennes battle in the winter of 1944/45.

At the end of the war Schonland believed that OR had influenced many aspects of 21st Army Group's operations, for instance the signals organization, which before the campaign began had largely ignored scientific advice, was later 'not too proud to ask for help when its rear communications had failed miserably!' An expert was summoned from home; he discovered that the system had been grossly overloaded and suggested a suitable remedy.

Conclusion

Despite the controversies surrounding the application of OR, there is little doubt that the small amount of staff involved made a contribution to winning the war out of all proportion to their size. In contrast, as Bernal pointed out, the German failure to make use of OR led to their failure to counter enemy weapons and to expend a disproportionate effort on weapons which OR would have shown to be useless. After the war OR became firmly established in both military and civilian organizations on both sides of the Atlantic. But the verve with which problems were tackled during the war evaporated. Not only had the original brilliant practitioners of OR, like E. J. Williams and Cecil Gordon, died or returned to civilian life, but the 'Cold War' with its underlying menace of nuclear exchanges encouraged the adoption of solutions to hypothetical situations instead of extrapolating from data culled from real events as in the recent war. A new and influential school of nuclear strategists (mainly American) emerged influenced by the theory of games which, as Blackett commented, was a 'branch of mathematics . . . almost wholly irrelevant to decision-making'. Ironically, it was Blackett, dubbed the 'father of operational research' who, in a trenchant article written in 1961, criticized the new strategists, reminding them that the (wartime) OR groups were 'simply an addition to, and not a substitute for, the exercise by the trained staffs of conventional military wisdom'.[48]

7

The Transformation of Military Medicine

Organization of medical research

Until the First World War disease in the form of epidemics such as typhus and plague had taken a greater toll of troops in the field than shot or shell, while malaria and dysentery temporarily incapacitated thousands of men. Medical science made great strides in that war particularly in the application of antiseptics and even a start was made on trying to understand psychiatric cases induced by what was then loosely termed 'shell shock'. Greater attention had already begun to be paid to the health of civilians as well as of the military and this interest continued after the war.

In Britain the Medical Research Council was created in 1920 replacing the Medical Research Committee in existence before the war and in time to give support to the military and civil authorities. The new MRC consisted of a number of small committees of specialists covering every kind of medical problem that might be encountered by the armed forces. It was financed by the government and answerable to the Privy Council.[1] Its Secretary, who was also Chief Medical Adviser to the War Cabinet, was 65-year-old Sir Edward Mellanby whose interests in medical research extended far beyond his own province of nutrition where he had made his name in the treatment of rickets.

An organization similar to the MRC was set up by Bush in July 1941 called the Committee on Medical Research (CMR) under which 41 sub-committees of eminent specialists dealt with problems passed to them by the armed forces.[2] Research was carried out either by members of a committee or farmed out on contract to one of the universities. Generous funding was provided by the Federal Government in Washington.

Collaboration with the British medical authorities took place quite independently from the links formed in the aftermath of the Tizard mission. After a period of confusion when the British Central Scientific Office in Washington, manned by physicists who were largely ignorant of medical science, was responsible for making contacts with the Americans, direct contact was established between the MRC and the CMR with representatives residing in London and Washington.[3] This arrangement worked satisfactorily until the end of the war.

But attempts, not only to discover Soviet advances in medical science, but to provide the Russians with the latest drugs and insecticides developed in the West, foundered on account of Russian suspicions of Allied intentions.[4] Several attempts by western scientists to send missions to Moscow failed to achieve their objectives and even led to recriminations between British and Americans as each nation independently tried to impress the Russians with its scientific achievements. It is probable that the Russian refusal to take advantage of western medical research cost them many lives, both on the battlefield and among the civil population subjected to devastating epidemics like typhus.

Healing the combatant: development of antibiotics

After the First World War advances were made, especially in Germany, in developing sulphonamide drugs for use in surgery. A number of them were already in circulation at the outbreak of the Spanish Civil War in 1936. Alexander Fleming's accidental discovery in 1928 of an antibacterial substance which he named penicillin because it was formed by the fungus *Penicillium notatum*, able to kill certain bacteria but non-toxic to humans and animals, attracted less attention. Since his discovery of lysozyme, an antibacterial enzyme, Fleming was convinced that antibiotics were probably more effective than chemically-synthesized antiseptics. However, it was generally considered that penicillin was too unstable to be cultivated for mass production as a drug.

It was only in 1938 that it attracted the interest of a research group at the Sir William Dunn School of Pathology at Oxford led by Professor Howard Florey, an Australian physiologist, and Ernst Chain, a refugee from the Nazis, experimenting with antibacterial substances.[5] Inspired by Fleming's account of his discovery, they began to investigate penicillin's chemical properties. By May 1940 they had produced enough to discover its remarkable therapeutic effects on animals infected with certainly fatal doses of various disease germs. Their success led Florey to request modest funds, especially from the MRC, to which was added a grant from the Rockefeller Foundation, to discover the effect on human beings. Early in 1941 tests on infected patients convinced him that penicillin might be a better remedy than sulphonamide drugs.

Florey was already working on wound shock for the MRC and he appreciated that if penicillin was to be used by the Army it would need to be produced on a massive scale. There were two methods of cultivating the penicillin fungus.[6] In the one used by Florey, known as surface or stationary culture, the fungus grew as a mat on the surface of the liquid medium which was about 1.6 cm deep. After ten days or so, the penicillin content of the clear liquid was poured off and its penicillin extracted and purified. In submerged or deep culture the fungus was cultivated in large fermenters, of up to 10 000 gallons or more, vigorously aerated by sterile air, and stirred with powerful stirrers operating at several hundred horse power. The fungus grew in small loose balls or pellets, and maximum penicillin yield was reached within one to three days. In both processes the strictest precautions to avoid bacterial contamination were essential. As the yield, per volume of fluid, was gradually increased from the one to two units of penicillin/ml obtained throughout the Oxford work eventually reaching an astonishing 40 000 units/ml or more, the need for the gigantic fermenters declined.

All this preparation was considered to be beyond the capacity of British pharmaceutical firms at that time. The War Cabinet Scientific Advisory Committee therefore authorised Florey and one of his workers, Norman Heatley, to tour the United States, then not at war, with a view to persuading the Americans to embark on mass production of the new drug.[7] Heatley and A. J. Moyer, an expert on fungal metabolism, went to work at the Northern Regional Research Laboratory of the US Department of Agriculture at Peoria. Here Moyer increased the yield of penicillin ten or twentyfold during the mid-July to mid-December 1942 period. No work whatever had been done on penicillin there before the end of 1941, apart from Moyer's valuable increase of yield. His work was done in small flasks and the penicillin formed was all discarded. Deep fermentation had been in use for some years for making citric acid, itaconic acid, etc., but whereas the yield of desired product of these would have been grams, the early yields from similar volumes of a penicillin plant would have been in milligrams. Thanks to Dr Newton Richards, chairman of the CMR, and a personal friend of Florey, arrangements were made to mass-produce penicillin by several leading American pharmaceutical companies. But the actual implementation proved to be a gigantic effort and many technical problems had to be successfully overcome.

Meanwhile in the summer of 1942 Mellanby and Florey appreciated that with the campaign in the Western Desert reaching a critical phase, the British forces would still have to rely on homemade stocks of the new drug for a while. Efforts to persuade firms to collaborate proved so difficult that Florey complained to Mellanby that they 'have been of practically no help to us and I could give you a very snappy judgement on the incompetence met almost everywhere.'[8] Florey was equally irked by the Americans failing to keep their promises, not only in the supply of stocks of penicillin, but not informing him of the results of their latest researches. At the end of 1942 there was still only enough penicillin in Britain to treat a hundred cases.

Fortunately British firms suppressed their desire to keep patents to themselves and after prodding from the MRC and the installation of special plant, Imperial Chemical Industries in conjunction with the Therapeutic Research Corporation had managed to produce 38 million units of penicillin (one unit equalled the amount of penicillin in a millilitre of the fermentation solution by mid-1943). These stocks were immediately sent to the British Army in North Africa.[9] (Florey himself and Brigadier Hugh Cairns had already gone out to see the results of administering the antibiotic at first hand. Their report 'Investigation of war wounds. Penicillin. A preliminary report to the War Office and the Medical Research Council on investigations concerning the use of penicillin in war wounds. War Office [AMD 7]' received the highest praise from the authorities.)

In August 1943 two senior British chemists, Sir Robert Robinson, a member of the Scientific Advisory Council, and Professor Ian Heilbron, scientific adviser to the Minister of Production, visited Washington to impress on the Americans the need to increase penicillin production, which had not come up to expectation, especially in view of the possibility of many casualties being incurred in an invasion of Europe.[10] Richards assured them that both research and production were being improved and promised that the US output of penicillin would be stepped up to 150 000 million units per month in the latter part of 1943 using *both* the surface and deep fermentation methods of culture. The Canadians, too, had offered to help and set up production plant at Montreal and Toronto.

Following this meeting, American production of penicillin began to accelerate so that by the time of the Normandy landings there was enough penicillin to treat all casualties requiring it. The flow of information on research between the two countries also prospered. In Britain, meanwhile, agreement was reached on the assignation of patents facilitating the rapid production of the drug.

For some time the Americans had been investigating the chemical properties of penicillin in the hope of synthesizing it and improving on biosynthesis. After much work a synthesis was achieved by V. de Vigneaud of Cornell University Medical College and colleagues, but the yield was minute and commercial prospects nil.[11]

The Allies took great pains to keep their methods of penicillin production secret. Although the Germans were aware of the existence of the drug, they made surprisingly little effort to exploit it, instead developing a simplified and less effective version called vivicillin. This proved to be no more than marfanil, a sulpha drug.[12]

Treatment of wound shock

Less spectacular, but nonetheless important, advances were made in the treatment of shock afflicting wounded soldiers.[13] Their condition could be quickly improved by blood transfusions. Transfusions provided by donor had already begun on a limited scale in the First World War, but by the opening of the Spanish Civil War it had become possible to store blood, and this saved the lives of many troops who had undergone operations in the most primitive circumstances.

It was found that treating casualties with whole blood as opposed to human blood plasma was more efficacious. This required much research in finding effective means of refrigeration, storage and supply. The latter was expedited by air transport which was able to transfer supplies to blood transfusion units in every theatre of war.

Strangely enough, the Germans never found a method of storing blood, most of their transfusions requiring an on-the-spot human donor, and it was only after the capture of British dried blood serum in the Western Desert in 1941 that the Germans began to use natural blood substitutes. Yet in the First World War the German Army medical service had been admired for exploiting new medical techniques. While wartime conditions may have caused delays in the availability of drugs and other medical supplies, the Nazification of the officer corps undoubtedly contributed to a decline in the quality of army doctors, added to which the high casualty rate led to shortened training courses for medical personnel.

Applications of psychiatry

Much had been done in the interwar years to advance the new sciences of psychiatry and psychology. Both became invaluable after 1939. By then treatment of 'shell shock' had been radically transformed. This was due to the widespread acceptance of neuropsychiatric treatment introduced by pioneers like W. H. R. Rivers in the First World War. In Britain it revolutionized the attitude of the high command towards men whose morale had broken down under enemy fire. In 1930 this led to the abolition of the death penalty for cowardice and desertion in the British Army (although strongly opposed by several senior wartime commanders).[14] Such extreme punishment did not exist in the US Army.

In the early stages of the war psychiatrists were trained to deal with symptoms caused in ground and air warfare, hazardous service at sea and extreme conditions of climate. Psychiatrists were posted to fighting formations of both the British and American Armies.[15] The hysterical symptoms characteristic of the First World War were superseded by less obvious disabilities such as anxiety and psychosomatic illnesses generally classified as combat fatigue. Many of the cases were men who were under fire for the first time. In Tunisia one-third of the US Army casualties were psychiatric. Following the Normandy landings, about 10 per cent of British Army casualties were attributed to some form of neurosis.[16] After a period of rest and recuperation behind the battle area most men were returned to their units, but many cases (far too many in the opinion of some medical officers) were sent home to non-combatant units.[17] Shortage of man power became serious in the latter stages of the campaign in north-west Europe and infantry units had to be reinforced from the technical arms and even from the Navy and Air Force.

The air war differed from ground operations in that after combat missions air crews were able to return to relatively comfortable quarters on their airfields, especially in the case of the strategic bomber forces operating from the United Kingdom or Italy. Anxiety symptoms were described as lack of moral fibre (LMF), but much of the documentation relating to it has still to be released. In the bombing offensive against Germany, a postwar RAF psychiatrist, examining the evidence concluded that 'despite the heavy losses and tremendous stress – the Eighth US Air Force reckoned that for every two aircraft lost one individual came off flying for nervous reasons – LMF accounted for less than 0.5 per cent of RAF air crews throughout the campaign.'[18] In fact, most LMF cases seem to have occurred among non-operational aircrew, indicating that many under training were frightened of flying.

The attitude of the Axis commanders to battle exhaustion and stress was altogether different from that of the Allies. German military psychiatrists believed that nervous breakdown was a military rather than a medical problem. Even so, on the Eastern Front psychiatric disorders became rampant especially in the withdrawal from Moscow at the end of 1941. About 7000 German soldiers were executed for desertion while the desertion rate among German troops increased dramatically in the latter stages of the war.

Defeating 'General Malaria': prophylactic treatment

Malaria was a major cause of sickness among troops and was rife on every battle front from the Arctic to the Pacific. While infrequently fatal, malaria cases filled hospital beds and reduced the fighting efficiency of whole formations. In the Macedonian campaign of 1916, Allied troops suffered grievously from what Sir Ronald Ross, identifier of the *anopheles* mosquito as the carrier of the infection, called 'General Malaria' who, he warned, would take the field against the Army at the right moment.

At the end of 1940, with campaigns taking place in the Middle East and East Africa, Mellanby repeated Ross's warning and called upon the War Office to order the increase of supplies of atebrine (or mepacrine) which together with plasmoquin (pamaquin) were the standard synthetic antimalarial drugs.[19] Normally they were manufactured by the Germans who had resorted to them after supplies of quinine (the original anti-malarial drug) had been cut off by the Allied blockade in the First World War.

When the Japanese overran the Dutch East Indies in 1942 the production of mepacrine became even more important. British pharmaceutical firms worked hard to close the gap. Both drugs were made by long and complicated processes and required the construction of special plant. In Britain mepacrine production was increased from a mere 22 lb in 1939 to 12 500 lb (equivalent to over 50 million tablets) in 1942; by the end of 1943 production capacity had increased to a rate of over 100 000 lb per annum.

The next stage was to convince commanders of troops fighting in malarious country that the highest priority must be given to the regular consumption of anti-malarial pills. In the spring of 1943 a letter from a medical officer in Burma was passed to the Lord President of the Council, Sir John Anderson (himself trained as a chemist), responsible for the MRC, which stated that unless something was done 'we shall have the Expeditionary Force in Burma immobilised in exactly the same way as the Allies were held up on the Salonika front.'[20] A few weeks later General Wavell, Commander-in-Chief, India, always conscious of the importance of hygiene, personally intervened and directed that preventive measures should be taken at once by the Indian Army. (Wavell appreciated that troops refused to take the drug in the belief that it led to impotance.)

An important meeting of senior medical officers and members of the MRC in London chaired by the Director General of the Army Medical

Services on 15 March 1943 confirmed that malaria should be regarded as 'Enemy No. 1' in tropical areas.[21] They reached two conclusions; first, that the most important factor in the prevention of malaria was personal prophylaxis which had to be enforced by commanding officers; secondly, the 'sheet anchor' in personal protection was the 'regular and unfailing use of ... mepacrine daily one week before entering and one month after leaving a malarious zone.'

What was now required was scientific evidence regarding the correct dosage of anti-malarials and the assessment of new synthesized anti-malarial drugs. This was done by a specialist in tropical diseases, Neil Hamilton Fairley. He had served in the Australian Army in 1916, joined again in 1940, serving on both occasions in the Middle East and acquiring an extensive knowledge of tropical diseases.[22] He then went to the Far East with Australian forces on the outbreak of war with Japan and had recently escaped from the hands of Japanese in Java by plane. Fairley became a director of the Land Headquarters Medical Research Unit in Queensland, Australia. He built up a complex unit staffed by specialists in protozoology, entomology, biochemistry and clinical medicine in which large scale experiments were carried out on volunteers from the Australian Army. The measures he proposed were adopted first by the Australian Army Staff and field commanders in the south-east Pacific area and then by South-East Asia Command.

The introduction of daily doses of mepacrine – with severe penalties for defaulters – brought a spectacular reduction in the rates of malaria admissions to hospital. In South-East Asia Command the ratio of malaria admissions to those admitted with wounds was 126:1 in 1943, but by 1944, due to mepacrine, it had been reduced to 19:1. It now became possible to operate in malarious areas where the Japanese, who relied on quinine, were greatly disadvantaged. Unlike the Allies, the Japanese did not enforce strict anti-malaria discipline and the rate of malarial infection early in 1945 was 30–50 per cent – equivalent to the rates of infection among British and Indian troops two to three years earlier.

Use of insecticides

Next to prophylaxis, the elimination of the malaria-carrying mosquito ranked at high priority. In the early years of the war several sprays were used to destroy breeding grounds. One was Paris Green, a poisonous arsenical substance derived from a pigment used for paints and the making of wallpaper; the other was pyrethrum made from ground flower heads which, until her entry into the war, had been exported by

Japan. While growing pyrethrum in Kenya was a possibility, it would entail the construction of expensive extraction plant.

A remarkable substitute came unexpectedly from neutral Switzerland. In 1939 Paul Herman Mueller, a staff chemist employed by the firm of J. R. Geigy at Basel, synthesized a derivative of the compound dichloro-diphenyl-trichloroethane (DDT).[23] It was extraordinarily effective as an insect killer and did not deteriorate when exposed to weathering. It enabled the isolated Swiss to increase their food crops by killing the Colorado potato beetle, and when refugees started pouring into the country, DDT was used to rid them of the lice they carried.

Geigy, being an international company, sent samples of DDT to its subsidiaries in the United States in late 1942 and 1943 (the Germans were also informed). The US Department of Agriculture began to use it instead of pyrethrum, then urgently required by the Army. The experiments took place at the Department's laboratory at Orlando, Florida. Within a short time DDT was found to be safe to use on man and was effective not only against lice but against mosquitoes. For the latter a larvicide spray was devised to saturate mosquito breeding grounds.

Similar experiments were conducted at the Geigy laboratories in Manchester and field tests were held at the Chemical Defence Experimental Station in Wiltshire. On 3 December 1943 Professor P. A. Buxton, head of the Entomological Department of the London School of Hygiene and Tropical Medicine who had an international reputation reported to the MRC that 'DDT represents the greatest advance that has ever been made in the discovery of new insecticides.'

The first important use of DDT was to curb an epidemic of typhus (caused in the first place by lice) in Naples in January 1944. Not only was the clothing of the civilian population dusted with DDT, but thousands of Angola shirts impregnated with DDT, intended for the invasion of Europe, were diverted to Naples for the use of Allied troops.[24] The new insecticide was later widely used in the south-east Asia and Pacific battle areas against mosquito breeding grounds and camp sites, though by the time it arrived mepacrine had already begun to reduce the number of malaria casualties.

Other scourges of war

Typhus

Long before the introduction of DDT, Buxton, aware of the likelihood of typhus epidemics as a result of war, began to seek ways of destroying lice and improving vaccines. In 1941 he spent some time in Egypt carrying out tests on a local labour force. He evolved a compound derived from the salt of thiocyanic acid which was used to impregnate clothing and body belts, but these were unpopular with the troops because of the unpleasant smell emitted; as soon as DDT arrived they were abandoned.[25]

Epidemics of typhus due to lice were a much greater threat in the primitive conditions on the Eastern Front. Indeed there were fears of widespread epidemics occurring all over the war zones in Europe. According to an American military observer in Moscow from 1941 to 1942, no effective treatment for typhus was discovered by the Russians, but several anti-lice insecticides were later produced. Nonetheless the Soviet authorities refused access to Buxton, who could have given invaluable advice, to visit Russia.[26] Both the Red Army and the German Army suffered from typhus outbreaks, but the civilian population in the war zone suffered far more as they had no access to prophylactics.

Another form of typhus – scrub typhus – carried by mites was virulent in the latter stages of the Burma campaign and in the south-west Pacific. Kenneth Mellanby, nephew of Sir Edward, who in the early part of the war proved that scabies (an infection common among men and women living in close proximity) was spread through personal contact and not by blankets as was commonly supposed, visited these areas and made a film demonstrating the correct method of applying the mite repellant called dibutylphthalide.[27] A severe outbreak of scrub typhus in Burma in December 1944 was quelled by the immediate dispatch from England by air of one and a half million doses of the appropriate vaccine.[28]

Dysentery

Bacillary dysentery seriously affected the efficiency of troops in the Middle East in the First World War putting men out of action for as long as three to four weeks. Similar epidemics were anticipated in 1940–41 in Greece and the Western Desert but they did not occur due to more care being taken over sanitation (in contrast to the Germans of the Africa Korps whose camp sites were conspicuously lacking in the disposal of human faeces) and to the reduction of flies due to the replacement of horses by mechanized transport and the absence of horsed cavalry.

The treatment of dysentery was revolutionized by a new drug called sulphaguanidine prepared by Dr Buttle from England and Dr E. K. Marshall of Johns Hopkins Hospital in the States.[29] Hamilton Fairley, then serving in the Middle East, discovered that by administering sulphaguanidine to a patient expected to die, the symptoms rapidly disappeared and in a short time the patient was convalescent.[30] Arrangements were made to American-produced sulphaguanidine to be sent from the Lederle Laboratories in New York direct to the Middle East. By mid-April 1941 (shortly after Rommel's arrival in the Western Desert) supplies of sulphaguanidine began to arrive.

Compared with the British, the German treatment of tropical diseases had been rudimentary since before the war and was further restricted when military needs became paramount. However, a new drug called Miracil was prepared for cases of schistosomiasis – a disease carried by worms and induced by bathing. Trials were to have been carried out in Egypt in the event of a German occupation.[31]

In New Guinea both the Australian and Japanese forces were ravaged by an epidemic of bacillary dysentery. Acting on Fairley's advice all available supplies of sulphaguanidine in Australia were rushed by air to New Guinea and every man who complained of diarrhoea was treated with this drug. Within ten days the epidemic was brought under control. The Japanese attempt to take Port Moresby failed; it was commonly said that 'sulphaguanadine saved Moresby.'[32]

Aids to efficiency

Equipment enabling men to fight more efficiently had now become, in many cases, so sophisticated and stressful that medical science was required to provide aids to enable the human physique to adapt itself to these technical improvements. On the ground armoured vehicles like tanks became a priority for research because of the difficulties of working under pressure in a confined space, the ability to see out of the machine, not to mention the vulnerability of the crew to an internal explosion. Likewise submarines were subject to similar stresses and also to the need for supplies of oxygen. As a senior RAF medical officer later remarked: 'the human element must be linked up with the mechanical otherwise the machine will outpace the men.'[33]

The most revolutionary changes were, in fact, to be found in operating modern aircraft capable of rapid acceleration causing the pilot pains and of reaching high altitudes where breathing was impossible without oxygen. The GAF was far in advance of other air forces in finding solutions to these problems (probably because of the *Wehrmacht's* decision that the ground forces should be supported by close support dive bombing). On a visit to research establishments in Berlin in 1937, Wing Commander Philip Livingston, recently appointed as consultant in opthalmology to the RAF and who had become interested in improving pilots' vision while stationed in Iraq, was amazed to find that the Germans were using low pressure chambers and centrifuges for testing pilots.[34] On his return to London he persuaded his superiors to bring aviation medicine up to date. His advice was not ignored. By early 1939 a Flying Personnel Research Committee of the MRC under Mellanby himself had been set up with distinguished specialists to cover physiological, neurological and opthalmic problems of flying. It was to make air operations safer and more efficient.[35] A comparable committee was set up in the CMR,[36] but unlike the American and Canadian aviation experts, the British committee enjoyed an unusual degree of independence; its recommendations were quickly approved and trials of new equipment carried out rapidly. A section of the RAF's Physiological Laboratory was moved to Farnborough where there was a decompression chamber to help pilots cope with very high altitudes.

Oxygen masks

The Germans were well ahead in the development of pilots' breathing equipment. By 1936 they had developed the first demand regulator mask enabling a pilot to control the flow of oxygen. He was already able to connect or disconnect the mask nose to the oxygen supply.[37] The RAF, on the other hand, was not used to flying much above 15 000 ft so that on the outbreak of war photo-reconnaissance pilots and bomber crews were the first to suffer from anoxia flying at altitudes of 30 000 to 40 000 ft and above where the atmospheric pressure is insufficient to maintain a pilot's full mental and physical efficiency.

In the west the Americans led the way providing military pilots with oxygen masks enabling them to engage in aerial combat at heights over 30 000 ft without succumbing to blackout. A team led by Cecil Drinker, Dean of the Harvard School of Public Health, after two months' study, designed a mask which withstood freezing and inward leaking of oxygen-free air at high altitudes.[38] It completely covered the face and included a mask microphone and a special rubber valve for exhaling immediately above the microphone able to withstand temperatures to minus 55° below 0° F without freezing. Certain features from the standard RAF mask, including a chamois lining, were incorporated in the design. Shortly before the end of the war a pressurized cabin was introduced in the Superfortress B-29 and in the photo-reconnaissance Spitfire allowing airmen to dispense with special equipment. This was more important for American heavy bomber crews operating at heights of 25 000 to 30 000 ft.

Countering the effect of high G forces

The force of gravity affects pilots of aircraft flying along a straight and level course and acts positively on the pilot from head to foot. But when the pilot performs sharp turns or other manoeuvres at high speed he encounters much higher head to foot forces over the normal force of gravity (1 G).[39] At 4–6 G his bloodstream and various organs in his body will suffer and in a short while he will lose consciousness altogether. Whether pilots could withstand such high pressures became an urgent subject for research, mainly using a centrifuge in which animals and humans were rotated. Drinker and other scientists discovered that a pilot lying on his side could barely tolerate high negative G forces (over 4.5 G) but when seated he could tolerate accelerations up to 16 G.

Eventually a G suit was invented to withstand high G forces. Known as the Franks suit, it was a non-stretch garment enclosing fluid-filled reservoirs covering the lower body; it exerted counter pressure automatically under G compression by simple hydrostatic force and raised the blackout threshold by at least 1.5 G in centrifuge tests; it could be worn quite comfortably in the confined space of a cockpit. Mustang pilots escorting US heavy bombers on long distance flights in 1944–45 found the Franks suit a great help.

Night vision

Improvement of aircrews' night vision was another topic for medical scientists. Radar could guide a pilot in a night fighter within range of his quarry, but he had to identify his target visually before making an attack. Bomb aimers needed to release their bombs accurately in the face of the dazzle and glare of searchlights and the bursting of anti-aircraft shells fired from the ground. Crews of maritime aircraft need to identify surfaced submarines or ships in darkness. On return from a mission landings had to be made on darkened airfields.

Livingston was the driving force behind the Night Vision Sub-Committee of the FPRC and made two important contributions.[40] The first was the design of a pair of goggles for aircrew based on his experience of combating glare from the sun while in Iraq. The goggles gave protection against air blast dust. They were fixed to the flying helmet and could be quickly adjusted. Filters or corrective lenses could be changed quite easily and the goggles had a forward visor which when tilted into position enabled the pilot to fly against the sun with a minimum amount of discomfort.

Secondly, Livingston invented an apparatus with which it was possible for pilots to discover their ability to see at night. This was a rotating hexagon drum, each face being similar and displaying a series of illuminated panels showing letters, figures and shapes which could be presented under various illuminations to simulate moonlight, starlight and dark sky, and which pilots had to identify. Six men could be tested at one time. By the end of the war 200 000 tests had been carried out. No pilot who had not scored over 13 in a single test was accepted for training as a night fighter pilot. Air gunners had to obtain a score of five or above.

One of the worst obstacles to night vision in bombing operations was the glare from searchlights, not only directly but also because the light was scattered by the aircraft windows and reflected from fittings within the aircraft.[41] It was found that the perspex windows of the bomber reduced the range of vision. A crude short-term solution was to cut a hole in the perspex window allowing cold air to enter. Alternatively, aircrew were expected to keep their windows clean. Another important innovation made at the end of 1942 was the provision of an extra crew member specifically for bomb aiming. Until then the navigator had been responsible for bomb aiming. When the time came he was night blind for some moments after leaving his well-lit navigation desk for the dark bomb-aiming position.

Conclusion

Compared with the First World War, the care of the sick and wounded from 1939–45 was infinitely better. This was due to recent important advances in surgery, the availability of new drugs like the sulphonamides and antibiotics, blood transfusions and the ability to store blood and carry it rapidly to the battle area. The most notable advance in what were later termed antibiotics was penicillin, the discovery of which had remained dormant until resurrected by the team at the Sir William Dunn School of Pathology, Oxford. Nevertheless the mass production of penicillin was slow in getting underway and a joint Anglo-US effort was required to ensure that there were enough supplies available for the casualties expected in the campaigns to liberate Europe.

As in past wars, illness of troops in the field continued to exercise the medical services. Malaria was one of the main causes of sickness. Both the British and American forces were severely handicapped. On the Indo-Burma front, for example, the incidence of some British units admitted to hospital from malaria was as high as 746 per 1000.[42] In the

US Army the incidence of malaria was very high in the South Pacific and Burma–China areas. The US forces suffered 500 000 cases in four years of war, the highest numbers being reported in 1943–44.

While drugs like mepacrine and the fortuitous arrival of DDT were made available as quickly as possible, the importance of individual prophylaxis of malaria was to begin with either ignored or not properly appreciated despite the known high sickness rate from this disease in the First World War. Reflecting on the connection between malaria and war, a leading British authority on tropical medicine declared forty years after the end of the Second World War:

> All individual methods of protection depend forcibly on the individual, be it wearing proper clothing, using repellants, or taking antimalarial drugs. Training in the use of these methods, supervision of medical authorities and responsibility of the commanding officer may secure success. Unfortunately one of the lessons of the past was that the value of these simple measures is fully recognised only after they have been disregarded.[43]

Penicillin, DDT and the new antimalarials were hailed by the general public as 'wonder drugs' as soon as the veil of secrecy was lifted. Even in the services, the reputation of DDT was such that in some units in Burma sanitary fatigues were believed to be no longer necessary. It was left to the scientists themselves occasionally to sound a note of caution warning that, for instance, DDT was no panacea 'to be broadcast indiscriminately to kill off all noxious pests. Much more research was needed to ensure that there was no serious effect on the "balance of nature" with subsequent disastrous effects.'[44]

Only twenty years after the end of the war was it realized that antimalarials and insecticides were either having less effect on the parasites they were intended to destroy or were adversely affecting the balance of nature. Perhaps the greatest shock was the discovery that *P falciparum* malaria had become resistant to mepacrine and its successors. This was the reason for as many as 26 000 cases of malaria during the Vietnam war.

Finally, the saving of lives and limbs as well as the reduction of illness in the Second World War depended not only on medical research but on the 'directives, organisation, cooperation, integration, training and skills, supply and transport'.[45] Fortunately the British and Americans, despite occasional misunderstandings, saw eye to eye over this necessity. The Russians, on the contrary, were blinkered by their antipathy to the capitalist West and failed to take advantage of new discoveries in antibiotics and insecticides.[46] As for the Axis powers health and sanitation was not always given a high enough priority. The Germans, who before the war had been in the forefront of medical research, although they made use of DDT, failed to exploit new antibiotics like penicillin and some of the sulphonamides.

8
Unacceptable Weapons: Gas and Bacteria

Developments in chemical warfare before 1939

Chemical weapons were never used in the Second World War. But the Allies believed that there was always a possibility that the Axis powers would resort to them especially as the Germans had been the first to use poison gas on the Western Front in the First World War while in more recent years the Japanese employed chemical and biological weapons against the Chinese in Manchuria, and there was no doubt that the Italians had used gas against the Abyssinians. The armed forces of the great powers therefore had to be able to protect themselves against chemical weapons while defence scientists sought to improve gases such as phosgene and mustard whose properties were well known from after 1915, and to examine the properties of new chemical compounds.

In fact, poison gas had failed to break the deadlock on the Western Front as the Germans had hoped. Their High Command did not have the confidence to exploit the factor of surprise, allowing the Allies to find countermeasures and, in the long run, to prove themselves more efficient at launching gas attacks, aided by the prevailing winds which were usually favourable to them. While gas-filled projectiles could be effective, they were only decisive in limited actions and they were no more lethal than bullets and high explosive shells. British gas casualties on the Western Front were about 180 983 of whom only 6062 died, or one in every thirty. American Army casualties were even lower: out of 74 779 casualties due to gas, 1400 died, or less than one in fifty. And that was when gas warfare was at its height.[1] After the war military thinkers like Liddell Hart even contended that gas was more humane than other weapons and that 'the suffering due to gas [was] not often as bad as the agony caused by a mangling bullet or shell wound.' Support for chemical weapons also came from the well-known scientist, J. B. S. Haldane, who, like Liddell Hart, had served on the Western Front.

Nevertheless in the minds of the general public (not to mention the conventional military) chemical weapons were held to be a barbarous method of waging war and this conception was expressed powerfully in postwar literature and art. Wilfred Owen, killed in action by small arms fire only a week before the Armistice, and whose poems were published posthumously, wrote from personal experience in *Dulce et Decorum est*:

> Gas! Gas! Quick boys! An ecstacy of fumbling,
> Fitting the clumsy helmets just in time:
> But someone still was yelling out and stumbling...
> In all my dreams, before my helpless sight,
> He plunges at me, guttering, choking, drowning...

Less convincing was Sargent's popular painting 'Gassed' which shows a single line of soldiers, hands on each other's shoulders, after a mustard gas attack. (In fact, the blindness would go and the blisters disappear after about a fortnight.) Even an eminent judge like Lord Halsbury, who had been head of the Explosives Department in the Ministry of Munitions, asserted that a single gas bomb dropped on Piccadilly would kill everyone in an area from Regent's Park to the Thames, and a well-known supporter of disarmament informed radio listeners that protection of the civil population from gas attack would be impossible (strenuously denied by government scientists).

The abhorrence (based mainly on misinformation) with which chemical warfare came to be regarded was exemplified in the Geneva Protocol of May 1925 signed by 41 powers including Britain, France, Germany, Japan and the United States, all of whom agreed not to use either chemical or bacteriological weapons. But neither Japan nor the United States ratified the agreement, the latter submitting to pressure from a military lobby led by the wartime commander of the Chemical Warfare Service.[2] As there were no means of enforcing the Protocol, it is not surprising that China and Abyssinia, lacking a chemical industry to enable them to retaliate, fell victim to aggressors.

After the Geneva Protocol, the industrial powers accepted that chemical warfare could not be ignored and, in general, adopted the policy that they would only use poison gas in *retaliation* against a surprise enemy attack. Britain, France and the United States already had experimental establishments kept up since 1918. In Britain the Chemical Defence Experimental Station was at Porton near Salisbury where the rolling downland bore a striking resemblance to the countryside round Ypres. The CDES was directed by a military commandant, but included a number of civilian scientists of whom the most senior had experience of chemical warfare in France.[3] Up to 1939 work on offensive weapons was constrained by the limited amount of money available as well as by the difficulty of anticipating what sort of weapons would be used in a future war. For the time being two gases were favoured, dichlorethyl-sulphide, commonly known as mustard gas, which was persistent, causing blisters, but was not necessarily lethal like the acute lung irritants, chlorine and phosgene. All three agents could be disseminated by artillery, mortars or aircraft. At the outbreak of war available stocks of toxic agents at the pilot plant of Sutton Oak in Lancashire amounted to no more than 500 tons.

Much more had been done on defence. Not only had the service respirator been greatly improved but respirators for the civilian population, regardless of age or infirmity, had been designed and mass production begun in 1937. Protection against non-persistent gases for 38 million people was available at the time of the Munich crisis in the following year, though they were blissfully unaware that their gas masks were useless against arsenical compounds (less lethal than phosgene) nor were they told how to take elementary precautions against mustard gas.[4]

The French chemical warfare centre was at Le Bouchet south of Paris and there was a testing ground in the Sahara desert. Unlike the British, they placed more reliance on artillery projectiles than airborne sprays to release poison gas.[5] Their policy for protecting civilians was based less on the issue of gas masks than on the construction of underground gas proof shelters, or the adaptation of the Metro for the protection of Parisians escaping from airborne gas bombs.

Far more ambitious were the Americans on account of their flourishing chemical industry. A poison gas factory and experimental centre were built at Edgewood on the Chesapeake River near Baltimore and which was combined with a large gas-filling plant. It became operational in 1918 and continued to be maintained after the war.[6] But in 1939 when war in Europe broke out again, the US armed forces were far from proficient in being able to engage in chemical warfare.

Under the terms of the Versailles Treaty, the Germans were, of course, forbidden to develop weapons for chemical warfare. But senior officers of the German Army, confident that gas would be an important weapon in a future conflict, made clandestine arrangements with the Soviet Union for German gas experts to work alongside Red Army chemical warfare specialists. The latter hoped to improve their own, rather primitive technology, and eventually to make use of the superior German chemical industry.[7] Collaboration, including the testing of gases, continued for ten years from 1923 to 1933. In the summer of that year Hitler abruptly ordered collaboration on chemical weapons with the Soviet Union to cease immediately and all German units to return home. Meanwhile foreign military observers, unaware of what had been happening, noted that in German Army manoeuvres anti-gas precautions were taken very seriously.

German reluctance to use gas in the early stages of the war

The German doctrine of *blitzkrieg* did not require the employment of chemical weapons, which would have been more of a hindrance than a help, requiring the transport of stocks of gas-filled projectiles only to be followed by the decontamination of ground covered in an advance. Neither Hitler, who became a casualty to mustard gas in the trenches near Ypres in 1918 nor the High Command were in favour of gas. There were other cogent reasons.[8] Gas warfare demanded the production of quantities of munitions which Germany could not provide. Finally, there was an underlying fear that, as in the First World War, initial success through a surprise gas attack would bring retribution to Germany on account of the greater industrial power of the United States.

But when the tide turned on the Eastern Front in 1942, chemical weapons were reconsidered. It was believed that for some years the Russians were investigating nerve gases. A surprise onslaught using phosgene or mustard might forestall these preparations and even retrieve the German fortunes at Stalingrad.

The British, who had been receiving little information on chemical warfare from Ultra intelligence, were worried not only by the possibility of the Germans using gas, but that Stalin might allege a German gas attack in order to compel the British to retaliate in kind. On 10 May 1942 Churchill in a forthright broadcast declared that the British would drop gas bombs on German cities should Hitler make an unprovoked gas attack against the Russians. This threat was followed on 5 June by President Roosevelt, after learning that the Japanese were suspected of using gas against the Chinese armies, and who also declared that the Americans would retaliate against the Japanese in kind.[9]

These warnings were probably in Hitler's mind at the Führer's Conference on 8 July 1942 when he ordered a review of German preparations for chemical warfare to be made.[10] Speer, his Minister for Armament Production, who had not been present at the meeting and who was unenthusiastic about using gas, although annoyed that he had not previously been consulted, ordered poison gas production to be raised from the low priority at which it had been placed since the beginning of the war. (At the end of 1939 the rate was 1500 tons per month.)

An event of greater significance was the beginning of the production of nerve gas. The German Army had learned about this possibility from Dr Gerhard Schrader, head chemist at the I. G. Leverkusen laboratories in 1936 when, in the course of work on insecticides, he discovered that a cyanogen phosphoric acid amide (an organic phosphorus compound) was highly toxic. It was of no use commercially and it was given the code name 9/91 and then called Tabun (later classified by the Allies as GA). Schrader and his colleagues were immediately taken over by *Waffenamt Prufwesen 9* (the experimental branch for chemical weapons) to continue their researches although on a low priority.[11] Schrader meanwhile had gone on to study an even more toxic substance called Sarin (GB) which was dispersed in a liquid form, but being non-persistent its effects were combined to a limited area (i.e. the area covered by a bursting shell or bomb). A third, and even more deadly gas called Soman (GD) was independently prepared by Richard Kuhn, a Nobel Laureate, in 1944, but there was no time to make a preliminary sample of the product.

Nerve gases in general were about ten times more effective than existing gases like phosgene because of the difficulty of detecting them and the rapidity with which they took effect. They caused death by inhalation and could also be absorbed through the skin. Side effects produced miosis or semi-blindness and other minor symptoms. A low-key postwar report by a Porton scientist concluded that the 'effects on the morale [of troops] of witnessing convulsive deaths in the field, and of uncertainty whether minor symptoms might not be the prelude to more serious consequences would undoubtedly be considerable.'[12]

The German High Command's reluctance to resort to using poison gas was further strengthened by two factors. First, the GAF from the beginning of 1944 was no longer in a position to bomb cities. Use of chemical weapons would therefore be restricted to artillery weapons in the field while in mobile warfare gas would be of doubtful benefit. (There were several occasions where the Germans *could* have used gas to their advantage, for example at Stalingrad, but this would merely have provided a reason for the Allies to retaliate wherever they wished. Secondly, the Allied bombing of German industry had increased in intensity and accuracy. By the autumn of 1944 the German army had withdrawn east of the Rhine. On 11 October Speer wrote to Field Marshal Keitel, Chief of the German High Command, requesting that the production of tabun and mustard gas should be cut drastically in favour of propellants and explosives badly needed for the hard-pressed army. By that date the total production of toxic agents had risen to 3800 tons a month and further expansion had been planned. However, little had been done to protect the civil population. Keitel agreed, but it was too late for any increase in conventional munitions to stop the Allied advance.[13]

When the Allies crossed the Rhine in March 1945 they were amazed to find no less than a quarter of a million tons of toxic munitions and bulk agents. Much of this was discovered at Raubkammer in north-west Germany, the German equivalent of Porton, but larger, covering an area of 50 square miles.[14] Its organization was similar to that of Porton. It was probably here that the British discovered gas-filled shells bearing an unfamiliar code mark (green rings) on their sides. They proved to be filled with tabun. The toxic group to which it belonged had been investigated and synthesized by British chemists but there had been no time for further development. The Russians meanwhile captured Dyhernfurth in Silesia where tabun was being produced and a number of German scientists were sent back to Russia, but whether or not existing stocks of tabun had already been destroyed remains a matter for conjecture.

The British consider retaliatory measures

The British preparations for chemical warfare were no more advanced than in Germany. An organization for research and development and for production of toxic agents had existed since 1923. In 1940 J. Davidson Pratt, an industrial chemist, who had held an important post in the Ministry of Munitions in the First World War, was appointed Controller of Chemical Defence Research and Development in the Ministry of Supply. The possibility of a German invasion in 1940–41 created a dilemma for the General Staff as under the terms of the Geneva Protocol Britain could not initiate chemical warfare. It was, however, Churchill, who had been responsible for gas supplies towards the end of the First World War, who transformed hesitant speculation into active measures. The production of mustard gas was increased and the embargo on the importing of American phosgene was lifted and shipments to Britain in foreign-registered vessels began. This gas would be used against German cities. By the end of 1941 the British had supplies of toxic agents not far short of 18 546 tons. Bomber Command had trained seven medium bomber squadrons to use chemical weapons.[15] In theory they were supposed to be able to launch a retaliatory strike at five hours notice.

On the scientific side some sixty chemists who had been working at the universities or in industry were commissioned as 'technical officers'; they included O. H. Wansbrough Jones, a Cambridge chemist (a postwar Chief Scientist in the Ministry of Supply), who had briefly known Fritz Haber after he had left Berlin for Cambridge in 1933. These officers were posted to formations at home and overseas but they regarded Porton as their alma mater.

Porton itself was inadequate for trials involving the release of very large amounts of some gases. Sir Frederick Banting, a Nobel prize-winner in medicine and the co-discoverer of insulin, was a member of the Canadian National Research Council and visited England early in 1940 mainly for the purpose of fostering Anglo-Canadian scientific cooperation, especially in chemical warfare.[16] This not only led to the exchange of information between the two countries but also to the despatch of the Superintendent of Experiments at Porton, L. Lloyd Davies, to Canada to find a suitable area remote from human habitation where trials of poisonous gases could take place. A site fifty miles by fifty miles was chosen at Suffield in Alberta and was called the Field Experimental Station. It was completed by the beginning of 1942 with civil and military divisions and a small runway for light aircraft. Professor Otto Maass of McGill University, known as the Canadian 'father of chemistry', directed the Canadian chemical warfare effort and Davies became Superintendent at Suffield.

Cooperation with the Americans, however, had its ups and downs. Chemical warfare weapons were not on the agenda of the Tizard Mission, but Lieutenant Colonel E. J. Barley, with first hand experience of gas in the trenches of Flanders, went to the States in August 1940 and was given full access to American research at Edgewood and elsewhere with the expectation that this would be reciprocated.[17] Sensing the Americans' disappointment over the lack of information on gas weapons, Tizard arranged with the Canadian NRC that Banting, Maass and another chemical warfare officer, F. A. Flood, should act as substitutes for the British. This proved acceptable for the Americans until January 1941 when the British Chemical Warfare Board decided to stop the exchange of information. Fortunately H. J. Gough, the Director of Scientific Research in the Ministry of Supply, was wise enough to appreciate that severing connections with the Americans would not only be politically disastrous but probably impossible. On 7 January 1941 Americans, British and Canadians confirmed that all information and chemical warfare materials and equipment would be shared between them.[18] In the meantime the British chemist, Professor R. P. Linstead, then appointed to the Chair of Organic Chemistry at Harvard, acted as unofficial liaison officer for chemical research problems. After the United States entered the war, the head of the US Chemical Warfare Service visited Porton and selected US Army officers began to work at the establishment.

As already observed, the German setbacks on the Eastern Front caused some anxiety amongst British Intelligence especially when Ultra transcripts revealed that modifications were being made to German Army anti-gas equipment.[19] A plan was drawn up that in the event of the Germans initiating a surprise attack on the Russians or elsewhere, Bomber Command would retaliate with a combined high explosive/phosgene attack on selected German cities. The scientist responsible for advising on the tactics of the plan was Professor David Brunt, a meteorologist and member of the Chemical Warfare Committee. Brunt had served in the former capacity in France in 1917 with the Independent Air Force and after the war had been responsible for forming a section at Porton to study problems of diffusion and turbulence about which nothing was known on the quantitative scientific plane. Modelling his calculations on the thousand bomber raid on Cologne, Brunt estimated that phosgene could be disseminated over an area of four square miles of a city centre at a rate of 10 tons per square mile per hour.[20] Another plan drawn up at Porton in December 1943 introduced persistent mustard gas in addition to phosgene, the target being 'immobilized' for more than 24 hours 'provided that the attack was delivered in sufficient weight.' (A force of 430 aircraft was envisaged.)

These proposals were criticized by the Air Ministry's Director of Bomber Operations. Gas, he said, was still an untried weapon in air warfare and while it might cause many casualties and upset morale, on its own it was unlikely to be able to inflict permanent damage to property or reduce the enemy's industrial potential.

Resort to using gas was, however, given more serious consideration when the flying bomb attacks against London got underway, with the prospect of them being followed by long-range rocket attacks. On 6 July 1944, after 2500 people had been killed or injured in three days of flying bomb attacks, the Prime Minister told the Chiefs of Staff:

> If the bombardment of London really became a serious nuisance and great rockets with far reaching and devastating effect fell on many centres of government and labour, I would be prepared to do *anything*

that would hit the enemy in a murderous place. I want the matter studied in cold blood by sensible people and not by that particular set of psalm singing uniformed defeatist which one runs across here and there.[21]

After the Chiefs of Staff had studied reports by the inter-service committees on chemical and biological warfare, they agreed unanimously on 26 July that nothing would be gained by resorting to either poison gas or bacterial weapons.[22] The use of gas against flying bomb launching sites would be ineffective without dropping high explosive as well; neither would gas help in breaking out of the Normandy beachhead; on the contrary, it would only restrict movement of the advancing troops. Then there was the question of the morale of the people of London. Neither the Germans nor the Japanese were likely to initiate chemical warfare, but a 'first strike' by the Allies would almost certainly invite retaliation and would probably cause resentment among the general public whose morale (as a result of the flying bombs) was less resilient than it had been. 'On balance', the Chiefs of Staff concluded, 'we do not believe that for us to start chemical or biological warfare would have a decisive effect on the result or duration of the war against Germany.'

Churchill was unconvinced by what he called 'this negative report', grumbling that he was unable to 'make head against the parsons and the warriors at the same time. The matter should be kept under review and brought up again when things get worse.'[23] Fortunately they did not. The defeat of the flying bombs and the capture of their launching sites in August and early September removed the threat against London (though not that of rockets, the warheads of which were, in any case, too small to hold adequate quantities of toxic agents). On 27 February 1945 the Prime Minister accepted the Chief of Staff recommendation that the production of gas and the charging of gas weapons should be discontinued as there were now enough chemical warfare agents and weapons stockpiled. He asked that all those who had worked on chemical weapons should be thanked for their efforts.[24]

The search for a biological weapon

Armies have resorted to bacterial agents for hundreds of years. In the fourteenth-century Mongol soldiers hurled plague-infested carcasses over a city's walls and a sixteenth-century tactical manual described how toxic-filled shells could be fired against an enemy. Although not used in the First World War, biological weapons were included in the 1925 Geneva Protocol at the insistence of the Polish government. The Japanese, never having ratified the Protocol, apparently developed bacterial agents and used them against the Chinese in the 1940s. The Italians were believed to have conducted trials in biological warfare (BW) in the late 1930s, but abandoned the project as being too dangerous. The French, who had been engaged in BW research since the 1920s, after hearing that the Germans were investigating anthrax, began research at Le Bouchet on anthrax, brucellosis and botulinus toxin as agents with which to charge aircraft bombs and hand grenades. Experiments were abandoned in 1940 after the General Staff had concluded that BW had no military value.[25] When France was occupied all the documentation on chemical and biological weapons at Le Bouchet was seized by the Germans, thus alerting them to the possibility that the Allies might be developing bacterial agents.

As we know, the British were especially concerned about the vulnerability of their cities to air attack and the thought of microbes descending on London was indeed alarming. In 1934 the government, after receiving intelligence reports that the Nazis were preparing for BW, referred the matter to a small group of bacteriologists. In 1936 Hankey, then Secretary to the Cabinet and the Committee for Imperial Defence, and who always kept an eye on the technical side of war, formed a small committee, including four bacteriologists and representatives from the fighting forces, to study the problem. On the outbreak of war this committee was upgraded and attached to the War Cabinet.[26] Hankey remained in charge after he left the Cabinet Office and became Chancellor of the Duchy of Lancaster, later being succeeded by Alfred Duff Cooper who had been Secretary of State for War during the prewar rearmament period.

However, the real force behind BW was Paul Fildes, son of Sir Luke Fildes, a fashionable Victorian portrait painter, who was regarded as the foremost bacteriologist of the day. Fildes, aged 56, had served as a doctor in the Royal Naval Volunteer Reserve in the First World War and was then working for the MRC. In the summer of 1940 he was put in charge of a small Biological Department at Porton. His earlier military experience had made him wary of bureaucracy and he persuaded the Ministry of Supply that he should continue to serve under the MRC but that his salary and expenses and those of his team would be paid by the Ministry.[27] The results of his work would be communicated direct to the War Cabinet Committee. Fildes was convinced that little could be done to protect human beings against bacterial agents, so it would be more sensible to concentrate on evolving an offensive weapon which could be used as a threat or in retaliation.

After considering various viruses and bacteria, Fildes chose *bacilus anthracis*, or anthrax, the spores of which are infectious to men and animals, and they are resistant to heat and to drying. Anthrax was given the code name N. He also investigated the botulinus toxin as an alternative. The next problem was to find a suitable projectile to carry the poison to the enemy. Three possibilities emerged: first, by contaminating bullets or shells; second, distributing the bacteria by aircraft bombs or artillery shells; three, using saboteurs to plant bacteria in enemy-occupied territory. The last was ruled out as being impracticable. The difficulty with missiles was to preserve the toxicity of the bacteria on the way to the target. Eventually, a small four-pound bomb, which would be dropped in clusters, was chosen.

Fildes and his eight colleagues worked under conditions of great secrecy in a small brick building, originally the animal house of the Department of Physiology. It was soon extended to provide more laboratory space. An American military observer visiting Porton in the spring of 1942 noted that, although he was responsible to the War Cabinet Committee, Fildes was, in fact, the 'guiding genius' of the establishment.

On account of the development work required for the filling of the N spores, the bomb was not ready until August 1942. It was first tested on the island of Gruinard off the north-west coast of Scotland. A small bomb, suspended from a gallows, was detonated near sheep tethered 250 yards away. A second trial was made in September. Fildes reported to the Cabinet Committee that 'the effects are of a completely different order of magnitude from those found with chemical weapons.'[28]

The Americans, since entering the war, had been following the British experiments with great interest, but had not yet taken any action to produce either BW agents or weapons. The effectiveness of the trials at Gruinard, where the ground was to remain contaminated for many years to come,[29] followed by an airborne trial at Penclawdd in south Wales, brought American scientists over to explore the results at first hand. Clearly it was beyond the British capability to mass produce the weapon. The Americans decided to go ahead with producing and improving N and a suitable projectile to carry it in September 1942. A research station was built at Camp Detrick in Maryland and a number of scientists of high calibre recruited to work there under the direction of Dr G. W. Merck, founder of the pharmaceutical firm of that name. (The organization was completely detached from the OSRD.) Conditions for testing BW weapons in secret were much more favourable than in

Scotland. Production of N was to take place at the Vigo Plant in Indiana. This was a cooperative enterprise conducted by the Americans and the Canadians and was administered by Dr Maass.[30]

However, the Americans, in spite of receiving a copy of the 'BW Bible' (or 'Green Book'), failed to reciprocate during the latter part of 1943 apparently because of difficulties in Washington and Fildes complained that American policy (as far as he could discover) differed so much from that of the British that it would be impossible for him to carry out his own government's instructions.[31] Lord Stamp, a bacteriologist who had been working as Director of the Emergency Public Health Laboratories at Epsom, was sent to the States to smooth out relations with the Americans.[32] On 8 February 1944 Stamp reported to Fildes that the 'political crisis' in the US organisation seemed to have died down. A pilot plant for the production of N had started at Camp Detrick. A week later British and Americans met there and agreed on a policy of retaliating in 'as short a time as possible' should the enemy commence BW. This, of course, needed the approval of the 'higher command.'[33]

That April Churchill asked for defensive measures to be driven forward in case the Germans retaliated after the Allied invasion of Europe.[34] No sooner had the flying bombs began to arrive than *offensive* action was planned and an order was placed for 500 000 N bombs to be manufactured by the Americans.[35] They would be used to saturate six German town and city centres including Berlin, Hamburg, Frankfurt and Stuttgart. Shortly after, the responsibility for BW was transferred from the War Cabinet to the Chiefs of Staff. A new inter-service committee was created under Air Marshal Sir Norman Bottomley, Deputy Chief of Air Staff. Although Fildes had flatly refused to serve under either the Civil Service or the armed forces, his masters, the MRC, had no desire to be so closely associated with a weapon of unparalled destruction. Bottomley resolved the matter by sending Fildes a telegram inviting him to join the new committee.[36] Fildes accepted; he and Davidson Pratt, later joined by Lord Stamp, sat as the only civilians. Fildes was somewhat mollified by the Air Marshal's offer to share his gin ration.

At the end of August 1944 Intelligence believed it unlikely that the enemy would resort to BW. It had also transpired that the production of N bombs had encountered difficulties and that they were unlikely to be available before the spring of 1945. Fildes had, however, made up his mind that his task was now to develop 'a specific defence against N and *not* to prove the practicability of other offensive weapons.'[37] The failure of the N bombs to materialize led Fildes to write on 7 December 1944 'I doubt whether the production of BW weapons is at present practicable by any country.'[38] But he did believe that BW research should continue after the war, concentrating on defensive measures linked closely with peaceful application, for too little was then known about the transmission of respiratory diseases.

The German reaction to biological warfare

It was clear that British Intelligence had exaggerated the German development of bacterial weapons both before and during the war. BW weapons were just as distasteful to the German High Command as nerve gases. After discovering the French work on BW, the Germans must have thought that the Allies were unlikely to resort to it. On the other hand, the Russians might, and for some time they had been suspected of secretly developing microbes or viruses as a weapon.[39] Even so, it was only in 1943 that a BW experimental centre was set up at Birnbaum between Posen and Frankfurt-am-Oder. On 30 April Professor Kurt Blome, head of the Department of Genetics, Population Policy and Racial Care in the RFR, was put in charge of bacteriological research by Field Marshal Keitel. The latter, appreciating that should the Allies launch BW attacks against Germany, epidemics might break out among the civil population, decided it was preferable that a civilian should be in charge of defensive and offensive measures. Blome had proved himself to be a good organizer but he was no bacteriologist and only worked half time on the project. When he was taken prisoner by the Allies he claimed that Keitel had told him that Hitler had strictly forbidden offensive BW measures to be taken, Keitel adding that, in his opinion, it was a foolish way of waging war.[40]

Not so for Himmler, head of the SS, who expressed a keen interest in using viruses against an enemy (his employment of low-grade poison gas as a means of eliminating occupants of concentration camps is too well known to need stressing) and wanted to carry out experiments with plague viruses on human beings. Objections by service officers, including the Surgeon-General of the GAF, were countered by Himmler's threat that refusal to allow experiments important to the war effort was a treasonable act. Fortunately, experiments made little headway and, like the Allies, Germany had no stocks of BW agents at the end of the war.

Conclusion

The possibility of retaliation by one side or the other made senior commanders on both sides seek reasons for not employing either poison gas or bacteria. Moreover, they were unreliable weapons and had never been tested properly in air warfare against a modern state (the bomber being the most likely vehicle to carry toxic agents to the enemy). In land warfare the need for laborious decontamination would be needed for mustard gas and N spores.

In spite of these reservations the use of nerve gases in the event of another war could not be ignored. Nerve and other lethal gases continued to be developed. In ground warfare the purpose was to produce the greatest effective concentration in the shortest possible time. In the battle area gas would be used, firstly, to immobilize tanks and, secondly, to disorganize personnel. Less progress was made with BW weapons. Ten years after the war, David Henderson, the Superintendent of the Microbiological Research Department at Porton, concluded that the most likely use of BW would be covert: the London Underground, for instance, could easily be contaminated by terrorists and this type of attack could be extended to other parts of the country. His American counterpart at Camp Detrick, G. W. Merck, warned that BW weapon development did not require a vast expenditure of money nor large production facilities and could easily take place under the guise of medical or bacteriological research.

9
Premature Weapons: the Rocket and the Jet

Introduction

Two revolutionary weapons emerged in the latter part of the Second World War – the long-range rocket and the jet-propelled aircraft. The arrival of the first was entirely due to the Germans while the second was developed in parallel secretly by both the British and the Germans. Neither the long-range rocket nor the jet fighter influenced the outcome of the war, but both were to change radically the face of warfare while their peaceful applications led, on the one hand, to the exploration of space and, on the other, to the transformation of air transport.

The long-range rocket: early development

Rockets were used as weapons of war as early as the fourteenth century; the Chinese even designed two stage rockets ultimately releasing swarms of arrows to harass hostile troop concentrations.[1] Military rockets were revived by European armies in the eighteenth and early nineteenth centuries but were soon superseded by artillery which, by the end of the 19th century, had achieved much greater accuracy of aim. In the first half of the twentieth century improvements in fuels and materials made rockets a more practical proposition. Three protagonists of long-range rockets, the Russian, Konstantin Tsiolkovsky, the Hungarian, Hermann Oberth and the American, Robert Goddard, provided theoretical studies, sowing a seed bed for more intensive development in the years before the Second World War.

Experiments with various types of rocket were made by the major powers; the British, because of the urgent need to strengthen their air defences, decided to concentrate on primitive ground to air weapons;

American engineers working on behalf of the US Army, influenced by Goddard, who had already fired a fuelled rocket in 1926, experimented with rockets designed to propel aircraft; in the Soviet Union a military rocket was launched in August 1933 reaching a modest height of over 1000 feet, inspiring a young scientist, Sergei Korolev, involved in the project, to write 'Soviet rockets must conquer space!'[2]

But it was the German Army, as described earlier, that took the lead in developing a supersonic rocket (the A4) with a range of over 200 miles, carrying a warhead weighing one ton to the target. Development took place at Peenemünde under the technical direction of von Braun. It was decided not only to develop the missiles but actually to build them *in situ*, quite independent of the Reich Research Council, ordnance branches of the Army and armament firms.[3] To achieve this von Braun made use of his contacts with the universities and institutes of technology and by the outbreak of war had teams working on propulsion, aerodynamics and guidance and control.

Difficulties encountered

However, despite von Braun's admirable foresight the Army rocket programme soon found itself handicapped by political indecision and technological setbacks. After the invasion of Poland in September 1939 increased funds became available for rocket research. This was largely due to the persistence of Colonel Walther Dornberger, who was in charge of von Braun's team, and who also was a close friend of Field Marshal Brauchitsch, Commander-in-Chief of the Army. Hitler's attitude towards the research at Peenemünde varied from unbounded enthusiasm to indifference, even hostility. Before the war he displayed little interest and in November 1939 ordered the steel quota for the rocket casing to be cut back. But this order was rescinded six months later and in August 1941, after being shown a film about the A4 by Dornberger and von Braun, he declared that the A4 was 'revolutionary for the conduct of war in the whole world' and instantly demanded the production of hundreds of thousands of missiles. On 28 August 1941 the A4 was given top priority in new weapons. But Hitler never grasped the complexity of rocket development and production and the numerous electronic components that would be required. His interest in the A4 was really aroused by the increasing weight and accuracy of Allied bombing and the inability of the GAF to retaliate. Long-range rockets, originally intended by the Army as being able to out-distance artillery thus became a weapon of revenge to be directed against centres of population.

A more valuable ally of Dornberger and von Braun was Albert Speer, Hitler's chief architect, who had had a hand in the construction of the Peenemünde installations. He became fascinated both by von Braun's team and the novel technology of the missile. When appointed Minister for Armaments and Munitions on 9 February 1942 he became directly responsible for Peenemünde.[4] One of his first actions, however, was to cut back the numbers of the construction force. The Peenemünde establishment was also used by the GAF which, in 1942, began its own long-range missile project in lieu of a bomber force – the flying bomb conceived by the staff of the air frame makers, Gerhard Fiesler. In the same year a joint Army–GAF team combined to develop a ground to air missile known as *Wasserfall*.

While *Wasserfall* brought fresh manpower and resources to the Army side at Peenemünde, it also complicated and therefore delayed the progress of the A4. A brief description of the rocket must now be given, Just over 45 feet in length, it had three important features requiring skilled staff and specialist manufacture. First, propulsion. This was provided by a motor running on alcohol and liquid oxygen which, in turn, was backed up by a second system using hydrogen peroxide and calcium permanganate to drive the fuel pumps. This work was supervised by Walther Thiel, formerly a member of the Research Section of the Ordnance Testing Division. Between 1936 and 1941 he was able to reduce the size of the engine but increase its thrust to 25 tons.

Secondly, special attention had to be paid to the aerodynamics of the fin and fuselage of the rocket making use of the wind tunnel. Rudolf Hermann, from the Institute of Technology at Aachen, was the supervisor. He had already been testing small rocket models and was attracted to Peenemünde by the promise of a much larger, world class supersonic wind tunnel completed in November 1939.

Thirdly, and most important, was the guidance system which became the responsibility of Ernst Steinhoff, another ordnance scientist and Professor Wolmann from the Dresden Institute of Technology. The system was preset with an integrating accelorometer to measure when the missile had reached the requisite speed to reach the target; the fuel to the motor was then cut off and the missile coasted along its ballistic trajectory to the target.

All these different components had to compete with other equipment priorities on an overstretched economy. Nevertheless Dornberger pressed ahead in the belief that it was better for the missile programme to advance rather than to shrink or to be cancelled.[5] But it inevitably affected the reliability of the A4. The engine was too complicated for cost-effective mass production and the guidance system too inaccurate. It was hardly surprising that the scientists, to Dornberger's irritation, turned to dreaming about rocket travel in space on occasion. In spite of all these difficulties, after two attempts, an A4 was successfully launched on 3 October 1942.

Intervention by Speer and Himmler

Further complications arose when Speer tried to rescue the production plans from 'the morass into which they had fallen' as he had successfully done with the fighter aircraft industry. Dornberger resented the intrusion of Speer's bureaucrats, who wanted to turn over the project to the great electrical engineering company, AEG. Instead, in May 1943 a realistic production programme was drawn up with the aim of increasing the number of A4s from ten at that date to 600 by September 1944. The Zeppelin works at Friedrichshafen was to be used as a supplementary production centre.

More intrusive and dangerous than Speer was Himmler who visited Peenemünde for the first time in March 1943. Although silent at the time, he was evidently impressed and from then on the SS attempted to wrest control of the establishment from the Army. An attempt to demonstrate their power was made early in 1944 after von Braun and several senior members of his team had refused to be taken over by the SS.[6] They were arrested but after some weeks were released due to the efforts made by Speer and Dornberger.

Peenemünde was not immune to the attention of British scientific intelligence as the Germans assumed it to be. By the summer of 1943 reports from secret agents and an indiscreet conversation between two German generals recorded while they were prisoners of war in England increased the likelihood of a surprise attack either by pilotless aircraft or by long-range rockets. On 18 June 1943 R. V. Jones at the Air Ministry scrutinizing aerial photographs of Peenemünde detected a rocket parked on a railway truck.[7] More substantial evidence was provided when a rocket launched from Peenemünde erroneously landed in Sweden. The wreckage was examined by British intelligence officers. Later further evidence was provided by Polish resistance fighters from the A4 proving site at Blizna south of Warsaw. Although there was some disbelief about the reality of the rocket threat from the countermeasures organization set up to deal with the new German weapons and, especially from Cherwell, enough evidence was at hand to justify a major attack on Peenemünde on the night of 17/18 August 1943 by RAF Bomber Command.

This raid marked a turning point in the history of the establishment. While severe damage was caused, particularly to the camp housing Russian and Polish workers, the test stands and special facilities such as the wind tunnel remained unscathed, and Dornberger reckoned that work could be resumed after a delay of only four to six weeks. But two leading scientists, Thiel and Helmuth Walther, an expert on rocket fuels, were killed in the raid.[8] As it happened, the development of the A4 had virtually been completed.

Production of the A4

The raid gave Himmler the opportunity to exercise greater control over the A4 and he persuaded Hitler to move production underground. An SS general, Hans Kammler, was put in charge and after looking at possible sites for a factory, he chose Nordhausen in the Harz mountains. The factory was named *Mittelwerke* and was to be entirely manned by prisoners from the concentration camps. By the end of September 1943 over 3000 were already at work preparing the underground site and this total was increased to 13 816 just over a year later. *Mittelwerke* became infamous for the cruelty to which the workers were subjected and the atrocious conditions in which they worked.

More and more, the A4 was regarded as a retaliatory weapon and in company with the flying bomb acquired the name of *Vergeltungswaffen* (retaliation weapons and known by the Allies as V weapons), especially after the devastating raid on Hamburg by Bomber Command in August 1943. A year later, after the assassination attempt on Hitler, the opportunity was taken by Himmler to absorb the rocket programme under the SS. Kammler became 'Special Commissioner for A4 matters' and as a result of the decline in the German Army's prestige Peenemünde was absorbed into a civilian organization headed by a director from Siemens. Kammler despised Dornberger for being what he called an 'armchair general' (to which rank he had by then been promoted) but allowed him to continue to direct the training and outfitting of the rocket troops.[9]

The A4 becomes operational

Mainly on account of inefficient administration exacerbated by the production of rockets *and* flying bombs, rocket troops were not deployed until August 1944, by which time British troops were overrunning the flying bomb launching sites in northern France. (One reason for the failure of the flying bomb offensive was described on page 44.) While the British press was elatedly announcing this victory, the first two rockets were fired against London from Wassenaar near The Hague on the evening of 8 September. They landed at Chiswick in west London and at Epping in east London. Rockets continued to be fired from the Netherlands and along the Rhine until shortly before the end of the war. As the rockets could be fired from a small pad of concrete easily camouflaged and were serviced by transportable equipment, they were very difficult to locate. It became possible, however, for a gunlaying radar located in the Thames estuary to detect the rise of a rocket after firing, though the range could not be estimated. At least a few minutes warning of the imminence of an attack could be given.[10]

Just over 2700 Londoners were killed and 10 000 injured by the rockets. The material damage was relatively slight. But the effect on the morale of a war-weary population was marked, giving them a taste of what future warfare might be like. On 17 March 1945 the last rocket was fired against London and targets in East Anglia. But far more grievous casualties were suffered by the citizens of Antwerp and Liège, both within close range of the rocket firers in the last three months of 1944.

Conclusion

Even such an enthusiast for the A4 as Speer had begun to have doubts about the potential value of the A4 as early as July 1943 and one of his colleagues confided six months later that the rocket was 'in no way a wonder weapon'.[11] The haste with which it was developed meant that it was extremely inaccurate (its error of aim was as high as seven miles) and with current technology it could never (as has often been assumed) have rivalled the bomber aircraft to destroy pinpoint targets. A far better weapon for development would have been an airborne guided missile carried by fighter planes which, had it been available in sufficient quantities, might have acted as a brake on the Allied daylight bombing offensive. But such a weapon would have been a *defensive* one and that was abhorrent to Hitler and his entourage.

It was, indeed, on account of Hitler's indecision that the A4 suffered from a lack of positive direction so that its priority alongside other new weapons was never secure. Even had this support been available the German armament industry could never have sustained not only two V weapons but a host of other complex weapons which proliferated in the latter stages of the war.

The subsequent use of the A4

Nevertheless the Allies were not slow in perceiving that the long-range rocket was a weapon of great potential, not only for use in the war against Japan but in the postwar era, because it was relatively immune from interception and was likely to be more accurate at long ranges compared with pilotless aircraft. The Americans were first off the mark. Within a few weeks of the end of the war against Germany specialist teams had seized most of the documents and key personnel, including Dornberger and von Braun, connected with the German Army missile programme in addition to parts and equipment for about 100 A4s. Much of this material had to be evacuated quickly from the Russian and the British zones of occupation.[12] In due course a total of 240 scientists and engineers, headed by von Braun, Arthur Rudolph, his chief Engineer, and Hermann Oberth, volunteered to go to the States where they believed they would enjoy better pay and living conditions than in England or France. They were earmarked for the US Army's guided missile research programme at Fort Bliss in Texas.

The Russians, too, were not slow in snatching the spoil. In July 1945, after searching for material at Peenemünde, they went on to examine Nordhausen. Helmuth Gröttrup, von Braun's deputy for production, who had decided to return to the Soviet zone and collaborate with the Russians, was able to help them redraw the A4's components. In a very short time the Soviets had replicated the technical documentation removed by the Americans. In October 1946 two hundred members of the German Army missile team headed by Gröttrup and their families were secretly transported to Moscow. Here Gröttrup and Sergei Korolev, who had become the leading Russian rocket expert, began work on their own version of the A4 known as the R-1 (*Raketa* 1).[13]

Although 184 German scientists and engineers arrived in England to provide information for British defence scientists (only to be sent home to their bitter disappointment after two years), the British missed out on this wholesale exploitation of German talent. However, a unique test firing by a German team of A4s took place at Cuxhaven on the shores of the North Sea in the British sector on 14 October 1945. The firings, designated Operation Backfire, were attended by representatives from the USA, the Soviet Union and France. Subsequently the British Special Projectile Operations Group produced a complete set of instructions of how to assemble, test and launch the A4 in the form of a five-volume handbook, the like of which had not even existed in Germany.[14] Thus Backfire marked a new phase in the development of the long-range rocket.

In the end von Braun and Arthur Rudolph achieved their dream of conquering space when they joined the National Astronautics and Space Administration (NASA) to lead the team working on the giant

Saturn rocket project responsible for the landing on the moon in 1969. Ironically, it was Korolev, who had learned so much from German experience, who designed the R-7 which 12 years earlier had both astonished and alarmed the world by putting the first *sputnik* into space and thus proving an intercontinental ballistic missile was possible.

Jet-propelled aircraft: early gas turbines

Like the rocket, the turbojet aircraft has a number of antecedents. Following water power machines, steam power began to be exploited in the Industrial Revolution; the steam turbine itself was first defined by a French engineer in 1822. As the nineteenth century progressed, more sophisticated turbines were designed; one of the most important was the brain child of the English engineer, Charles Parsons who, in the 1880s, designed axial flow and centrifugal turbines for propelling ships.[15]

By the early 1930s research, conducted mainly in Europe, on compressors, combustion chambers and outlet nozzles enabled the internal combustion gas turbine to become a practical proposition only awaiting an inventor to design a light and efficient power unit (a turbojet) for an aircraft. Already it had been found that aircraft could be accelerated by rearward pointing jets. The principle of the turbojet engine was for a quantity of air to be drawn in, compressed in an axial or radial rotor, mixed with suitable fuel in a combustion chamber and expanded through a turbine which provided sufficient power to drive the compressor and then to be expelled through the power jet nozzles. It was possible to choose from two types of compressor – axial or centrifugal.

Early British turbojet development

Research and development of gas turbines for aircraft took place mainly in England and Germany, though useful contributions were made by the French; for example, in 1921 Charles Guillaume patented a complete axial flow turbojet in very nearly its modern form. Research on gas turbines in the United States concentrated more on a turbo-supercharger than on a self-contained gas turbine prime mover.

In 1921 W. J. Stern, a British Air Ministry engineer, wrote a report on the use of gas turbines as prime movers for aircraft, and suggested that what was needed was an efficient lightweight compressor which would be incorporated in a turboprop engine.[16] Stern's proposal was further developed by A. A. Griffith, who had arrived at RAE Farnborough with a distinguished degree from Liverpool University but who had chosen to work his way up from the shop floor to a senior scientific officer in the Physics and Instruments Department. In 1926 Griffith outlined a theory for axial turbomachinery whereby the blades were shaped as aerofoils using experimental and theoretical data on aerofoil design. The Aeronautical Research Committee (ARC) was sufficiently impressed and authorised the making of two test rigs, one for testing cascades of aerofoils and the other consisting of a coupled axial compressor and turbine rotor.

In spite of the success of the ensuing experiments, Griffith's subsequent proposal to develop an aircraft power plant was rejected, though further experiments on components were recommended by the ARC. But Griffith, discouraged by this verdict, abandoned work on the gas turbine as a power plant at RAE until 1936, though work on superchargers and exhaust turbines was continued. Tizard, the chairman of the ARC, then recommended that RAE should develop a turboprop engine as part of the rearmament programme.[17] Griffith was now joined by Hayne Constant, a Cambridge graduate in the mechanical sciences who had joined RAE in 1928 and worked on engine vibration problems. From 1936 to the outbreak of war when Griffith left RAE (Constant then took charge of the team), all types of turbine engines, especially the performance of multistage axial compressors and turbines were investigated. Construction and testing of components were undertaken by several engineering firms, including Metropolitan Vickers, which later produced an axial flow engine called the F-2, but it played no part in the war.[18]

Entirely different was the line taken by a young RAF officer, Frank Whittle, son of an engineer who ran a small business in Coventry. Whittle early displayed an interest in mechanics and when old enough was determined to join the RAF. At first rejected because of his physique, Whittle embarked on a course of physical development which enabled him to be accepted for an RAF apprenticeship in 1923. After going as a cadet to the RAF College, Cranwell where he learned to fly, he set out his ideas for improving aircraft propulsion in a remarkable thesis entitled 'Future Development in Aircraft Design'. At that time he was unaware of the RAE project and he apparently never revealed when he first heard about the gas turbine. On 16 January 1930 Whittle, then aged 22, filed a patent embodying the principles of a gas turbine turbojet engine. While his ideas attracted no support from industry or the Air Ministry (then preoccupied with modernizing conventional aero engines to meet the German threat), his inventive energies were recognized and he went with the backing of the RAF to Cambridge where he took first class honours in the Mechanical Sciences Tripos in 1936. He continued to work on his engine design until five weeks before his final exam.[19]

In 1935 Whittle obtained the backing of several friends who formed a private company called Power Jets. It was established in an unused shed at the engineering firm of British Thomson Houston at Rugby. Power Jets was largely dependent on this firm for services and components. The RAF continued to take an interest in jet propulsion and transferred Whittle to the Special List enabling him to devote his energies to improving his invention.

It was a tragedy that a major invention like Whittle's was dependent upon a financial backing not exceeding £20 000 (£800 000 would be its current value).[20] In spite of this handicap, the technical ability of the Power Jets' team was sufficient for it to place an order for an experimental engine from BTH early in 1936. It failed to come up to expectation. But in June 1939 after the development and testing of three centrifugal engines, supervised by Whittle himself, a test run of 20 minutes produced a maximum speed of 16 000 rpm. Among those watching the trial was the Director of Scientific Research at the Air Ministry. Hitherto sceptical, he was so convinced by this performance that a fortnight later a contract was placed with Power Jets for a centrifugal engine – the W1 – and with Gloster Aircraft Company for an experimental aircraft with the specification E28/39.[21]

Early German turbojet development

German interest in jet propulsion was rather more active than in England. As noted earlier, German engineers were not only interested in rocket propulsion but also in pulse and ram jet engines (without compressors). At Göttingen, the well-known centre for aeronautical research, Albert Betz and W. Encke were investigating axial compressors at the same time as Griffith's team at RAE. Unknown to them, a young physics student, Hans von Ohain, son of a retired army officer who had become a light bulb distributor in Berlin, began to design a turbojet engine in the autumn of 1933. He had no knowledge of either Whittle's or Guillaume's patents, but he was fully aware of the studies being made by Betz and Encke.[22] Having no engineering experience, he engaged a motor mechanic to help him build a test engine for which he took out a patent in 1935. Unfortunately the engine was defective and never really ran properly. Ohain recognized that he was unable to afford full-scale development and would have to seek external support.

In 1936 Ohain managed to convince his professor of the potential value of his turbojet and, armed with an introduction, Ohain met Ernst Heinkel, the enterprising aircraft manufacturer. Heinkel had been obsessed for some time with the design of high speed aircraft. He immediately became enthusiastic over Ohain's proposal and provided him with ample funding and first class facilities. By September 1937 a hydrogen-fuelled demonstration engine was being run on the bench. These experiments were a private venture of Heinkel and were not disclosed to the *Reichsluftfahrtministerium* (RLM), the German Air Ministry. Ohain was, however, not alone in thinking about jet propulsion. There were several members of the *Deutsche Versuchsanstalt für Luftfahrtforschung* (the German Research Institute for Aeronautics) sponsored by the RLM. One of them was Helmut Schelp who had studied engineering in the United States and specialized in gas turbines. Schelp appreciated that propeller-driven aircraft would become inefficient at speeds over 480 mph and concluded that jet-propelled aircraft would fill the gap.[23] In August 1937 Schelp was assigned to a special jet propulsion office in the RLM where he learned about Heinkel's turbojet experiments and also the work being done on axial compressors at Göttingen.

Meanwhile Ohain's engine (classified as He-3B) was fitted into a specially designed aircraft, the Heinkel 178; the engine gave a thrust of 1000 lb at 13 000 rpm and weighed only 800 lb. Early in the morning of 27 August 1939, only four days before the outbreak of the Second World War, the Heinkel took off from Marienehe, a lonely airfield near the German port of Rostock and made the first jet-propelled flight lasting six minutes. Some weeks later Hitler watched a demonstration flight but was apparently unimpressed, merely enquiring why it was necessary to fly faster than sound.

Notwithstanding Hitler's discouraging reaction, General Ernst Udet, Chief of Development in the GAF, who had witnessed the first flight, instructed that development of a high-speed turbojet fighter should go ahead. Even Göring was apparently not told of this order. Following his success, Heinkel designed a successor to the experimental He-178, the He-280, the first twin-jet engined machine which flew in April 1941, a month before the Gloster E28/39.

But Schelp and his colleagues decided, after investigating the possibilities of several aircraft engine makers, to give a contract for a twin-engine aircraft fitted with axial jets to Willy Messerschmitt, maker of both engines and air frames.[24] This became the Me-262; it was intended to have a speed of 528 mph and an endurance of one hour, thus giving it a higher performance than the best German fighter – the Me-109. The engine chosen was the Jumo-004, designed by Anselm Franz of the Junkers Engine Division. It was an axial engine which had a smaller frontal area than a centrifugal engine, giving the Me-262 an advantage over the Meteor, the British equivalent. A prototype was first flown in

July 1942 but failed to attract the attention of senior GAF officers until almost a year later. Schelp had also taken the precautionary measure of inducing another firm, the Bavarian Motor Works (BMW) to design its own axial engine.

Development and production of British and German turbojet fighters

The Gloster Whittle E28/39 did not fly until 15 May 1941, nearly two years after the Heinkel 178. Whittle watched the flight, made appropriately at Cranwell. The delay was largely due to the failure of industry and the Air Ministry to appreciate the importance of the turbojet. However, in January 1940, Air Marshal Tedder, then Director General of Research and Development at the Air Ministry, accompanied by Tizard, visited Power Jets where they were given a demonstration of Whittle's engine. Tedder later recalled how impressed he was by the

glowing combustion chamber and the blazing blue jet flame roaring out into the open, added to which the fact that the thrust developed was considerably more than optimism had suggested. Here was another gamble, a real war winner justifying the manufacture of an initial batch of engines and aircraft to match, straight off the drawing board.[25]

Further encouragement for the project came from Cherwell who visited RAE that September and was convinced by Constant's and Whittle's arguments for introducing the new aircraft.

But Power Jets was far too small to manufacture engines and relations with BTH had become strained, so a search was made for another maker of power plants. Since the leading aircraft engine manufacturers were heavily committed to the war effort, Rover, the motor car makers, was chosen. Whittle's latest design – the W2 – was handed over to it and work began at the shadow factory at Barnoldswick in the Midlands in the spring of 1941. Unluckily relations between Power Jets and Rover also turned out to be unsatisfactory. According to Whittle, the engineers at Rover's did not follow Power Jet's advice and drawings sufficiently closely and gave the impression that they wanted to strike out on a different course with an eye to postwar development.[26] Moreover, Power Jets had to depend on Rover for a supply of components, many of which proved to be defective. While these criticisms were to some extent prejudiced, much of the trouble was due to the somewhat vague policy contained in the words 'off the drawing board' expressed by Tedder and to the ambiguous terms of reference which allowed some junior

officials in the MAP, who regarded Power Jets as a 'bunch of gifted ama-
teurs',[27] to give Rover undue latitude in design.
In the meantime the nature of the air war had changed. The defensive tactics employed in the Battle of Britain had been superseded by
aggressive measures against the GAF which took the form of long-range
sweeps over northern France. High altitude interceptors were no longer
needed but fighters capable of high speed and endurance at comparatively low altitudes. It was therefore possible to devote more time to
improving Whittle's gas turbine. An overdue reorganization also took
place on 1 April when Rover's function was taken over by Rolls-Royce.

Rolls-Royce with its reputation for high engineering capability in
design, development and production took over the Barnoldswick factory
and became responsible for development and production of the W2B
engine while Power Jets started work on a new engine – the W2/500 and
subsequent engines. Rolls-Royce's policy was that the gas turbine was
not a secret weapon but just 'another way of pushing an aeroplane along
except that at the present time it is not as good as with the conventional
engine.'[28] Intensive tests were therefore made to eliminate known weaknesses in the engine. In a short time (June 1943) a prototype aircraft –
the F9/40 (later known as the Meteor) fitted with W2B/37 engines (the
Derwent Series 1) based on Power Jets' W2/500 – was flown.

By the autumn of 1943 intelligence reports on new German weapons
were giving anxiety to the British government. Churchill, suspecting
that the Air Staff was too complacent about a threat from German jet
aircraft, privately commissioned a report from Duncan Sandys, his son-
in-law, who had recently been selected by the Air Staff to investigate
the possibility of rocket attacks on the UK. Sandys contended that the
Germans might well have a small force of jet fighters and bombers by
the end of 1944 and recommended speeding up turbojet development
by the Allies. The Air Staff being sceptical about the emergence of jet
propelled aircraft in general managed to intercept Sandys's report and
Portal, the Chief of Air Staff, asked for it to be toned down. However,
Sandys communicated his fears privately to Churchill who then
ordered Portal to exert pressure on the lagging British jet development.[29] In consequence, a force of 100 operatives were detached for
the purpose of completing 120 Meteors I (the outcome of the F9/40).
In comparison, the Messerschmitt work force at that time numbered
around 1400.

As early as 1941 Tizard had wisely attracted the interest of a number of
well-known aero engine designers and other experts to apply themselves
and the resources of their firms to gas turbine design. This move had

been successful and by 1942, in addition to Power Jets, 10 firms were engaged in work on turbines in one form or another. One of the most advanced was the de Havilland H-1 engine which was designed by an experienced engineer, Frank Halford, also using a centrifugal compressor.[30] By 1943 de Havilland's had progressed sufficiently for H-1 engines (later called the Goblin) to be fitted in the Meteor I, though early Goblin engines had powered the F9/40 before the Derwent engine was ready.

But when the flying bomb attacks began in June 1944, the Gloster Meteor powered by the W2B/23 engine giving a maximum speed of 410 mph at 30 000 ft was the only jet fighter available. It went into action against the flying bombs in July, shooting down its first on 4 August, but the operations of its successor, the Meteor III, against the GAF on the continent were only on a small scale and there is no record of any combat between Meteors and Me-262s taking place.

The Germans, too, had their problems. The Messerschmitt engineers encountered many difficulties with the Jumo-004 engine. While superior to the BMW version, its compressor and turbine designs were inferior to the Metro-Vick F-2 engine; and it had a very high fuel consumption. When the Me-262 eventually became operational, it was found necessary to provide spare pairs of engines for every aircraft in case of failure. All these failings came after nearly four years of well-funded research and development. It was only at the end of the war that the Germans developed an axial compressor that approached, but not equalled, the RAE equivalent.

The Me-262 aircraft also had a chequered career. General Adolf Galland, the celebrated fighter pilot, then head of the German fighter force, had flown the prototype in May 1943 and reported that it offered 'completely new tactical possibilities'.[31] Just as it became possible in the autumn of 1943 for production to begin, Hitler intervened and ordered the Me-262 to be produced solely as a bomber. As the Allied air offensive gathered momentum in the spring of 1944, Galland again renewed his demand that the Me-262 should be a fighter in order to combat both the number and the superiority of the Allied planes. 'At the moment', said Galland, 'I prefer one Me-262 to five Me-109s'.[32] It was only towards the end of 1944 that Hitler allowed himself to be convinced of the need for a high performance fighter and his order was rescinded. By then it was too late. The first Me-262 squadron went into action in December 1944 and was later enlarged into a wing. When the GAF attempted to stage a 'come back' in support of the counter-offensive in the Ardennes, the majority of its fighters were Me-109s and FW-190s.

Recent research reveals that the Me-262's development as a fighter was not held back by Hitler's wish to have a bomber version as has often been suggested. It appears that all types, day fighter, night fighter, bomber, reconnaissance aircraft, had equal priority. Furthermore, the Me-262 was probably no more retarded than any other wartime development, while its engine defects made it unlikely that it could have been available to the GAF any earlier. From an operational point of view the Me-262 was a difficult aircraft to fly and so required experienced pilots, then in short supply.

Turbojet development in the United States

As the Americans had no equivalent of a Whittle or Ohain, development of an aircraft gas turbine was slower than in England and Germany. Leading aircraft engineers were, in any case, more interested in the possibilities of rocket-propelled aircraft. It was only in the spring of 1941 that senior American Air Force officers visiting England learned of the existence of the Whittle engine.[33] They found the British cooperative and in July 1941 Power Jets was instructed by MAP not to withhold any information to the Americans on jet development. In October a W1X engine and drawings of the W2B engine were despatched to America under US diplomatic seals. After difficulties with the US Customs at Washington National Airport, the engine was handed over to General Electric (GE) at Schenectady by the US Army Air Force for further development. Although the GE engineers had little experience of aircraft engineering, they had their own centrifugal test engine running on 18 March 1942. It was then installed in a Bell XP-59 fighter which made its first flight in October 1942, before either the production of the British Whittle engines had begun or the first flight of the Meteor made. Thereafter progress was delayed by the same teething problems that beset the British engineers.

By then collaboration on jet propulsion had been firmly established between the two countries, especially after a visit by Whittle in June 1942.[34] He noted that while the Americans were then experiencing the same difficulties which had now been overcome in England, British development was suffering from the lack of materials like heat-resisting alloys (later solved in part by the nickel-chromium alloy called Nimonic 80).

At the same time the Americans had begun to develop an axial flow engine. (Information about German development of this type of engine had come through US intelligence reports.) Testing and production was entrusted to the Westinghouse Electric Corporation, a firm considered by British observers to be superior in engineering skills to GE, though not quite in the same class as Rolls-Royce. Westinghouse produced its first axial engine for the US Navy Corsair fighter in January 1943 but full-scale production did not get underway before the end of the war. When the war ended, centrifugal engines were largely forsaken for axial flow engines. But the Americans received no help from the British (unlike the centrifugal engine) on the F-2 axial engine, presumably because there were plans for large-scale postwar commercial development. Top priority was still given to conventional aircraft with long-range capability as the war against Japan had been expected to go on much longer than it did.

Conclusion

Britain was still, in 1945, well ahead of the United States in aircraft gas turbines.[35] But the organization for research and development badly needed overhauling. Power Jets had always been an anomaly, being halfway between a research establishment and a commercial firm. Its attitude of 'prickly independence' annoyed the authorities. Even within the company skilled workers complained of inefficient management. The Government therefore decided to convert the company into a research establishment directly under its control. Early in 1946 Power Jets became the National Gas Turbine Establishment at Pyestock not far from RAE.

Whittle, who had fought hard to preserve his company, resigned together with most of his staff. After a short (unhappy) time as adviser to the Ministry of Supply, he went on to work for several aircraft companies and then, somewhat embittered, retired to live in the United States. In the words of *The Times* obituarist, Whittle 'had an individuality and quixoticism bordering at times on the eccentric'[36] and to the end of his life believed that if only the Air Ministry had listened to him earlier, jet fighters would have flown in the Battle of Britain. But the difficulties outlined above in developing not only British but German jet engines make it an unlikely claim. Similarly his contention that the W2B was the 'only jet engine which made any contribution at all to the war effort [the shooting down of 13 flying bombs] and all other work was a detraction from it' was perhaps excusable on account of the great stress to which he had been subjected. In the war against Japan the production of the de Havilland Vampire in the role of a naval jet fighter would have been invaluable if the atomic bomb had not been dropped.

The jet fighter was a premature weapon both for the Allies and for the Germans. The air war was won by aircraft with reciprocating engines and the threat from German jet aircraft was, like the A4 rocket, greatly exaggerated. Comparing the development of jet propulsion in Britain and Germany, Ohain was fortunate in obtaining the backing of Heinkel. Whittle's insecure financial backing and the indifference of the authorities were a severe handicap in promoting the W1 engine. The Germans, on the other hand, never waivered in their intention to develop a 525 mph aircraft and concentrated on the Me-262 (although the slower Arado-234 bomber-reconnaissance aircraft went into service in small numbers). Contrary to the development of the rocket, the aircraft engineers did not suffer from political interference. They were fortunate in being supported by respected industrialists like Heinkel and Messerschmitt, particularly the latter who had an intuitive approach based on sound engineering experience which enabled the German turbojet to go into operation.

After the defeat of Germany work on jet propulsion naturally came to a halt. Ohain, who had continued to work for Heinkel on gas turbine projects throughout the war, opted, like von Braun, to put his knowledge at the disposal of the Americans. He became chief scientist at the United States Air Force base at Dayton, Ohio, and later held posts in several research institutions. In retirement he met and became friends with his rival, Sir Frank Whittle. Schelp and other senior engineers concerned with the administration of the turbojet programme likewise joined him in the States.

10
The Ultimate Weapon: the Atomic Bomb

Conception of the bomb

Soon after the beginning of the twentieth century scientists began to speculate that the atom, being a source of energy, might be used as a weapon of war. In 1904 the Canadian physicist, Frederick Soddy, a one-time colleague of Rutherford, wrote that atomic energy only awaited a 'suitable detonator to cause the earth to resort to chaos'. In 1922, four years after the First World War, F. W. Aston, a Nobel Laureate in chemistry, caused a minor sensation when he asserted that should atomic energy ever be released in a practical form 'the human race will have at its command powers beyond the dreams of scientific fiction.'[1] Other scientists were sceptical, however. Rutherford, despite his experiments in artificially disintegrating the atom in 1919, to the end of his life pooh-poohed claims made for atomic energy as being no more than 'moonshine'.

Yet perceptive writers like H. G. Wells, who followed recent advances in physics, sensed the potential power of the atom. Wells in his book *The World Set Free* published early in 1914 anticipated a European nuclear war at some future date. Winston Churchill, author and politician, was even more percipient when in September 1924, converting atomic energy into military terms, wondered whether 'a bomb no bigger than an orange [had] a secret power to blast a township at a stroke?'[2] (The size of an orange was roughly the size of the plutonium core of the bomb exploded in the New Mexican Desert in July 1945.)

Feasibility of fission

In September 1932, only a year before Rutherford's oft-quoted remark, James Chadwick, one of his colleagues at the Cavendish, had discovered the neutron which, having no electrical charge, could penetrate any of the elements. The neutron and the discovery of artificial radioactivity two years later by Irène Curie (the daughter of Marie Curie) and her husband, Frédéric Joliot, at the Radium Institute in Paris provided the means for irradiating, or bombarding, the elements, especially the heaviest, uranium.

One of the experimenters, Enrico Fermi, leader of a team of young Italian physicists, inspired Otto Hahn, professor of chemistry at the Kaiser Wilhelm Institute in Berlin, and his long-standing collaborator, the Viennese physicist, Lise Meitner, to irradiate uranium in the hope of discovering new and heavier transuranic elements. Unfortunately their partnership ended when Meitner, who since the German occupation of Austria in March 1938 had technically become a German citizen, was forced to flee the country on account of her Jewish blood. Hahn continued experimenting with his colleague Fritz Strassmann. In mid-December 1938 they tried to separate irradiated radium from inactive barium ballast by fractional crystallization (a technique of chemical analysis which 45 years earlier had enabled Marie Curie to isolate radium). They were unable to separate the radium from the barium and were forced to conclude that the radium was not radium at all but barium. During neutron bombardment the uranium had split into medium weight elements, one of which was barium while the other turned out to be krypton.

Although Hahn did not immediately appreciate the significance of his discovery, he told Meitner, who was spending Christmas in Sweden with her nephew, Otto Frisch, also a physicist working with the famous Niels Bohr in Copenhagen. In February 1939 *Nature* published two letters entitled 'A New Type of Nuclear Reaction' signed by Frisch (who in the meantime had confirmed Hahn and Strassmann's results by other means) and Meitner, explaining the process of nuclear fission (the name being borrowed from the biological process by which single cells divide into two).[3]

Shortly after this discovery, Bohr suggested that fission was much more likely to occur in the light isotope of uranium U-235 than in U-238. For natural uranium contains only 0.7 per cent U-235 whereas nearly 99.3 per cent is U-238 which made it seem unlikely or impossible that a uranium bomb was feasible because it would have to be so enormous. Bohr later expanded these ideas in a paper published only two days before the outbreak of war in September 1939. He had in the meantime retailed the discovery of nuclear fission to the American Physical Society. Almost at once the small community of nuclear physicists in Europe, America and the Soviet Union appreciated that if enough neutrons were produced, it would be possible to make a self-sustaining energy-producing chain reaction.

Before that could be achieved, however, a number of problems had to be solved relating to the ability of neutrons to hit a U-235 nucleus when passing through a mass of uranium. This may be compared with the collision that occurs when a bullet hits its target. Fermi discovered that nuclear targets could be measured in terms of an area called a nuclear cross-section. Measurements of cross-sections varied from one element to another in an apparently random manner. Another essential was to discover the minimum, or critical, amount of fissile material needed before a self-sustaining chain reaction could be established. This critical mass depended on the purity and density of the uranium and the concentration of it in U-235, among other things. It also depended, especially, upon the speed of the neutrons producing fissions, because nuclear cross-sections were generally much larger for slow than for fast neutrons.

Joliot, with his co-workers, the Austrian, Hans Halban, and the Russian, Lew Kowarski, were the first to exploit the Hahn-Strassmann experiment. During the summer of 1939 they attempted to achieve a chain reaction through slow neutrons. The reaction would be moderated by heavy water (water consisting of molecules in which the hydrogen is replaced by deuterium) to limit the multiplication of neutrons, so producing a nuclear furnace or boiler. This was intended to produce power and as the scientists were not required for defence work and the experiments had no military value they were continued until the collapse of France.[4]

Feasibility of a bomb established

At the beginning of the war, as we have seen, the leading British physicists were fully occupied in developing the highly important defensive measure of radar. But there were a few scientists who had been following Joliot's experiments, notably G. P. Thomson, Professor of Physics at Imperial College, Chadwick, Professor of Physics at Liverpool, and Oliphant at Birmingham. They were, in general, sceptical about the possibility of making a bomb with a chain reaction of fast neutrons and even if possible, development would take too long to be of use in the present war. These views were shared by the leading scientists in government, Lindemann and Tizard.

Their reservations were suddenly dissipated in March 1940 by a report entitled 'On the construction of a Super Bomb based on a nuclear chain reaction in Uranium'[5] from the Department of Physics at Birmingham. Although Oliphant was preoccupied with radar, he had two scientists working on isotope separation who were the authors of the report. One was Otto Frisch, who had left Copenhagen because of its proximity to Germany and who had been invited by Oliphant to remain in Birmingham; the other was another German émigré, Rudolf Peierls, who knew Oliphant from Cambridge and had recently applied for the Chair of Applied Mathematics at Birmingham.

Frisch and Peierls had reconsidered Bohr's paper of September 1939. They speculated what might happen if a lump of pure U-235 rather than natural uranium enriched by a greater-than-natural percentage of U-235 was considered. This led them to consider the cross-section of pure U-235. They discovered (Peierls doing the mathematics) that the critical mass of U-235 was very much lighter than had previously been assumed and that the critical mass for a super atomic explosive would be no more than 5 kg. This was small enough to make separation of U-235, though difficult, worth pursuing. (In fact, Peierls' first calculation of the critical mass was too low, but this was an added incentive for considering a bomb. It was not sufficiently far out when compared with other scientists' calculations and estimates to matter very much.) Peierls and Frisch concluded their memorandum by outlining a scheme for separating U-235 and giving a warning about the hazards of radiation. Short though it was, their paper was the key to the whole development of the atomic bomb; it enabled the problem to be assessed in terms of men, cost and materials.

Oliphant sent the memorandum to Tizard, who in turn, forwarded it to Thomson, now responsible for uranium research. Spurred on by anxieties that the Germans might start work on an atomic bomb, the MAUD Committee was formed to coordinate all aspects of physics and chemistry in developing a nuclear weapon. Thomson was chairman and his members included Chadwick, Cockcroft, Oliphant and Blackett. Work was to be continued at Birmingham (later removed to Liverpool under Chadwick) on isotope separation, on chain reactions at the Cavendish, and separating isotopes by gaseous diffusion at the Clarendon Laboratory, Oxford.

The Cambridge team led by Norman Feather and a Swiss physicist Egon Bretscher, an able experimenter who had been on the staff of the Cavendish for some years, had been reinforced by Halban and Kowarski who continued their experiments of producing power in the boiler using the heavy water they had brought with them from Paris. Feather and Bretscher were soon to make a contribution almost as significant as Frisch and Peierls. Halban and Kowarski had shown how fission could be achieved with slow neutrons. But two Americans,

E. M. McMillan and P. H. Abelson had just found out that when an atom of U-238 absorbed a neutron it formed a new isotope, U-239; its particles formed a new artificial element called 94 which was radioactive and long-lived. Bretscher and Feather surmised that 94, which they named plutonium, would be fissionable by fast neutrons even more effectively than those of U-235. Plutonium could be used as an efficient super explosive, thus providing an alternative to U-235 for making a bomb. It had the advantage of saving raw materials since it would be possible to use for fission not only the minute fraction of U-235 in natural uranium but the much more plentiful U-238, while the large-scale separation of isotopes would be unnecessary.

Plutonium was also discovered by the American Glen Seaborg who bombarded uranium with deuterons (the nuclei of an atom of deuterium) in March 1941 in Ernest Lawrence's cyclotron at Berkeley.[6] Four months later, Lawrence, a pioneer of nuclear physics, reached the same conclusion as Feather and Bretscher that a super bomb could be produced with plutonium. Like the British, the Americans gave the same name to the new substance.

Meanwhile the Clarendon team led by Francis Simon, a specialist in low temperature physics, which included the Hungarian, Nicholas Kurti and an American, H. S. Arms. Their aim was to find an economical method of separating isotopes through gaseous diffusion. Simon recalled a system of metal mesh or membranes used in a German laboratory a decade earlier for separating neon isotopes. He decided to use as test material a mixture of water vapour and carbon dioxide, later superseded by the volatile gaseous compound, uranium hexafluoride manufactured by ICI. The team was soon able to draw up a plan for producing concentrations of U-235 on a large scale quite quickly, while the overall cost would not be much more expensive than building a large munitions factory or a battleship.

Despite the Battle of Britain and the Blitz all these studies had by July 1941 reached a point at which the MAUD Committee could state that a bomb using the separated isotope, U-235, was feasible and worth pursuing and that the government should step up the pace of research.[7] The Committee optimistically believed that the fissile material could be ready by the end of 1942. It was Blackett, supported by a majority of the Committee, who advised that the production plant should be erected in the United States. Thus while the MAUD Report was approved by the Scientific Advisory Committee of the Cabinet and an organization set up that October to continue work on the atomic project under the cover name of Tube Alloys, it was the United States with its great scientific and industrial resources that now became responsible for the development and production of the atomic bomb.

Convincing the Americans

Compared with the vigorous prosecution of research in Britain, American scientists appeared to have no inkling of the importance of fission. Pushed by the Hungarian physicist, Leo Szilard, who for some time had been warning other scientists of the perils of an atomic bomb, Einstein wrote a letter to President Roosevelt on 2 August 1939. The outcome was the appointment of an uranium committee whose chairman, on receiving a copy of the MAUD Report, put it in a safe where it remained unread. No substantial action was recommended. When Conant, Bush's deputy, visited London in March 1941, he evinced no interest when Cherwell patiently tried to explain to him the significance of the Frisch-Peierls memorandum on the grounds that Cherwell was 'conveying secret information to me without authorisation'.[8]

As the MAUD Committee had received little information on the extent of American nuclear research, Thomson suggested to Oliphant, about to visit the States on radar business in August 1941, that he should find out what was going on. After unfruitful talks with Lyman Briggs, the chairman of the Uranium Committee, Bush and Conant, as well as with Fermi now at Columbia University, who was even sceptical of the theory of fission, Oliphant found a more receptive ear in his friend Ernest Lawrence. In no uncertain terms Oliphant told him that 'the preparation of a nuclear bomb, if this is possible, should be undertaken at once and on the very highest priority'.[9]

It was not until 9 October 1941 that Bush and Conant grasped the grim implications of the MAUD Report's conclusions. Nearly two years after reading Einstein's letter, Roosevelt gave the go-ahead on an American uranium project. Even so, it was only the day before the attack on Pearl Harbor on 7 December that the President authorized large sums to Lawrence's studies on the electromagnetic separation of isotopes and for reactor materials and other work at Columbia and Princeton.

The Manhattan Project

As the summer of 1942 approached, Bush informed the President that pilot plants should be built to test production processes. Scientists had neither the knowledge or experience to manage such large-scale engineering activities, nor were the US Army Engineers, heavily committed at the beginning of a war, keen on tackling a project whose outcome was so uncertain.

After 17 September 1942 the situation was radically transformed when Brigadier General Leslie Groves, who had vast experience of construction and project management, was put in charge of what was called the Manhattan Project because of its office in Manhattan near Columbia University. Groves was disliked by many of the scientists while he was antipathetic towards the British, greatly underestimating the importance of their contributions to the project. In a memorandum written shortly after the end of the war he claimed that 'the scientific contribution of the British was . . . in no sense vital and actually not even important . . . it is true that without any contribution at all from the British the date of our final success need not have been delayed by a single day'[10] – a statement that was undoubtedly untrue. Yet 15 years later he would write in his book *Now It Can Be Told* that 'without active and continuing British interest [especially from Churchill] there probably would have been no atomic bomb to drop on Hiroshima'.

Meanwhile it was necessary to obtain positive proof of a self-sustaining chain reaction. Fermi was put in charge of the project named the Metallurgical Laboratory, or Metlab, in Chicago. He decided to use purified graphite as a moderator for the pile in the form of bricks; they were interspersed with sealed cans containing uranium oxide powder and some blocks of natural metal. The pile was built in an improbable site under the University of Chicago football stadium in the middle of the city. Fermi was confident that his control rods of cadmium and other techniques to soak up excess neutrons would be able to regulate the pile. On 2 December 1942, witnessed by a small group of co-workers, Fermi removed the control rods one by one until the pile became critical. Even though the amount of power was minute – only half a watt, it led to the first plutonium-producing reactors, not to mention the thousand megawatt postwar reactors for the generation of electricity.[11] Bush advised the President that full size reactors should be constructed as quickly as possible. The President approved on 28 December, thereby committing the United States to making nuclear bombs.

The way was now open for the various stages required to develop a bomb. A huge electromagnetic separation plant and gaseous diffusion equipment was built at Oak Ridge, code-named K-25, a prewar depressed area in Tennessee which had benefited from the power provided by the Tennessee Valley Authority. The installations required more electricity than most American cities. Much of the large equipment had to be made on assembly to high standards of vacuum tightness. Although the

British were not allowed to work at the gaseous diffusion plant, they were able to provide a special type of nickel powder for the separating membranes, or barriers, as they were called by the Americans, and which were vital to the success of the programme. High quality nickel powder was unobtainable in the States and was provided by the International Nickel Company's plant at Clydach in South Wales. This and other modifications enabled the gaseous diffusion plant to be completed by the end of 1944.[12]

British scientists were, however, able to participate in the electromagnetic separation process. Oliphant early on had inspired Lawrence to convert his cyclotron to develop the industrial process. Subsequently 35 British scientists were assigned to that process and were completely integrated into the technical and policy implications of it. Later Oliphant and Chadwick persuaded Groves to stage the production processes in tandem. Had that not been done, the completion of the Hiroshima bomb would have been delayed significantly.

Production of plutonium took place in a remote desert valley at Hanford, Washington where abundant hydroelectricity was provided by two dams on the Columbia River.[13] Three water-cooled reactors were built, starting in April 1943, and two pairs of chemical separation plants were located some ten miles away from the nearest reactor. Each reactor building was like a huge windowless box, 120 ft tall enclosing lattices of graphite blocks containing fuel rods encased in aluminium. The irradiation process caused a great deal of heat and the system had to be cooled by pipes through which large quantities of water were pumped.

The chemistry of plutonium had been determined from microscopic samples in the laboratory. This laboratory process was now scaled up a billion times in mammoth concrete canyons that housed the chemical separation apparatus. One of the advantages of plutonium was that it could be separated from irradiated uranium because uranium and plutonium were different elements, whereas isotopes of uranium cannot be separated chemically because they are the same element. Chemical separation was thus much easier than isotopic separation.

As we have seen, the assembly of the bomb took place in the desolate country of Los Alamos, New Mexico under the direction of Robert Oppenheimer. He had been selected by Groves (with whom he got on remarkably well) as being the best of all available candidates although he lacked the experience of other project leaders and the prestige of a Nobel Prize. Most of the American scientists were theoreticians and included Robert Brode and Edwin McMillan from Berkeley, Edward Teller from Hungary, Fermi and Hans Bethe from Germany as well as young unknown physicists such as Richard Feynman who became leader of the Theoretical Computations Group.

After a long delay in reaching an agreement on Anglo-US collaboration on atomic energy, a team of 19 British scientists led by Chadwick arrived at Los Alamos early in 1944 (though excluded from Hanford, others were working throughout the project).

They included a number of leading European Scientists such as Bohr, who had escaped from Denmark and now carried the alias of Nicholas Baker, Peierls, Frisch, Geoffrey Taylor, the hydrodynamics expert, and Klaus Fuchs, another refugee from Germany who had been working under Oliphant at Birmingham. The suspicions that appertained at the policy-makers level did not exist on the *mesa* and Peierls noted with satisfaction that no distinction was made between the American and British teams, the work being guided 'by the necessity to get the best answer in the shortest possible time rather than by questions of formal organisation and prestige'.[14]

The tasks confronting them were threefold. First, they had to confirm that a chain reaction was possible with fast neutrons. Related to this was the need to know how rapidly the neutrons were released in each fission. Speed was essential to maximize the number of generations of fission and thus the energy liberated before the bomb pieces were blown too far apart to react further. Secondly, they had to determine the quantity of scarce U-235 and plutonium needed for a supercritical mass;* using too little would be pointless, while too much would be wasteful. Thirdly, and this was more in the area of applied science, it was necessary to design the geometry of the weapons and plan their delivery.

A major problem was how to keep the U-235 and plutonium in a subcritical condition until ready for detonation. The solution was to construct the heart of each weapon in two pieces. With uranium this was not difficult; one half was made into a 'slug' for a 'gun' which fired the slug at the other half as a target. The gun method was not possible with plutonium which was prone to fission spontaneously. The process of implosion was suggested – a technique never used before. It involved placing a sphere of high explosive around a small ball of plutonium. When the chemical explosive was ignited uniformly a pressure wave would compress the centre from all sides, squeezing the plutonium into a much smaller and denser lump – a supercritical mass. In order to generate a uniform pressure wave, the core of the bomb was surrounded by

---

* This was the quantity exceeding the critical size of fissile material. The explosion was caused by quickly converting a subcritical system of fissile material into a supercritical one.

many sections of high explosive which were cast into special shapes (similar to glass lenses of different shapes and materials used to focus light waves). The shock waves shaped by the explosive lenses would exert enormous pressure upon the plutonium core, shrinking it into a supercritical mass.

The implosion method was the responsibility of the British team. Fuchs and Peierls made the implosion possible, according to a Los Alamos secret memorandum, while James Tuck, an explosives expert, contributed to the lenses and to the initiating process for the bomb reaction. Frisch, with his familiarity with nuclear theory, was also indispensable.[15]

At the end of 1944 the electromagnetic plant at Oak Ridge overcame most of its operating difficulties and began to produce substantial amounts of fairly pure U-235, while the gaseous diffusion plant was producing even more highly enriched material in U-235 before the end of January 1945. But serious difficulties were encountered in the production of plutonium at Hanford. However, all three reactors were operating by early 1945, small amounts of plutonium being sent by road to Los Alamos under armed guard.

As is well known, the plutonium bomb was tested on a steel tower on 16 July 1945 at the Alamogardo bombing range under the code name of Trinity ten weeks after the end of the war in Europe. Not only had implosion worked but it had produced a much larger explosion, equivalent to about 20 000 tons of TNT, than most of the scientists had expected. A week later the plutonium core for the first true bomb was machined into shape and the following day the U-235 parts for the first gun-type bomb were ready.

Roosevelt's death in April and Churchill's resignation on 26 July, only 10 days after Trinity, somewhat confused the policy on the bomb after the German defeat. However, on 1 June the British government concurred with President Truman's decision that the bomb should be used against Japan as soon as possible.

The Soviet connection

Anglo-US cooperation with the Soviet Union on scientific matters excluded anything on an atomic bomb. Bohr made a brave but fruitless attempt to persuade both Churchill and Roosevelt of the imperative need for international control of atomic energy; this would mean divulging information to the Soviet Union but not necessarily providing details of the bomb. Nevertheless Soviet agents were able to extract the most valuable information which was then passed on to Soviet scientists already, as explained earlier, on the threshold of atomic discoveries but which had been violently disrupted by the German invasion in June 1941.

Most senior physicists like Peter Kapitsa and Igor Kurchatov believed that the technical difficulties of utilizing atomic energy for a weapon precluded a quick solution. A colleague of Kurchatov, Georgii Flerov, thought otherwise.[16] Observing that publication on nuclear fission had dried up in the west, he suspected that uranium research was being conducted for use in a bomb. In a long letter to Kurchatov in December 1941 Flerov described how a chain reaction could be made by using U-235, remarkably similar to that suggested by Frisch and Peierls. However, Kurchatov ignored the letter. The indefatigable Flerov then wrote to Sergei Kaftanov, the State Defence Committee's plenipotentiary for science. With the German army at the gates of Moscow, it was hardly surprising there was no answer.

Meanwhile the Soviet secret agents had not been inactive. An agent of the NKVD (The People's Commissariat on Internal Affairs) in London acquired knowledge about decisions on the MAUD Report taken by the War Cabinet Scientific Advisory Committee in September 1941.[17] His source of information seems likely to have been John Cairncross recruited by Guy Burgess while an undergraduate at Cambridge in the 1930s. In 1941 Cairncross was private secretary to Hankey, chairman of the Scientific Advisory Committee and would have had access to the MAUD Committee papers. Another agent was Fuchs who had been working on the Technical Sub-Committee of MAUD. After the German invasion of the Soviet Union he decided to inform the Soviets about the atomic bomb. He was to work with the GRU (the Chief Intelligence Directorate of the General Staff) and a rival organization to the NKVD. Even so, Fuchs as a scientist would have been better able to evaluate the information for Moscow.

Nuclear matters were inevitably submerged in the crisis of the German invasion. It was only after the Soviet counter-offensive at Stalingrad (curiously codenamed Uran which could be interpreted as uranium) that a decision was taken to launch a uranium project. By then two things seemed clear, one, that Germany could lose the war, and the other, that the construction of a German nuclear weapon was improbable. Kurchatov was put in charge of the project and early in 1943 assembled a team of scientists and engineers to work on the design of an atomic bomb. A laboratory was found for them in Moscow and given the cover name of Laboratory No. 2.[18] But they were considerably handicapped by the lack of requisites such as uranium, heavy water, graphite and a cyclotron to work with. Kurchatov himself was uncertain whether a bomb could be built or, if it could, how long it would take.

Fortunately for the Russians in March 1943, Molotov, the Minister for Foreign Affairs, was able to show Kurchatov the intelligence reports on British nuclear research acquired by Soviet agents. From them he obtained much essential information on isotope separation, gaseous diffusion, and on the possibility of using plutonium instead of U-235 for making a bomb. Kurchatov was now able to work out a programme of research. A cyclotron was assembled from parts found in Joffe's Institute at Leningrad. It began to operate in Moscow on 25 September 1944. A more serious problem was to obtain uranium and graphite for a pile. Uranium compounds were even purchased from the United States (the sale was permitted for fear that refusal would alert the Soviets to the US atomic project) and uranium deposits in Central Asia were investigated. But Kurchatov became increasingly frustrated by the slow progress of the project and felt that he was not receiving enough from the government compared with the support given to the Manhattan Project about which information was now trickling through. Kurchatov knew about Seaborg's discovery of plutonium but possibly not about Fermi's self-sustaining chain reaction.

However, the work of the bomb group was transformed early in 1945 by information from Fuchs at Los Alamos.[19] He gave a Soviet agent full details of the bomb including the aluminium shell and the high explosive lens system described above. A further report in June stated when and where the Trinity test would take place. But most important was the data supplied by Fuchs on the fission cross-sections of U-235 and plutonium 239 for fast neutrons since they made it possible to define the critical dimensions of an atomic bomb.

When the European war ended, like their Western allies, Soviet missions went into Germany to discover progress made by German nuclear scientists. Like the British and the Americans, they soon discovered they had little to learn. What was more important was the discovery of 100 tons of uranium oxide that had been hidden away. Later, the Soviets acquired extensive uranium deposits in East Germany.

Even so, the slow progress made by Kurchatov's group was not speeded up by the acquisition of German scientists and material. In spite of urgent requests by Kurchatov the Soviet leaders did not treat the project as an urgent priority. Although warned by Fuchs that if Trinity was successful the Americans proposed to use the bomb against Japan, neither Stalin nor Beria, the political head of the atomic project, nor Molotov, had any conception of the role that the atomic bomb would play in future international relations. It was only when the bomb had dropped on Hiroshima that Stalin, encouraged by Kapitsa, took immediate steps to give the Soviet atomic project a more urgent priority.[20]

German failure to achieve fission

When news of the Hiroshima bomb on 6 August 1945 was heard over the radio by ten of the leading German scientists who had been working on their atomic project and who were then interned in Farm Hall, a country house north of Cambridge, they were flabbergasted. Only after several days were they able to reason how the Americans had built a bomb within such a short space of time and their disbelief turned to mutual recriminations. Why had the German scientists, of whom there were a number of the highest quality still working in the Reich, not been able to develop an atomic bomb?

The HWA had, in fact, been studying with interest the scientific papers on fission that had been published since the disclosures by Frisch and Meitner, and shortly after the outbreak of war formed a group of physicists known as the *Uranverein*, or Uranium Club, to investigate the possibility of making a bomb. One of them, Friedrich von Weizäcker, a young physicist whose father was a senior official in the German Foreign Office, and who was not unsympathetic towards the Nazis, urged Hahn to put his laboratory at the disposal of the HWA.[21] While Hahn was reluctant to become involved with weapon-making, he was keen to pursue his nuclear research and badly needed to build a cyclotron similar to one recently built for the neighbouring KWI for Physics. After some doubts, Hahn agreed that the work on fission should become a war aim, thus guaranteeing the existence of his Institute. In July 1940 the HWA began to construct a building for nuclear research in the grounds of the KWI for Physics, known as the Virus House in order to discourage visitors.

The leader of the Uranium Club was the most distinguished physicist still working in Germany – Werner Heisenberg. He had, as noted earlier, been turned down for an appointment at Munich University after being accused by the Nazi press of Jewish sympathies and for some years had been in charge of the Institute of Theoretical Physics in Leipzig. Like Hahn, he was a close friend of Weizsäcker. Heisenberg who had just written two papers on fission decided that the group should find out, first, how to separate U-235 and, second, how to build a chain-reacting pile.[22] Heavy water obtained from Norway was to be used as a moderator rather than graphite which in Germany was of poor quality.

This work continued at a leisurely pace throughout 1940 and 1941. However, when the German Army began to retreat on the Eastern Front the HWA realized that it was unlikely that nuclear research would have any impact on the war and in December 1941 decided to turn over the project to the Reich Research Council.[23] Seven months later it was transferred again, this time to the Aviation Ministry. Meanwhile Heisenberg continued to direct the work though officially he was not in charge of the group.

The limited knowledge of the Uranium Club was remarkably revealed by their conversations at Farm Hall which were picked up by microphones hidden in the rooms and recorded. Unlike the Allied scientists, Heisenberg failed at the outset to calculate properly the critical mass of U-235 required for a bomb. It was only on 6 August 1945 that Heisenberg declared that 'if the bomb had been done with U-235 we should be able to work it out. It just depends whether or not it is done with 50 or 500 or 5000 kg and we do not know the order of magnitude.'[24] Peierls, who at one time had been a student of Heisenberg, years later explained that though he was a brilliant theoretician, Heisenberg was always very casual about numbers. 'When he first heard of the reality of the Hiroshima bomb, he at last thought though the question of critical mass seriously and came up with a reasonable answer.'[25] The Germans also failed to appreciate, unlike Francis Simon, that large-scale separation of uranium isotopes was technically and financially feasible. Thus Hahn was recorded as saying 'I think it is absolutely impossible to produce one ton of U-235 by separating isotopes.'[26]

The German scientists had also failed to exploit the alternative method of using plutonium instead of U-235 as an ingredient for the bomb. Plutonium, of course, needed the design and construction of large reactors and methods for cooling them, while the problem of extracting the plutonium from the highly radioactive fuel would have had to be solved. All this would, as we have seen with the development of the V weapons, have imposed an intolerable strain on the war economy. Finally, they would have had to have worked out a method for detonating plutonium, the hardest of the problems solved at Los Alamos.

After the development of a bomb had been abandoned, the Uranium Club concentrated on an energy-producing reactor which might be used for ship or submarine propulsion. Funds were provided by Speer to build an underground bunker to house the reactor at the KWI for Physics. But the work proceeded with 'glacial slowness' owing to a running argument between Heisenberg and his colleagues over the design of the pile.[27]

Meanwhile, as the Allied bombing of Berlin gathered in intensity in 1943, plans were made to evacuate the Uranium Club and its equipment to the countryside south of Stuttgart where it would at least be out of reach of the Red Army. During the move, which began in the spring of 1944, two air raids virtually destroyed the chemistry laboratory and severely damaged the physics block, though the underground bunker with its uranium pile remained intact. Hahn's team continued their work in a disused textile factory at Tailfingen while Heisenberg, as late as March 1945, made his eighth and final attempt[28] to establish a self-sustaining chain reaction at Haigenloch nearby with heavy water and uranium oxide brought in trucks from Berlin. A month later an Anglo-American intelligence team discovered the pile consisting of a shell of graphite blocks but no heavy water or uranium. Within a few weeks the members of the Uranium Club were rounded up and the most important flown to England for interrogation.

Conclusion

The uranium bomb (Little Boy) that exploded over Hiroshima was responsible for killing 78 150 and injuring 51 048, though many victims were later to die through the delayed effects of radiation exposure, leukaemia and other cancers. At Nagasaki the plutonium bomb (Fat Man) caused the deaths of 70 000, less than Hiroshima because the city was protected by the slopes of the steep hills on which it was built thus confining the enormous explosion. Terrible though these figures were, it must be remembered that the American conventional bombing of mainland Japan during the previous eight months had been far more punishing; in one incendiary attack on Tokyo on 9–10 March 1945 alone, 84 000 Japanese died.

The news of the first bomb was received with mixed feelings. At Los Alamos Frisch would later remember 'the feeling of unease, indeed nausea'[29] when he saw his friends rush to book tables at the hotel in Sante Fe in order to celebrate. At Farm Hall in England, Hahn, the discoverer of nuclear fission, was 'shocked and depressed at the deaths of so many innocent women and children'. But when a young American officer who had survived the German war only to be sent to the Pacific theatre heard that the invasion of Japan would not after all take place, he and his platoon 'cried with joy and relief.'[30] (American staff officers had estimated that the invasion of Japan would cost 105 000 casualties though General MacArthur did not anticipate such a high loss rate.)

As a scientific enterprise, the making of the atomic bomb was probably the most sophisticated large-scale effort ever made by man. It cost at least $20 billion in present money terms and the work force was more than 600 000. It could not have been achieved without the collaboration that was eventually established between American and British scientists, nor without the remarkable insight of Peierls and Frisch. This was in stark contrast to the half-hearted efforts to achieve fission by the German scientists (Heisenberg's claim that moral scruples prevented him and his colleagues from developing a bomb has, since the publication of the Farm Hall transcripts, been exposed as a myth). More concerned about the effect of the bomb on mankind was Oppenheimer. In an eloquent farewell speech to the Los Alamos staff on 2 November 1945 he urged that the scientists should play a constructive part in establishing a

> pilot plant for a new type of international collaboration . . . because it is quite clear that the control of atomic weapons cannot be in itself the unique end of such operation. The only unique end can be a world that is united, and a world in which war will not recur.[31]

The political implications of the decision to drop the two bombs on Japan are not the concern of this book, but they will be debated for many years to come. It only remains to comment that in the 53 years following Hiroshima and Nagasaki, in spite of the crises caused by the Cold War, neither atomic weapons nor the hydrogen bomb – a thousand times more terrible – were ever used. Surely the image of the mushroom cloud must have deterred responsible statesmen, however much provoked, from unleashing these immeasurable forces of destruction.

Conclusion

The effect of science on the Second World War and its aftermath

While the great land campaigns of the Second World War in Russia and north-west Europe were mainly fought without the aid of science, medical research providing antibiotics, sulphonamide drugs and insecticides saved many lives and maintained the operational efficiency of units in the field. Thus Tizard could confidently assert after the war that 'So far as we can see, we need not fear that disease will be a matter of major importance in war.'[1]

Physical science, on the other hand, was indispensable for the rapid development of radar evolving from the rather crude CH stations to the sophisticated magnetron (an invention probably even more important than the atom bomb), fitting in the palm of a hand and generating more power at a hundred times the frequency than a CH transmitter using valves which a man could just manage to lift. Fitted in an aircraft or installed in a naval escort vessel, microwave radar was the most effective counter to the U-boat since the Germans were not able to develop suitable countermeasures in time. The Germans were, however, more successful in interfering with Allied offensive radar thus introducing the new technique of electronic warfare in which attackers and defenders strove to outwit each other. For distant targets the Allied strategic bombers had to depend on airborne radar (H2S) which five years after the end of the war still lacked adequate definition of a target.[2] It was admirable as a navigational aid, but once switched on it could betray the position of the bomber.

Accurate attacks on pinpoint targets could only be made accurately after postwar advances in solid-state physics whereby valves were replaced, first by transistors and then by integrated circuits which, instead of being soldered, could be manufactured much more cheaply by etching or printing onto silicon chips. This led to the precision-guided missile (PGM) using infra-red as well as radar for guidance. A forerunner of the PGM was the proximity fuse introduced at the end of the war.

The parallel development of jet propulsion in England and Germany had no effect on the outcome of the war, but its novelty should not over-shadow a decisive engineering feat – the piston-engined Mustang long-range day fighter. Originally rejected by the Americans, who designed it, when powered by Rolls-Royce Merlin engines, it could outmanoeuvre the best German interceptors and equipped with long-range fuel tanks could escort day bombers up to at least 600 miles from their base. There was, unhappily for the RAF, no equivalent escort for the night bomber force.

Bullard was one of the British scientists who regarded the development of the V2 in the Germany of 1942–44 as 'an almost unbelievable achievement'.[3] Its payload, its liquid fuel and its inertial navigational control system were an immense advance on any rocket hitherto developed. Nevertheless as a weapon of war its inaccuracy and lack of destructive power could not at that time compete with the manned bomber.

Operational or operations research (the latter as it was known in the United States) became a permanent feature in all the services. But increasing dependence on computer programming instead of the 'back of an envelope' calculations which produced such remarkable results in the war tended to generate laborious and complex reports. In Britain OR percolated into industry and commerce rather than into civil administration, but in the States academic and quasi-academic institutions like the Rand Corporation, supported by the military, explored and analysed the implications of thermonuclear weapons. Inevitably, as Blackett foresaw, their studies became ever more theoretical leading to attempts to rationalize war by scientists like Herman Kahn, parodied in the film *Dr Strangelove*, while the application of systems analysis of the Vietnam war led to body counts and truck kills to measure progress.

Effect of the war on scientists

Just as warfare was influenced by science, so young scientists who had been working in university laboratories without even access to a tele-phone suddenly found themselves in the arcane world of strategy and tactics. Early in the war a senior officer in the Royal Navy was astonished that a lecturer in physics could do a staff officers' job. After the war when scientific advice had become acceptable, General Eisenhower, then Chief of Staff of the US Army, wrote that scientists are 'more likely to make new and unsuspected contributions to the development of the Army if detailed directions are held to the minimum.'[4] Bernal thought that the war taught scientists not only to work but to think in a new way, firstly, by making contact with all ranks and, secondly, while this was going on, the subject of research was being integrated into an analysis and recommendation for a certain course of action. The war, Bernal continued, was an educative period for scientists that 'few who took part in it will come to regret.'[5] Moreover, after the war scientists were able to convert military equipment like radar to, for example, instruments for the new field of radio astronomy, while the Colossus and ENIAC computers became models for the first digital computers with stored programs, so leading to the technological revolution of the 1960s and 1970s.

The political implications of scientific advice

Never before had scientists provided advice to operational commanders and heads of state (though not to the leaders of the Axis powers). This would continue into the postwar era. Cherwell was always at hand to provide Churchill with facts and advice. During six years of war he sent the Prime Minister approximately 2000 minutes, or roughly one a day. Roosevelt, however, did not have Churchill's fascination with the scientific side of war and did not ask Bush for advice on a regular basis. According to the latter, he failed to grasp what might be involved in the crucial matter of the atomic bomb, though later he did act vigorously. Cherwell probably had a bigger impact on *events*, though, as we have seen, Tizard, Blackett, Fowler, Geoffrey Taylor, A. V. Hill and Chadwick had a bigger impact on British scientists as a whole. It was, indeed, those scientists and others less well known who built up the remarkable collaboration with the Americans. There were moments when political motives brought cooperation to a temporary standstill. Yet the most outstanding example of large scale collaboration to that date in which British and American teams of physicists and chemists developed a close sense of community was the Manhattan Project. As the Australian physicist, Harrie Massey, explained, 'they were actively involved in so many technical discussions and other activities that, despite their numbers [and nationality] they got to know each other very well.'[6] That feeling of mutual identity would continue, with occasional breaks, into the years of the Cold War and would also provide an example for peaceful organizations like the European Organization for Nuclear Research (CERN).

Notes

The following abbreviations have been used for the location and designation of documentary sources.

Cherwell Papers, Nuffield College, Oxford
Public Records Office (PRO):

ADM Admiralty
AIR Air Ministry
AVIA Ministry of Aviation
CAB Cabinet Office
DEFE Ministry of Defence
FD Medical Research Council
T Treasury
WO War Office

Introduction

1. CAB103/205, *Science at War*, Memo for ACSP, 8 October 1947.

Chapter 1 Organization of Science for War

1. Editorial, *Nature*, 17 June 1915.
2. John Bradley, *History and Development of Aircraft Instruments, 1909–1919*, PhD thesis, 1994, Science Museum Library.
3. L. F. Haber, *The Poisonous Cloud. Chemical Warfare in the First World War*, Clarendon Press, Oxford, 1986, p. 273.
4. Monika Renneberg and Mark Walker (eds), *Science, Technology and National Socialism*, Cambridge University Press, 1994, p. 88.
5. Ibid., p. 9.
6. Ibid., pp. 81–2.
7. Ibid., p. 6.
8. Ibid., pp. 53–8.
9. Ibid., p. 51.
10. David Holloway, *Stalin and the Bomb. The Soviet Union and Atomic Energy, 1934–1956*, Yale University Press, 1994, p. 146.
11. Ibid., pp. 21, 145.
12. Andrew Brown, 'Blackett at Cambridge, 1919–1933', *Blackett Centenary Conference*, 24 September 1998.
13. Sir Henry Tizard, 'Science and the Services', *RUSI Jnl.*, vol. XCI, no. 563, August 1946, p. 338.

14. Peter Hennessy and Sir Douglas Hague, 'How Hitler Reformed Whitehall', *Strathclyde Papers on Government and Politics*, no. 41, 1985, p. 8.
15. Ibid., p. 19.
16. Solly Zuckerman, *From Apes to Warlords, 1904–46*, London, 1978, App. 1, 'The Tots and Quots'.
17. Anon, *Science in War*, 'Penguin Special', Penguin Books, 1940.
18. Vannevar Bush, *Pieces of the Action*, London, 1972, p. 74.
19. Ibid., p. 36.
20. James Phinney Baxter, *Scientists Against Time*, MIT Press, paperback edn, 1968, chs I and VIII.
21. David Zimmerman, *Top Secret Exchange, The Tizard Mission and the Scientific War*, McGill-Queen's University Press, 1996, chs 1–7.
22. Henry E. Guerlac, *Radar in World War II*, New York, American Institute of Physics, 1987, ch. 9.
23. Jeremy Bernstein, *Experience of Science*, Dutton Paperback, New York, 1978, p. 93.
24. F. E. Terman to A. P. Rowe, 23 July 1962 (author's collection).
25. A. P. Rowe, *One Story of Radar*, Cambridge University Press, 1998, pp. 84–6.
26. A. P. Rowe, 'From Scientific Idea to Practical Use', *Minerva Quarterly Review*, Spring 1946, pp. 309–10.
27. John Bradley, op. cit.
28. Ralph Benjamin, *Five Lives in One, An Insider's View of the Defence and Intelligence World*, Parapress Ltd, 1996, p. 28.
29. Bush, op. cit., p. 279. ADM I/10459, Statistical Branch Admy. Lindemann as Head of S Branch.
30. Sir Frederick Brundrett to A. P. Rowe, 21 September 1962 (author's collection).
31. Lord Hankey, 'Technical and Scientific Manpower', *The Worker in Industry*, HMSO, 1952.
32. Alice Kemball Smith and Charles Weiner, *Robert Oppenheimer Letters and Recollections*, Harvard University Press, 1980. Letter to James Conant, 1 February 1943.
33. Holloway, op. cit., pp. 74–5.
34. Ulrich Albrecht, *The Soviet Armaments Industry*, Harvard Academic Publishers, USA, 1993, p. 58.
35. Holloway, op. cit., p. 206.
36. Ibid., pp. 138–41.
37. Ibid., pp. 148–9.
38. K. H. Ludwig, *Technik und Ingenieure im Dritten Reich*, Dusseldorf, 1979, p. 28.
39. AVIA 39/4, German Academic Scientists and the War by Major I. W. B. Gill.
40. ADM 213/611, Scientific Research in Germany: Establishments and Organisation, W. Osenberg, 1945.
41. Thomas Powers, *Heisenberg's War: The Secret History of the German Bomb*, p. 501.
42. AVIA 39/4, op. cit.
43. Guy Hartcup and T. E. Allibone, *Cockcroft and the Atom*, Hilger, Bristol, 1986, p. 83.

Chapter 2 Radar: Defence and Offence

1. S. S. Swords, *Technical History of the Beginnings of Radar*, Peter Peregrinus, London, 1986, p. 43. See also R. W. Burns, *Radar Development to 1945*, Inst-

itute of Electrical Engineers, 1988, ch. 40, 'Who invented radar?' by Prof. C. Susskind.

2. David Pritchard, *The Radar War. Germany's Pioneering Achievement, 1904–45*, London, 1929, p. 57 et seq.

3. Swords, op. cit., p. 141.

4. Sir Philip Joubert, 'Science in Planning for Defence, Review of *Science and Government* by C. P. Snow', *Daily Telegraph*, April 1961.

5. T 161/855; T 161/891.

6. J. E. Allen to author, 22 December 1980.

7. B. T. Neale, 'CH, The First Operational Radar', *GEC Journal of Research*, Special issue on radar, vol. 3, no. 2, 1985.

8. RAF Hist. Soc., *The Battle Rethought. A Symposium on the Battle of Britain*, 25 June 1990, p. 10. Contains much useful material on radar's effect on the battle.

9. Sir Mark Oliphant, 'Comments on C. P. Snow's *Science and Government*', reviewed by P. M. S. Blackett in *Scientific American*, September 1966.

10. R. W. Burns, op. cit., 'The Background to the Development of the Cavity Magnetron', ch. 19.

11. Russell Miller, 'Secret Weapon: How Two British Inventors Helped to Win the Battle of the Atlantic', *Sunday Times Magazine*, 7 September 1975, pp. 8–15.

12. Burns, op. cit., p. 277.

13. R. W. Clark, *Tizard*, London, 1965, p. 268.

14. AIR 19/517, Director of Radar. Consideration of A. P. Rowe. Correspondence between Col J. T. C. Moore-Brabazon and Sir Archibald Sinclair, May 1941.

15. Sir Bernard Lovell, *Echoes of War*, Hilger, Bristol, 1991, p. 41.

16. E. G. Bowen, *Radar Days*, Hilger, Bristol, 1987, p. 69.

17. Ibid., p. 181.

18. Robert Buderi, *The Invention that Changed the World. The story of radar from war to peace*, London, 1997, p. 124.

19. RAF Hist. Soc., *Seek and Sink. A symposium on the Battle of the Atlantic*, 21 October 1991. Very good on the technical side.

20. Ibid., p. 50.

21. Ibid., p. 32.

22. Rowe, 'From Scientific Idea to Practical Use', op. cit., pp. 306–7.

23. CAB 47/15 Butt Report.

24. Lovell, op. cit., p. 95.

25. Ibid., p. 150.

26. Pritchard, op. cit., p. 91.

27. Lovell, op. cit., p. 184 et seq.

28. Buderi, op. cit., pp. 188–9.

29. Derek Howse, *Radar at Sea. The Royal Navy in World War 2*, London, 1993, p. 68.

30. Ibid., p. 147, AVIA 46/36 Radar History. Interview with Charles Wright. 'The 271 Set was one of the outstanding achievements of the war'.

31. Howse, op. cit., pp. 156–7.

32. Ibid., p. 96.

33. Ibid., pp. 158–9.

34. D. H. Tomlin, 'The Origins and Development of the UK army radar to 1946', in Burns, op. cit., *Radar Development to 1945*, ch. 20, p. 292.

35. Buderi, op. cit., pp. 131–4.
36. Hartcup and Allibone, op. cit., pp. 109–10.
37. Pritchard, op. cit., pp. 48–50.
38. Ibid., p. 65, 73.
39. Ibid., pp. 155, 165.
40. Howse, op. cit., pp. 45–9.
41. Pritchard, op. cit., p. 195.
42. Guerlac, op. cit., ch. 18.

Chapter 3   Diverse Applications of Radio and Radar

1. Capt. Geoffrey Bennett, RN, 'The Development of the Proximity Fuse', *RUSI Jnl.*, March 1976.
2. R. V. Jones, *Reflections on Intelligence*, London, 1989, p. 229 et seq.
3. AIR 40/2572, The Oslo Evidence, Scientific Intelligence sent to Naval Attaché, Notes by R. V. Jones. See also R. V. Jones, *Most Secret War*, London, 1978, ch. 8.
4. Guy Hartcup, *The Challenge of War. Scientific and Engineering Contributions to World War Two*, David & Charles, 1970, pp. 173–6.
5. T 169/39, Royal Comm on Awards to Inventors. Transcripts of Claim by Cobden Turner for PF. See also T 166/25.
6. Baxter, op. cit., p. 223 et seq.
7. WO 163/205, Weapon Development Cttee, 'VT fuses: development and production in UK' by H. Gough.
8. Hartcup and Allibone, op. cit., pp. 110–11.
9. Gen. Sir F. A. Pile to *The Times*, 5 April 1946.
10. CAB 122/365, Armament Programmes – VT fuses, 22 November 1945.
11. A. O. Bauer, 'Receiver and Transmitter Development in Germany, 1920–1943', pp. 76–82, *Instn of Electrical Engineers Int. Conference on 100 Years of Radio*, 5–7 September 1995.
12. Ibid., E. B. Callick, *VHF Communications at RAE, 1937–42*, pp. 153–60.
13. CAB 102/641, History of Development Production of Radio and Radar, p. 78 et seq.
14. Ibid., Radio at Sea, p. 11 et seq.
15. F. A. Kingsley (ed.), *Radar and Other Electronic Systems in the Royal Navy in World War 2*, P. G. Redgment, 'HF DF in the RN. Development of Anti-U-boat Equipment, 1941–45', London, 1995.
16. Howse, op. cit., pp. 142–6.
17. ADM 220/1486, C. Crampton et al., 'HF DF in HM Ships'.
18. C. Crampton, 'Naval Radio Direction-Finding', *Jnl Instn of Electrical Engineers*, vol. 94, pt IIIA, nos 11 and 15, 1947.
19. AVIA 46/37, Interview with Crampton, Admiralty Signal Estab.
20. ADM 220/291, 'Appreciation of the German *Kurier* System of telegraphy and the intercept problem', 20 August 1948. Reprint of report dated 1945.
21. Jürgen Rohwer, *Critical Convoy Battles of March 1943*, London, 1977. RAF Hist. Soc., *Seek and Sink*, op. cit., Rohwehr, 'A German perspective', p. 59. Kingsley, *Radar and Other Electronic Systems*, op. cit., Relation between DF and Ultra.

22. ADM 220/234 Signal Intelligence Board. D. F. Sub Cttee, 1944–45, Visit to USA by W. Rose, Admy. Sig. Estab., 13 February 1945.
23. Philip Warner, *The Story of Royal Signals, 1945–85,* London, 1989, Lieut-Col H. Winterbotham on HF DF.
24. Hartcup, *The Challenge of War,* op. cit., pp. 182–7.
25. AVIA 23/612, Communications trials of No. 9 Set in a tank with aircraft, March 1935.
26. M. D. Fagen (ed.), *A History of Engineering and Science in the Bell System, 1925–75,* New York, 1977, ch. 5, p. 319 et seq.
27. Warner, op. cit., pp. 237–8.
28. Hartcup, *The Challenge of War,* op. cit., pp. 187–9.
29. AVIA 7/968. 'Jamming from ships', 8 June 1938.
30. Jones, *Most Secret War,* op. cit., chs 11, 15 and 16.
31. Ibid., pp. 84–5, ch. 17.
32. Ibid., pp. 243–4.
33. Howse, op. cit., pp. 51–2.
34. Ibid., p. 212.
35. AVIA 7/2713, A Note on the Technical Problems associated with RCM, October 1942.
36. *Operational Research in Bomber Command* (Air Historical Branch monograph), ch. 16, Miscellaneous investigations concerning bomber issues.
37. AVIA 26/1872. Technical Report of the German RDF equipment captured at Bruneval, 28 February 1942.
38. *OR in Bomber Command,* op. cit., ch. 17, 'Radio Aids to the Defence of Bombers'; R. V. Jones, *Most Secret War,* op. cit., pp. 388–9 and 390–2.
39. *OR in Bomber Command,* op. cit., ch. 17.
40. Jones, op. cit., pp. 39–40.
41. Ibid., ch. 33, passim.
42. *OR in Bomber Cmd,* op. cit., ch. 17, 'The Final Fight for Introduction of Window'.
43. Ibid.,
44. Ibid., Dates of introduction of radar aids.
45. Ibid., Window for Overlord. Final Scheme.

Chapter 4   Acoustic and Underwater Warfare

1. Willem Hackmann, *Seek and Strike. Sonar, Anti-Submarine Warfare and the Royal Navy 1914–54,* HMSO, 1984, p. 7.
2. Ibid., pp. 77–83.
3. Ibid., pp. 83–9.
4. Ibid., p. 92.
5. Ibid., pp. 122–3.
6. Ibid., pp. 171–80.
7. Ibid., pp. 184–7.
8. Ibid., pp. 216–19.
9. Ibid., pp. 197; ADM 219/334.
10. Ibid., p. 196.
11. Ibid., pp. 131–2.
12. Ibid., pp. 192–5.

13. Cherwell Papers, Memo on ASDICS, 1939, PERS. QE (currently missing).
14. ADM I/15197 Admiralty Advisory Panel on Scientific Research, Fowler's visit to Fairlie, 16 June 1941.
15. ADM 116/4585 Case 4178, vol. 117. Homing Torpedoes, March 1940.
16. RAF Hist. Soc., *Seek and Sink*, op. cit., p. 70.
17. ADM I/15197 op. cit., Blackett to Wright, 27 September 1941, Wright to First Sea Lord, 27 November 1941.
18. Gerald Pawle, *The Secret War 1939–1945*, London, 1956, p. 31.
19. J. D. Scott and Richard Hughes, *The Administration of War Production*, London, 1956, p. 132.
20. Hackmann, op. cit., pp. 281–3.
21. Ibid., p. 321.
22. Ibid., p. 335.
23. Sir Bernard Lovell, *P. M. S. Blackett. A Biographical Memoir*, The Royal Society, London, 1976, p. 56.
24. John Herrick, Sub-Surface Warfare. The History of Division 6. NDRC Dept. of Defense, Research and Development Board, Washington DC, January 1951.
25. Hackmann, op. cit., pp. 288–9; Herrick, op. cit.
26. AIR 65/268, Tactical use of the passive directional radio sonobuoy, 6 March 1950.
27. C. H. Waddington, *OR in World War 2: Operational Research against the U-boat*, Elek Science, London, 1973, ch. 7, 'The Principles of Depth Charge Attacks'; ADM 213/93, The explosive efficiency of 'lean torpex', September 1946.
28. ADM 189/175, Technical History of Anti-Submarine Weapons, pt 1.
29. Pawle, op. cit., ch. 12.
30. ADM 189/175, op. cit.; ADM 219/251, R and D in relation to ahead-thrown anti-submarine weapons.
31. RAF Hist. Soc., *Seek and Sink*, op. cit., J. Rohwer.
32. Ibid., Lt-Cdr W. S. R. Gardner, 'The Course of the Battle', p. 34; ADM I/17667, Walter to Dönitz on *Schnorkel*, 20 February 1944.
33. ADM 116/4685, Homing Torpedoes.
34. ADM I/17671, Mark 24 Mine.
35. ADM 213/618, German torpedo docs. History of the Chemical and Physical Exptl Estab of the German Navy.
36. Hackmann, op. cit., pp. 311–12.
37. Ibid., pp. 318–20; Buderi, op. cit., pp. 160–3.
38. ADM I/22283, Countermeasures to Gnat. Arrangements for speeding completion of Publican; ADM I/17179, Publican.
39. G. R. Lindsey, *Tactical Anti-Submarine Warfare: The past and the future*, Adelphi Papers no. 122, International Institute for Strategic Studies, London, 1976.
40. Albert Wood Memorial No., *Jnl. Roy. Naval Scientific Service*, vol. 20, no. 4, July 1965, p. 84.
41. C. F. Goodeve, 'The Defeat of the Magnetic Mine', *Jnl. Roy. Soc. of Arts*, vol. XCIV, January 1946, p. 81.
42. *Jnl. RNSS*, no. 4, July 1965, op. cit., pp. 91–2.
43. Ibid., p. 92.
44. Stephen Roskill, *The War at Sea*, vol. 3, pt 2, HMSO, London, 1961, p. 140.

Chapter 5 The Acquisition of Signals Intelligence

1. Guy Hartcup, *The War of Invention, Scientific Developments, 1914–18*, London, pp. 125–7.
2. David Kahn, *Seizing the Enigma. The Race to Break the German U-Boat Codes, 1939–1943*, Arrow Books London, 1992, p. 31.
3. F. H. Hinsley and Alan Stripp (eds), *Code Breakers. The Inside Story of Bletchley Park*, Oxford University Press (paperback edn), 1993, ch. 11.
4. FO 966/1059, Chief Clerk's Dept., Domestic File, September 1939.
5. Marian Rejewski, 'How Polish Mathematicians deciphered the Enigma', *Annals of the History of Computing*, vol. 3, July 1981, pp. 211–34.
6. F. H. Hinsley et al., *British Intelligence in the Second World War. Its Influence on Strategy and Operations, 1979–1988*, vol. 1, app. 1, London, pp. 491–2.
7. Andrew Hodges, *Alan Turing: the Enigma*, London, 1983, pp. 96–110.
8. Gordon Welchman, 'From Polish Bomba to British Bombe: the Birth of Ultra', *Intelligence and National Security*, January 1986, pp. 71–110.
9. Hodges, op. cit., p. 181.
10. Ibid., pp. 182–4.
11. Hinsley, op. cit., vol. 2, p. 748.
12. Ibid., p. 163 et seq.
13. Hodges, op. cit., pp. 219–21.
14. Hinsley, op. cit., vol. 2, pp. 179 and 747–4.
15. Ibid., op. cit., p. 750; Kahn, op. cit., pp. 220–7.
16. Hinsley, op. cit., pp. 750–2.
17. Ibid., p. 752.
18. Ibid., vol. 3, pt 1, app. 2, *passim*; Hinsley and Stripp, op. cit., pp. 141–8.
19. Thomas H. Flowers, 'The design of Colossus', *Annals of the History of Computing*, vol. 5, no. 3, July 1983, pp. 239–52.
20. Hinsley, op. cit., vol. 2, pp. 29–30; Hinsley and Stripp, op. cit., ch. 21 by Gil Hayward, 'Operation Tunny', pp. 175–92.
21. Flowers, op. cit., pp. 244–5.
22. Ibid., pp. 245–9.
23. Hinsley, op. cit., vol. 3, pt 1, p. 479 et seq.
24. Hinsley and Stripp, op. cit., p. 163.
25. Hinsley, op. cit., p. 779.
26. Hinsley and Stripp, op. cit., p. 147.
27. J. D. Andrews, 'Discussion on Flowers' Lecture on Colossus', *Annals of the History of Computing*, vol. 4, no. 1, January 1982, p. 51. See also B. Randall, 'The Colossus', in J. Howlett, G. C. Rota and N. Metropolis (eds), *A History of Computing*, New York, Academic Press, 1980, pp. 47–92.
28. James R. Chiles, 'Breaking Codes Was This Couple's Lifetime Career', *Smithsonian Magazine*, June 1987, pp. 128–44.
29. David Kahn, *The Codebreakers* (revised edn), New York, 1996, p. 20.
30. Louis Kruh, 'Reminiscences of a Master Cryptologist' (interview with Frank Rowlett), in Cipher A. Deavours et al., *Cryptology Yesterday, Today and Tomorrow*, Artech House Norwood, MA and London, 1987, p. 105.
31. Bradley F. Smith, *The Ultra–Magic Deals and the Most Secret Special Relationship, 1940–46*, Presidio, 1993, pp. 55–6, 74.

32. Kahn, op. cit.; *Kahn on Codes Secrets of the New Cryptology*, New York, 1983, pp. 276–7, 331.
33. Hinsley and Stripp, op. cit., App. Japanese naval codes and ciphers, pp. 276–81.
34. Carl Boyd, *Hitler's Japanese Confidant, General Shima Hiroshi and Magic Intelligence, 1941–1945*, passim.
35. Hinsley and Stripp, op. cit., p. 275.

Chapter 6   Birth of a New Science: Operational Research

1. C. H. Waddington, 'Science Outside the Laboratory', *Polemic*, no. 4, July–August 1946, p. 53.
2. Lord Zuckerman, *Six Men out of the Ordinary*, London, 1992, p. 22.
3. ADM I/15197, Admiralty Advisory Panel on Scientific Research, Blackett to Wright, 27 September 1941.
4. P. M. S. Blackett, 'Scientists at the Operational Level' – see app. 1, *The Origins and Development of Operational Research in the Royal Air Force*, HMSO, London, 1963.
5. WO 291/1911. P. M. S. Blackett, 'A Note on certain aspects of the methodology of Operational Research'.
6. Edward Meade Earle, *Makers of Modern Strategy*, Princeton University Press, 1944, p. 37.
7. A. V. Hill, *The Ethical Dilemma of Science*, Oxford University Press, 1960.
8. R. V. Jones, 'A Concurrence in Learning and Arms', Blackett Memorial Lecture, *J. Opl. Res. Soc.*, vol. 33, no. 9, 1982, pp. 780–1.
9. B. H. Liddell Hart, 'Early Efforts towards Military (Operational) Research', Liddell Hart Centre for Military Archives, Kings College London.
10. *Origins and Development of Operational Research in RAF*, op. cit., pp. 6–7.
11. M. Kirby and R. Capey, 'The air defence of Great Britain, 1920–1940: an operational research perspective', *J. Opl. Res. Soc.*, vol. 48, 1997, pp. 563–4.
12. *The Times*, Obituary of Harold Larnder, 24 August 1981.
13. *Origins and Development of Operational Research in RAF*, op. cit., pp. 16–17.
14. F. L. Sawyer et al., *J. Opl. Res. Soc.*, vol. 40, no. 2, 1989, 'Reminiscences of Operational Research in World War II by some of its Practitioners', p. 117.
15. Ibid., p. 119.
16. Lovell, 'P. M. S. Blackett', op. cit., p. 59; Waddington, op. cit., ch. 6.
17. Waddington, op. cit., ch. 7, 'The early attacks (December 1939)'.
18. Ibid., ch. 3, 'The general theory: organisation of flying'.
19. Jonathan Rosenhead, 'Operational Research at the Crossroads: Cecil Gordon and the Development of Post-war OR', *J. Opl. Res. Soc.*, vol. 40, 1989, pp. 4–9.
20. Rosenhead, op. cit., p. 23.
21. Ibid., p. 9.
22. Solly Zuckerman, *From Apes to Warlords, 1904–1946*, London, 1978, pp. 113–30.
23. Ibid., pp. 139–48.
24. M. Kirby and R. Capey, 'The area bombing of Germany in World War II: an operational research perspective', *J. Opl. Res. Soc.*, vol. 48, 1997, p. 666.
25. Freeman Dyson, 'The Flying Coffins of Bomber Command', *The Observer Magazine*, 28 October 1979, p. 69.

26. *OR in Bomber Command,* op. cit., ch. 3, 'The Study of Night Bombing Techniques'.
27. Ibid., ch. 14, 'The Operational Use of Oboe'.
28. ADM 219/209. Leon Solomon, 'Some Problems of Naval Operational Research', 14 September 1945; PREM 3/414/3, Progress of Analysis of the value of Escort Vessels and Aircraft in the anti-U-boat campaign (Blackett).
29. Michael Howard, *Grand Strategy,* vol. V, HMSO, London, 1972, pp. 303–4.
30. ADM 205/30, First Sea Lord's Records, 1931–45, Papers by Williams and Blackett, 22 March 1943.
31. Ibid., First Sea Lord's arguments for Bay offensive, 31 March 1943.
32. Ibid., Slessor to Pound, 4 April 1943.
33. Ibid., Slessor to Pound, 16 April 1943.
34. Ibid., Note by First Sea Lord on Bay Offensive, April 1943.
35. Zuckerman, op. cit., p. 266.
36. P. M. S. Blackett, on E. J. Williams, Obit. notices of FRSs, vol. 5, 1944–45.
37. Hackmann, op. cit., pp. 254–6; Buderi, op. cit., pp. 161–3.
38. Hackmann, op. cit., p. 256.
39. AIR 52/154 Methods of OR (US); Guido Pereira, *History of the Organization and Operation of the Cttee of Opns Analysts,* 1945, Air Force Hist. Div. Bolling A. F. B., Va (microfilm).
40. Zuckerman, op. cit., chs 8–10.
41. *Origins and Development of Operational Research in the RAF,* op. cit., p. 129.
42. Zuckerman, op. cit., chs 12–13.
43. J. G. Crowther and R. Whiddington, *Science at War,* HMSO, 1947, pp. 107–13.
44. WO 291/1301, Operational Research in the British Army, 1939–45.
45. Terry Copp, 'Scientists and the Art of War, Operational Research in 21 Army Group', *RUSI Jnl.,* Winter 1991, p. 66.
46. P. Johnson to author, 'The Use of GL MKIII for Mortar Location', 8 November 1965.
47. Terry Copp, op. cit., pp. 67–9.
48. P. M. S. Blackett, 'Critique of Some Contemporary Defence Thinking', *Encounter,* vol. XVI, April 1961, p. 9.

Chapter 7 The Transformation of Military Medicine

1. F. H. K. Green and Sir Gordon Covell, *Medical Research,* London, 1953.
2. Irvin Stewart, *Organizing Scientific Research for War.* Boston, Little Brown, 1948, ch. VII.
3. FD 1/6578, British and USA collaboration with research problems 1940–41; FD I/6721, FD I/6723, Medical Liaison with Canada and USA.
4. FD 1/6781, Scientific Cooperation with Russia; FD I/6783 Scientific Cooperation and Liaison with Russia, vol. III, 1943–45.
5. Green and Covell, op. cit., p. 264 et seq.
6. Norman Heatley to author, 1 April 1989.
7. Leonard Bickel, *Rise up to Life. A Biography of Howard Walter Florey who gave penicillin to the world,* London, 1972, p. 141 et seq.
8. FD I/6831, Penicillin Production, Florey to Mellanby, 11 December 1942.
9. FD I/6875, Army research – penicillin trials, April 1943.

10. FD I/6732, Report on Mission to the US and Canada undertaken by Prof. I. M. Heilbron and Sir Robert Robinson, August to September 1943.
11. John P. Swann, 'The Search for Synthetic Penicillin during World War II', *British Jnl. for the History of Science*, vol. 16, 1983, p. 164.
12. FD I/7004, Vivicillin. Cutting from *Time*, 22 May 1944. See also ADM 213/ 45, Interrogations of German scientists concerned with physiological and psychological research.
13. FD I/5260, Committee on Shock, vol. 1, 10 June 1941.
14. Anthony Babington, *Shell Shock. A History of the Changing Attitude to War Neurosis*, London, 1997, p. 137.
15. R. H. Ahrenfeld, *Psychiatry in the British Army in the Second World War*, London (RKP), 1958, *passim*; John R. Neill, 'How Psychiatric Symptoms varied in World War I and World War II', *Military Medicine*, vol. 158, March 1993.
16. David French, 'Tommy is no soldier. The Morale of the Second British Army in Normandy, June to August 1954', *Jnl. of Strategic Studies*, vol. 19, no. 4, December 1996.
17. Capt. H. J. C. J. L'Etang, 'A Criticism of Military Psychiatry in the Second World War', *Jnl. RAMC*, vol. XCVI, January 1951, pp. 316–27.
18. Prof. Brandon, LMF policy, *Reaping the Whirlwind. A Symposium on the Strategic Bomber Offensive*, 1939–45, RAF Hist. Soc., 1993, p. 63.
19. FD I/6604, Anti-Malaria Measures in the British Army, 5 November 1940.
20. Ibid., Letter to Sir John Anderson, 21 January 1943.
21. Ibid., Prevention and Treatment of Malaria, 15 March 1943.
22. John Boyd on Neil Hamilton Fairley, *Biographical Memoirs of Fellows of the Royal Society*, vol. 12, November 1996, pp. 134–8.
23. John H. Perkins, *Insects, Experts and the Insecticide Crisis*, Plenum Press, London, 1982, ch. 1; Kenneth Mellanby, *The DDT Story*, London, 1992, ch. 4.
24. WO 32/9797, Prevention of Typhus Fever, 1941–48, 9 June 1948.
25. FD I/5976, P. A. Buxton, Lice and Typhus, 8 December 1941.
26. FD I/6781, Scientific Cooperation with Russia, 6 October 1941 et seq.
27. FD I/6641, K. Mellanby's visit to America.
28. FD I/6612, Typhus Committee, 7 December 1944, FD I/6635, Typhus Research in SEAC.
29. FD I/6643, Sulphaguanidine, 17–24 August 1941.
30. Boyd, op. cit., p. 134.
31. FD I/5835, German Medical Research, Field Information Agency Technical (British Section).
32. Boyd, op. cit., p. 134.
33. Allison Boyle, *A History of Aviation Medicine in the Second World War*, Dissertation, Wellcome Institute, 1989, p. 11.
34. Sir Philip Livingston, *Fringe of the Clouds*, London, 1962, pp. 159–72.
35. Boyle, op. cit., pp. 12–16.
36. Kenneth Birgin, *Aviation Medicine*, Bristol, John Wright & Sons, 1949, p. 7.
37. D. H. Robinson, *The Dangerous Sky. A History of Aviation Medicine.* G. T. Foulis, Henley on Thames, 1973, pp. 167–9.
38. FD I/5354, Flying Personnel Research Committee, Recent Developments in Aviation Medical Research in US and Canada, 10 April 1941.
39. Robinson, op. cit., pp. 140–2.

40. Livingston, op. cit., pp. 189, 194; T. M. Gibson and M. H. Harrison, *Into Thin Air. A History of Aviation Medicine*, London, 1984, pp. 197–8.
41. Gibson and Harrison, op. cit., p. 199.
42. L. J. Bruce-Chwatt, 'Mosquitoes, Malaria and War: Then and Now', *J R Army Med. Corps*, 1985, vol. 131, pp. 85, 90–1.
43. Ibid., p. 95.
44. Mellanby, op. cit., p. 61.
45. Bruce-Chwatt, op. cit., p. 93.
46. E. H. Beardsley, 'No Help Wanted. Medical Research Exchange between Russia and the West during the Second World War', *Medical History*, vol. 22, 1978, pp. 365–77.

Chapter 8   Unacceptable Weapons: Gas and Bacteria

1. Basil Liddell Hart, *Thoughts on War*, London, 1944; Haber, op. cit., pp. 243–4.
2. Haber, op. cit., p. 296.
3. G. B. Carter, 'The Chemical and Biological Defence Establishment, Porton Down, 1916–1991', *RUSI Jnl.*, Autumn 1991, pp. 66–8; WO 188/802, CBDE: History of Porton by Lieut-Col A. E. Kent.
4. Haber, op. cit., p. 304.
5. WO 188/687, Biological Warfare Repts (Int.), Visits to French Targets, August–October 1944.
6. WO 188/802, CBDE History of Porton by Lieut-Col A. E. Kent, ch. XIV. Haber, op. cit., p. 303.
7. Albrecht, op. cit., p. 63 et seq.
8. WO 208/2124, Chemical Warfare. Interrogations of German generals.
9. Edward M. Spiers, *Chemical Warfare*, London, 1986, p. 73.
10. WO 208/2124, op. cit.
11. WO 208/2183. Investigation into Tabun and Sarin products and Anabasine; Haber, op. cit., p. 306.
12. WO 195/10429, Appreciation of potential CW value of nerve gases based on information up to 30 June 1949.
13. WO 208/2124, op. cit.
14. WO 188/802, op. cit., ch. XVI.
15. AIR 2/8658. The use of phosgene by the RAF.
16. AVIA 22/2282, NRC Canada, Liaison Policy; Mel Thistle (ed.), *The Mackenzie – McNaughton Wartime Letters*, University of Toronto Press, 1975, pp. 20–2, 58.
17. AVIA 22/2286, Scientific Liaison with USA. Policy 1940–45.
18. AVIA 22/2282, Exchange of letters between H. J. Gough and C. J. Mackenzie, January 1941.
19. Hinsley, op. cit., vol. 2, app. 6 and p. 116; CAB 121/100, A/Policy, Chemical Warfare, 18 March 1942.
20. AIR 2/8658, op. cit., Memo by Brunt, 22 October 1942.
21. CAB 121/101, A/Policy, CW1 (vol. 2), PM's Personal Minute, D217/4, 6 July 1944.
22. Ibid., Military considerations affecting the initiation of chemical and other special forms of warfare, 26 July 1944.
23. Ibid., PM's Personal Minute, 29 July 1944.

24. WO 193/712, Chemical Warfare Policy – Offensive, 11 September 1942–20 September 1945.
25. WO 188/687, op. cit.
26. CAB 121/103, A/Policy/CW2/2; FD I/5535, BW Committee, 18 January 1940 and 7 February 1940.
27. G. P. Gladstone on Paul Gordon Fildes, *Biog Mem Roy Soc*, vol. XIX, 1973; G. B. Carter, 'Biological Warfare and Biological Defence in the UK 1940–1979', *RUSI Jnl.*, December 1992, p. 68.
28. WO 188/699, B. W. USA and Canada Correspondence, 10 August 1942.
29. G. S. Pearson, 'Gruinard Island returns to civil use', *ASA Newsletter*, 90–5, no. 20, 6 October 1990, pp. 8–9 and 14.
30. WO 188/699, Mtg held on 28 April 1943 to discuss Cdn cooperation in dev. of BW weapons; see also Fildes to Maj. Gen. Waitt (US Army), 13 September 1943.
31. Ibid., Fildes to Col Thompson, War Cabinet 1 February 1944.
32. Carter, op. cit., p. 70.
33. WO 188/699, op. cit., Mtg, 11 February 1944.
34. WO 188/657, War Cabinet BW Cttee, 1943–44, 11 April 1944.
35. CAB 121/103, op. cit., 16 June 1944 and BW (44) 1st Mtg, 8 July 1944.
36. Ibid., BW (44) 2nd Mtg, 30 August 1944.
37. Ibid., Fildes' Note on Present Possibilities of BW, 21 July 1944.
38. WO 188/699, op. cit., Fildes to Lieut-Col James H. Defendorf, US Army Sanitary Corps, 7 December 1944.
39. WO 208/3972, Investigation of BW targets, 17–20 June 1945.
40. WO 208/3974, Interrogation of Dr Kurt Blome.

Chapter 9   Premature Weapons: the Rocket and the Jet

1. Joseph Needham, *The Guns of Khaifêng-fu; China's Development of Man's First Chemical Explosive*, Creighton Lecture, University of London, November 1979.
2. R. Amman et al., *The Technological Level of Soviet Industry*, Yale University Press, London, 1987, p. 78.
3. Renneberg and Walker, op. cit., pp. 56–7 (M. J. Neufeld, 'The guided missile and the Third Reich').
4. Ibid., pp. 61, 65.
5. Ibid., p. 62.
6. Ibid., p. 65.
7. Jones, op. cit., p. 340.
8. Dieter Hölsken, *V Missiles of the Third Reich. The V1 and V2*, Sturbridge, Mass., 1994, p. 90 et seq.
9. Ibid., p. 98.
10. *Origins and Development of OR in the RAF*, op. cit., pp. 151–5.
11. Hölsken, op. cit., p. 305.
12. Hölsken, op. cit., p. 313; T. Bower, The Paperclip Conspiracy, London, 1987.
13. Amman, op. cit., pp. 79–84.
14. C. W. Lloyd, 'Pioneering Rockets', Letter to *The Times*, 8 May 1995.
15. E. W. Constant, *The Origins of the Turbojet Revolution*, Johns Hopkins University Press, 1980, p. 69.

16. W. Bailey, 'The Early Development of the Aircraft Jet Engine', 1995 (unpublished thesis held by the Roy. Aero. Soc.), p. 2.
17. CAB 102/393, Development of the Jet Propulsion and Gas Turbine Engines in the UK, Narrative by C. Keppel, para. 41.
18. Bailey, op. cit., p. 2.
19. F. Whittle, *Jet. The Story of a Pioneer*, London, 1953, chs 8–9; Obit. of Sir Frank Whittle, *The Times*, 10 August 1996.
20. Bailey, op. cit., p. 14.
21. Ibid, pp. 21, 71.
22. E. J. Ermenec (ed.), *Interviews with German contributors to Aviation History*, Meckler, London, 1990, Ohain interview, pp. 6–37.
23. Ibid, p. 101.
24. Bailey, op. cit., pp. 81–4.
25. Lord Tedder, *With Prejudice*, London, 1966, p. 11.
26. CAB 102/394, Development of Jet Propulsion and Gas Turbine Engines in the UK, C. Keppel narrative, para. 70 et seq.
27. CAB 102/394, op. cit., Whittle's comments on narrative.
28. M. M. Postan et al., *Design and Development of Weapons*, London, 1963, p. 122.
29. Bailey, op. cit., pp. 85–6; Bower, op. cit.
30. Postan, op. cit., p. 200.
31. W. Baumbach, *The Broken Swastika*, New York, 1992.
32. Ibid.
33. AIR 62/1009, 25 July 1941; Constant, op. cit., p. 222.
34. AIR 62/1010, Whittle's report on visit to USA, 8 August 1942.
35. AIR 62/1013, Roxbee Cox's report on visit to USA, November 1945.
36. *The Times*, Whittle Obituary, op. cit.

Chapter 10   The Ultimate Weapon: the Atomic Bomb

1. F. W. Aston, *Isotopes*, London, 1922, p. 104.
2. Martin Gilbert, *Winston S. Churchill: The Prophet of Truth*, vol. V, *1922–1939*, London 1977, pp. 51–2.
3. Hahn and Meitner, articles in *International Atomic Energy Agency Bulletin, Special Number*, 2 December 1962, pp. 6–11.
4. Spencer Weart, *Scientists in Power*, Harvard University Press, London, 1979, ch. 7.
5. Margaret Gowing, *Britain and Atomic Energy, 1939–1945*, London, 1964, app. 1.
6. Glenn Seaborg in *IAEA Bulletin*, op. cit.
7. Gowing, op. cit., app. 2, The MAUD Reports.
8. Arnold Kramish, No. 62, *The Nuclear Motive: In the Beginning*, International Security Studies Program, The Wilson Center, Washington, DC, 1982, p. 5.
9. Ibid., p. 5; Stewart Cockburn and David Ellyard, *Oliphant*, South Australia, 1981, ch. 8.
10. Kramish, op. cit., p. 2.
11. Laurence Badash, *Scientists and the Development of Nuclear Weapons. From Fission to the Limited Test Ban Treaty*, Humanities Press International, 1995, p. 36.
12. Kramish, op. cit., p. 9.
13. Badash, op. cit., p. 39.
14. Gowing, op. cit., p. 62.

15. Kramish, op. cit., pp. 10–11.
16. Holloway, op. cit., pp. 76–9.
17. Ibid., pp. 82–4.
18. Ibid., pp. 96–103.
19. Ibid., pp. 106–8.
20. Ibid., p. 129.
21. Renneberg, op. cit., p. 275.
22. Powers, op. cit., p. 98.
23. Ibid., pp. 135–6.
24. Sir Charles Frank (ed.), *Operation Epsilon: the Farm Hall Transcripts*, Soc. of Physics, Bristol, 1993, p. 73.
25. Rudolf Peierls, 'The Bomb that Never Was', review of Powers' *Heisenberg's War, NY Rev. of Books*, 22 April 1993.
26. Frank, op. cit., p. 73.
27. Powers, op. cit., pp. 322–3.
28. Ibid., p. 409.
29. Otto Frisch, *What Little I Remember*, Cambridge, 1979, p. 176.
30. Richard Rhodes, *The Making of the Atomic Bomb*, Penguin, London, 1988, p. 736.
31. Kimball Smith, op. cit., p. 320.

Conclusion

1. O. H. Wansbrough Jones, quoted in 'Present Science and Future Strategy', *Jnl. RUSI*, vol. 95, August 1950, pp. 405–23.
2. AIR65/335, Bombsights and Development Policy, October 1950.
3. Sir Edward Bullard, 'Effect of the War on the Development of Knowledge in the Physical Sciences', *Procs. Roy. Soc.*, A342, 1974–75, pp. 222–3.
4. Buderi, op. cit., p. 471.
5. J. D. Bernal, 'Lessons of the War for Science', *The Freedom of Necessity*, London, 1949. See also *Procs. Roy. Soc.*, A342, op. cit., pp. 555–74.
6. Sir Harrie Massey, 'Atomic Energy and the Development of Large Teams', *Procs. Roy. Soc.*, op. cit., p. 492.

Bibliography

Ahrenfeld, R. H., *Psychiatry in the British Army in the Second World War*, London, 1958.

Air Ministry, Air Publns 3368, *The Origins and Development of Operational Research in the RAF*, London, 1963.

Anon., *Science in War*, Penguin Special, London, 1940.

Barnett, Correlli, *The Audit of War. The Illusion and Reality of Britain as a Great Nation*, London, 1986.

Baxter, James Phinney, *Scientists against Time* (paperback edn), MIT, Boston, 1968.

Bernal, J. D., *Freedom of Necessity*, London, 1949.

Bickel, Leonard, *Rise up to Life. A Biography of Howard Walter Florey who gave Penicillin to the World*, London, 1972.

Birkenhead, Earl of, *The Prof in Two Worlds*, London, 1961.

Blackett, P. M. S., *Studies of War*, London, 1962.

Bowen, E. G., *Radar Days*, Bristol, 1987.

Boyle, Allison, *A History of Aviation Medicine in the Second World War*, Wellcome Institute, London, 1989.

Brown, Andrew, *The Neutron and the Bomb. A Biography of Sir James Chadwick*, Oxford, 1997.

Buderi, Robert, *The Invention that Changed the World. The Story of Radar from War to Peace*, London, 1997.

Burns, Russell, *Radar Development to 1945*, IEE, London, 1988.

Bush, Vannevar, *Pieces of the Action*, London, 1973.

Clark, Ronald, *Tizard*, London, 1965,

Clark, Ronald, *The Greatest Power on Earth*, London, 1980.

Cockburn, Stewart and Ellyard, David, *Oliphant*, Adelaide, Australia, 1981.

Constant, E. W., *The Origins of the Turbojet Revolution*, Johns Hopkins University Press, 1980.

Creveld, Martin, *Technology and War from 2000 BC to the Present*, London, 1991.

Crowther, J. G. and Whiddington, R., *Science at War*, London, 1947.

Edgerton, David, *England and the Aeroplane. An Essay on a Militant and Technological Nation*, Manchester, 1991.

Fagen, M. D. (ed.), *A History of Science and Engineering in the Bell Systems*, vol. II, *National Service in War and Peace, 1925–75*, New York, 1978.

Forman, Paul and Ron, José-Manuel Sanchez, *National Military Establishments and the Advance of Science*, Dordrecht, 1996.

Frank, Sir Charles (ed.), *Operation Epsilon: the Farm Hall Transcripts*, Bristol, 1993.

Frisch, Otto, *What Little I Remember*, Cambridge, 1979.

Gardner, W. J. R., *Decoding History: the Battle of the Atlantic and Ultra*, London, 1999.

Glasstone, Samuel, *Sourcebook on Atomic Energy*, London, 1967.

Goldsmith, Maurice, *Sage. A Life of J. D. Bernal*, London, 1980.

Gowing, Margaret, *Britain and Atomic Energy, 1939–1945*, London, 1953.

Green, F. H. K. and Covell, Maj. Gen. Sir Gordon, *Medical Research*, London, 1953.

Groves, Leslie, *Now It Can Be Told*, New York, 1962.

Guerlac, Henry E., *Radar in World War II*, 2 vols, New York, 1987.

Hackmann, Willem, *Seek and Strike*. *Sonar, Anti-Submarine Warfare and the Royal Navy, 1914–54*, London, 1984.

Harrod, R. F., *The Prof. A Personal Memoir of Lord Cherwell*, London, 1959.

Hartcup, Guy, *The Challenge of War*. *Scientific and Engineering Contributions to World War Two*, Newton Abbott, 1970.

Hartcup, Guy and Allibone, T. E., *Cockcroft and the Atom*, Bristol, 1985.

Hezlet, Vice-Admiral Sir Arthur, *The Electron and Sea Power*, London, 1975.

Hinsley, F. H. and Stripp, Alan, *Codebreakers*. *The Inside Story of Bletchley Park*, Oxford, 1993.

Hinsley, F. H. et al., *British Intelligence in the Second World War*. *Its Influence on Strategy and Operations*, 3 vols in 4 parts, London, 1979–88.

Hodges, Andrew, *Alan Turing: the Enigma*, London, 1983.

Holloway, David, *Stalin and the Bomb*, New Haven, Conn. and London, 1975.

Hölsken, Dieter, *V Missiles of the Third Reich*. *The V1 and V2*, Sturbridge, Mass., 1993.

Howse, Derek, *Radar at Sea*. *The Royal Navy in World War 2*, London, 1993.

Institute of Electrical and Electronic Engineers, Procs. of, *Fifty Years of Radar*, vol. 177, no. 2, 1985.

Jones, R. V., *Most Secret War*, London, 1978.

Jones, R. V., *Recollections of Intelligence*, London, 1989.

Kevless, Daniel, *The Physicists*. *The History of a Scientific Community in Modern America*, New York, 1979.

Kimball Smith, Alice and Weiner, Charles, *Robert Oppenheimer*. *Letters and Recollections*, Cambridge, Mass. and London, 1989.

Lovell, Sir Bernard, *Echoes of War*, Bristol, 1990.

Postan, M. M. et al., *Design and Development of Weapons*, London, 1963.

Powers, Thomas, *Heisenberg's War: the Secret History of the German Bomb*, London, 1993.

Price, Alfred, *Instruments of Darkness*, London, 1967.

Price, Alfred, *Aircraft versus Submarine*, London, 1980.

Pritchard, David, *The Radar War*. *Germany's Pioneering Achievement, 1904–45*, London, 1989.

Renneberg, Monica and Walker, Mark, *Science, Technology and National Socialism*, Cambridge, 1994.

Rhodes, Richard, *The Making of the Atomic Bomb*, Penguin Books, London, 1988.

Rohwer, Jürgen, *The Critical Convoys of March 1943*, London, 1977.

Rowe, A. P., *One Story of Radar*, Cambridge, 1948.

Royal Society, Proceedings of, *Science in the First and Second World Wars*, A342, no. 1631, 1975, pp. 439–591.

Smyth, H. D. *Atomic Energy for Military Purposes*, Princeton, NJ, 1945.

Spiers, Edward M., *Chemical Warfare*, London, 1986.

Stewart, Irvin, *Organizing Scientific Research for War*, Boston, Mass., 1948.

Swann, B. and Aprahamian, F., *J. D. Bernal. A Life in Science and Politics*, London, 1999.

Swords, S. S., *Technical History of the Beginnings of Radar*, London, 1986.

Waddington, C. H., *OR in World War 2. Operational Research against the U-boat*, London, 1973.

Watson-Watt, Sir Robert, *Three Steps to Victory*, London, 1957.

Weart, Spencer R., *Scientists in Power*, Harvard University Press, Cambridge, Mass. and London, 1979.

Webster, Sir Charles and Frankland, Noble, *The Strategic Air Offensive against Germany, 1939–1945*, London, 1961.

Whittle, Sir Frank, *Jet. The Story of a Pioneer*, London, 1953.

Wilson, Thomas, *Churchill and the Prof*, London, 1995.

Zimmerman, David, *Top Secret Exchange. The Tizard Mission and the Scientific War*, Stroud, 1996.

Zuckerman, Solly, *From Apes to Warlords, 1904–46*, London, 1978.

Zuckerman, Lord, *Six Men out of the Ordinary*, London, 1992.

Note   The Centre for the History of Defence Electronics at Bournemouth University has compiled an oral history of radar.

Index